SPIRIT OF LIBERALITY

SPIRIT OF LIBERALITY
COLLECTED ESSAYS

George Newlands

⁌PICKWICK *Publications* · Eugene, Oregon

SPIRIT OF LIBERALITY
Collected Essays

Copyright © 2014 George Newlands. All rights reserved. Except for brief quotations in critical publications or reviews, no part of this book may be reproduced in any manner without prior written permission from the publisher. Write: Permissions. Wipf and Stock Publishers, 199 W. 8th Ave., Suite 3, Eugene, OR 97401.

Pickwick Publications
An Imprint of Wipf and Stock Publishers
199 W. 8th Ave., Suite 3
Eugene, OR 97401

www.wipfandstock.com

ISBN 13: 978-1-62564-561-6

Cataloguing-in-Publication Data

Newlands. G. M., 1941–

    Spirit of Liberality / George Newlands

    xii + Y p. ; 23 cm. Includes bibliographical references and index.

    ISBN 13: 978-1-62564-561-6

    1. Liberalism (Religion). 2. Theology, Doctrinal. 3. Human rights—Religious aspects—Christianity. I. Title.

BT28 N495 2014

Manufactured in the U.S.A.

Permissions

I am grateful for these permissions to use previously published material.

"Luther's Ghost—*Ein gluehende Backofen voller Liebe.*" In *Theology as Conversation: Essays for Daniel Migliore*, edited by Bruce McCormack and Kimlyn Bender, 273–93. Grand Rapids: Eerdmans, 2009.

"Public Theology in Postfoundational Tradition." In *The Evolution of Rationality: Essays in Honor of J. Wentzel van Huyssteen*, edited by F. LeRon Shults, 394–417. Grand Rapids: Eerdmans, 2006.

"Humane Spirit." In *Religious Pluralism in the Modern World: An Ongoing Engagement with John Hick*, edited by Sharada Sugirtharajah, 153–63. London: Palgrave Macmillan, 2012.

"Christianity and Culture—WARC at the Millennium." In *Crossroad Discourses between Christianity and Culture*, edited by J. D. Gort et al., 563–78. Amsterdam: Rodopi, 2010.

"Adolf von Harnack." In *The Routledge Encyclopedia of Modern Christian Thought*, edited by Chad Meister and James Beilby, 117–26. London: Routledge, 2013.

"John Macquarrie in Scotland." In *In Search of Humanity and Deity: A Celebration of John Macquarrie's Theology*, edited by Robert Morgan, 17–24. London: SCM, 2006.

"John McIntyre and History." *Theology in Scotland* XIV.2 (2007) 19–32.

"Incarnation." *Doctrine Committee of the Scottish Episcopal Church, Grosvenor Series*, 1–8. Edinburgh, 2011.

For my students in sundry places, with thanks and admiration.

Contents

Preface | ix

Abbreviations | xi

1   The Spirit, the Academy, and the Vertical City | 1
2   Faith after Faith—Perplexed and Unperplexed | 22
3   Luther's Ghost | 37
4   Humane Spirit | 58
5   Christianity and Culture | 70
6   Public Theology in Postfoundational Tradition | 85
7   John Macquarrie in Scotland | 110
8   John McIntyre and History | 115
9   Religion and Democracy | 125
10 Incarnation | 142
11 Adolf von Harnack | 149
12 Faith, Slavery, and Human Rights | 162
13 Affirmation Scotland, Gay Christians, and Equality | 178
14 In Church | 184
15 Christian Futures | 213
16 A Journey into Theology | 222

Author Biography and Bibliography | 237

Bibliography | 241

Index of Names | 249

Preface

Spirit of Liberality

THE PIECES HERE CONTINUE in the liberal tradition of theology represented in *Traces of Liberality*, my essay collection of 2005. Theology has moved on since then, and in the present volume I try to reflect and assess developments in theology and the churches and in their diverse relationships.

Ten years ago it seemed to many observers that the liberal traditions in church and academy and in the public square were finally entering on their much prophesied demise. But prophets in history have very often been quite wrong.

Especially in the United States, it has been well noted that there continues to be a rich and inclusive stream of liberal theology in the academy. It has been realized that the numerical decline in the mainline churches has not taken due account of the wide reaching role of liberal Christian values on the embedding of a culture of human rights and concern for human dignity and for social justice in society, at a local and an international level.

Without attempting the prophetic, and sticking to the present, it seems to me that many of the luxuriant blooms of post-everything theology and church have not been as long-lived as had been expected. They have, however, provided a salutary reminder that the Christian faith can always be articulated in diverse manners, and that monocular visions, including monocular liberal versions, will always be of limited value. None of us can see the whole horizon; we can only try to bring to a conversation what we can ourselves imagine, and hope to encourage to conversation, and not simply on our own terms.

I have tried to indicate that liberal theological perspectives are to be found not only in professedly liberal projects, but throughout the rich history of Christian tradition, from the biblical narratives to the present, from Origen and Augustine, to Barth and Schillebeeckx. Good liberal Christian theology should be radically inclusive, not with the exclusiveness of indifference, but with the inclusiveness of Jesus Christ.

Inclusiveness will always be less than real until it is embedded in Christian community, in a church open to the world. This is the crucial challenge to churches which are often as obviously out of touch with a younger generation as they have ever been. Challenges are perhaps best met by considered and effective action, rather than embarrassed wringing of ecclesiastical hands.

It goes without saying that in producing these papers I have been deeply indebted as always to colleagues, friends, family, and the Pickwick publishing team. In particular, I am deeply grateful to Dr. Anthony Allison for extensive and careful scrutiny of the text, not least where consistency was complicated by the different publishing conventions of the volumes in which many of the pieces originally appeared.

—*George Newlands*
Edinburgh and Cambridge, 2014.

Abbreviations

ARG	*Archiv fuer Reformationasgeschichte*
CSEL	*Corpus Scriptorium Ecclesiasticorum Latinorum*
DSCHT	*Dictionary of Scottish Church History and Theology*
NEW DNB	*New Dictionary of National Biography*
RGG	*Die Religion in Geschichte und Gegenwart*
RSCHS	Records of the Scottish Church History Society
SST	Society for the Study of Theology
TRE	*Theologische Encyclopaedie*
WA	*Weimarer Ausgabe (Luther Werke)*

1

The Spirit, the Academy, and the Vertical City

Society for the Study of Theology, Nottingham, April 2013.

This paper is not about Theology and Education, though perhaps we may find some connections. When I began to think of writing a paper it seemed to be worth trying to suggest at least some sense of a continuing SST conversation over the years. I'm going to take a traditional presidential liberty to speak about something other than Education, and try to pick up the themes of SST 2012, on the Holy Spirit—with a few variations for 2013.

Part I: Cityscape and Spiritscape

For thousands of years there have been cities. Megacities have grown, in an accelerating drift, from countryside to city. Faith is also a major fact of our time. Weak in some countries, strong in others, the question of God remains both a unifying and an explosive force. There remains too a yawning gap between serious academic theology and faith communities. This paper aims to conduct a conversation with the image of the contemporary city in the background.[1]

---

1. Huge thanks to Ma Jun, Hai Wang, and Zhongwen Zhang for patience and illumination—they are in no way responsible for my own eccentric reflections.

Cities

> Approaching the city from the north, one passes through a tunnel in southernmost Marin county that leads on to the famous bridge. To the southeast lies the city, clustered on the peninsula between the bay to the east and the Pacific to the west. It was one of these summer evenings that I would come to know and never ceased to savour over the years. The night-time fog cools the city and the bay as far as the Oakland hills, only to burn off at midday, leaving the air and the land scrubbed clean and bathed in a shimmering, glad summer light. . . . It was the mythic city of the Gold Rush, the Dharma Bums, and the Grateful Dead.

> Telegraph Avenue, in Berkeley, like Haight Street in San Francisco, is one of those meccas of deeply committed oddity. . . . Then as now, straight, squeaky clean Cal students in slacks and Windbreakers mingles with aged hippies and burned out people talking to themselves in brain-addled confusion. Adolescent runaways with sickly complexions and greasy hair lounged on the sidewalk, begging spare change, their stray mongrels sitting at their side. Street vendors sold hash pipes, tie-dyed T-shirts and Vietcong flags that smelled of patchouli and verbena.[2]

There you have it. The vision of the dream city of a young struggling composer arriving in San Francisco in 1971, and the squalid reality which often underlies the dream, the reality of poverty. The city, in very different shapes, has long been both a huge threat and an awesome promise.

Creative minds have meditated on the city. From Augustine's *civitas terrena* and *civitas caelestis*, to the Free Cities of medieval Europe, to the New York of Michael Pye's *Maximum City*, cities have drawn fascinated scrutiny and masses of people. Churchmen reflected extensively on the City—in New York, Henry Sloane Coffin and Paul Moore Jr. Guidebooks exhaust the city's contents. Novelists like Dickens, memorialize it. Cities, like people, have lives written—Peter Ackroyd on London. The modern city, from Dohlian to Abu Dhabi, is increasingly the hub of society.

When Christians come to think of the Spirit of God, they don't always consider the role of the Spirit in and for people who live mostly in the city. Books on theology, especially on spirituality, are more likely to stress the solitude of the desert or the abstract air of the academic seminar

---

2. Adams, *Hallelujah Junction*, 64–66.

than the quotidian actualities of city life. Of the actualities—between Elysian heaven and urban hell—there have long been many variations.

Many people who work in cities do not live in city centres. Suburbs may not seem romantic, but much of what is important happens in suburbs. Modern gated communities become suburbs in themselves, distinguished more by conveniences of transport than anything else. All of this affects religious practice. Churches built in city centres can be emptied as people live further from the centre, and such mundane matters as parking restrictions make access to worship services difficult. There are exceptions. Great cathedrals attract worshippers to city centres because the quality of worship outweighs the inconvenience of accessing them.

The city encompasses a variety which stretches from compact Dunedin to Los Angeles, itself a conglomerate of more than ninety cities. The advent of mass communication, the internet, and the exigencies of contemporary employment, bring almost everyone into the world of "the city," the globalized world. Businesswomen may do their stock trading from laptops based on island communities, but this is still plugged into cities, while unskilled building workers commute by air to construction sites, leaving home for six months at a time. The cellphone is a great but ambiguous leveller.

So far the city. How about the Spirit? We come across jarring contrasts and constructive interactions between the gentleness of the Spirit and the harshness of much urban life. How might we explore the tradition of the Spirit for the welfare of the city?

Spirit in Theology

One of the most interesting modern studies of the Spirit is Michael Welker's *God the Spirit*. For Welker, many theologies of the Spirit provide no plausible account of a realistic relationship with the Spirit in contemporary life. They may envisage the Spirit as a unifying force—this can lead to domination and imperialism. They can be general and unspecific, captured by extraneous dialectics. They have little biblical foundation. They fail to take account of the value of complexity and otherness—a pretty sobering indictment. I don't expect for a moment to pass the Welker test myself, but perhaps I can drive you to enough frustration to encourage you to take up the challenge for yourselves.

Some basic parameters. Spirit in Christian tradition is often understood as the means through which God becomes present as a living reality, in the church, but also in relating to all persons, created in the divine image. Through the Spirit faith is created, sustained, and nurtured —contrasting with the often expressed sense of the disappearance of God as a living reality.

The Scope of the Spirit

For Christian faith, the Spirit of God, as the Spirit of the risen Christ, is promised in the New Testament to all believers. The Spirit is experienced in the community of Christ's body, in the fellowship of word, sacrament, discipleship, and service. Community is open, the church is there as the servant of the world for the sake of the gospel. In encounter between Christians and non-Christians—not always a hard division—there is a meeting of God's Spirit and human spirit.

The Bible suggests that the Spirit acts in, with, and under the history of the created order. The historicality of the Spirit is centrally related to the historicality of God in Christ. Through the events concerning Jesus, life, death, and resurrection, cosmic redemption have happened. But the work of the Spirit is not complete. All human beings, made in the divine image, are called to act, in contemporary society, as instruments of God's unconditional love. The Spirit is there, in the city for the city.

In the New Testament, the Spirit is giver and gift. The Spirit bears witness, touches, heals, works, imparts, prays, and wills. The Creator wills to be with us as a loving, active presence through the Spirit. From these focal points of biblical narrative, and continuing experience, theologians develop conceptions of the dynamic, complex nature of God—doctrines of Trinity. These have produced spiritual growth, understanding, argument, and violence. Formulas imposed in one generation as totalitarian decrees, can be construed as beautiful aids to devotion in another. Trinitarian thinking about Spirit can help us to imagine the self-dispossessing, self-differentiating God. This insight into the divine *kenosis* has not a monopoly of Trinitarian conceptuality and may be subverted. The non-coercive nature of the Trinity—so often an instrument of coercion, was long since well expressed by David Jenkins: "The Trinity symbolises the discovery of love which is both transcendent and committed to being at work in history and in human beings. The shape of the Trinitarian symbol also indicates that in the end identity is not to be had at the cost of other identities but by being the fulfilment of them."[3] The church of the Spirit is committed to the concrete of the city in the most literal sense. The production of concrete is an environmentally wasteful process which produces harmful by-products. Yet concrete buildings survive earthquakes much better than brick constructions, and concrete foundations resist pressure when silt bases slide. God is committed, to real cities lived in by people who live real, untidy, often fragile lives, with all the ambiguity which this involves. Beyond the ambiguity of ever squabbling denominations, the Spirit is the spirit of the vulnerable God.

The religious are called to maximize the reconciling dynamic and to minimize the divisive. The secular are called to bring their gifts of humane insight. Justice and mercy are values foundational to the Creator Spirit, uniquely instantiated by the crucified God. Jesus was crucified outside the city, an event not unrelated to inner-city politics, and to the marginalized of every city. Constantly we are reminded that Jesus did not confine his concern to his own natural constituents. If we look for an indication of Jesus' engagement with other faiths, improbable conversation partners, and the people at the edges of the city, this is as clear as anything in the tangled traditions of the gospel. Not every spirit—an exclusive spirit is not the spirit of Christlikeness.

Neanderthal Dogmatics of Transcendence

Where does human thinking about Spirit begin? In the beginning, in Launcelot Andrewes' majestic rendering, the Spirit of God moved upon the waters. After the resurrection of Jesus Christ, the Spirit descended on the nucleus of the Christian community. In the end, all will be gathered up into eternal life in the Spirit. God is in time, before time, and after time. We are gradually getting used to the idea of universes without end, quantum vacuums, and the like. Evolution in its kaleidoscopic and random variety, is a servant of God. The Spirit is the spirit of cosmic development.

Land masses evolve and with them life, culminating in the emergence of human beings. The shape of bodies, eyes, and brains mould human interaction. Societies of widely differing sorts emerge. Habits of the heart form, privileging some groups, disprivileging others. Men do well,

3. Jenkins, *The Contradiction of Christianity*, 57–58.

women less well. Meat eaters gain strength. Cannibalism is good for you, up to a point. A certain sociality encourages survival.

Cave paintings depict images to denote ideas of transcendence—arising, perhaps, in bursts of reflective activity over a comparatively short period. Today, contemporary invocations of Spirit appear in the liturgies of the major religions, and in such contexts as in the Spirit music of the native peoples of North America: from spirituality to spiritualism. Everything that we say packages these phenomena in the categories of our own time.

The religions of the ancient Near East develop notions of transcendence—Mycenean civilizations. There are interruptions—early Greek religion, an amalgam of ideas borne by different trade routes. Within this culture develop notions which we know as the work of "the Presocratics"—not unconnected with the rise of cities. The legendary seven sages of early Greek thought were each connected with a small but recognizable city. Intellectual development comes too through other channels—poets and dramatists.

When these people thought of the gods they reflected on the nature of transcendence. Why is there something and not nothing? Empirical objects had the quality of being. Did the transcendent realm also have being, and, if so, what sort of being? Spirits, ghosts? You know the story in the West, from Plato to NATO. For the Fathers of the church, the Hellenic heritage was fertilized by the creation narratives of the Bible. Platonic tradition influenced patristic and medieval thought, the Middle Ages, Reformation, Enlightenment thought—all leading in varied directions.

What did Christians mean by the fruits of the Spirit? No Luther and Calvin without the treasury of medieval theology. For Luther, it was impossible to speak of gifts of the Spirit apart from speaking of Jesus Christ, present in Word and Sacrament. Ever suspicious of "enthusiasm," he maintained that everything said about the Spirit, apart from the Word and Sacrament, is of the devil—salutary warning. When church committees produce reports based on weak arguments they tend to end with the assurance of the guidance of the Holy Spirit.

Luther's formula was not infallible. The Spirit works in the sanctuary and in the market place, in relation to all humankind and, indeed, to the whole cosmic order. The light of the Spirit of the risen Christ shines in the darkness, and the fruits of the spirit are peace, love, joy, forgiveness, and reconciliation, often in the teeth of suffering. The spirit's presence is not always signalled by an improbable euphoria. It may be experienced as a presence through pain. It is not always signalled by suffering—there can be an unnecessary preoccupation with suffering as an occasion for spiritual insight. But Spirit has been experienced as a calming presence in the midst of the most trying or chaotic circumstances. There is here something of the hiddenness of grace, given to be given away. Calvin links the presence of the Spirit with the preaching of the Word. In the name of the spirit of love, they damn the Anabaptists in unison.

Lutheran pietism led to a new emphasis on the fruits of the Spirit. How was this related to the gift of grace? New and risk-laden paradigms become possible when the Spirit is liberated from exclusive union with the Bible or the church. Barth's solution was to stress the relationship of the Spirit with the word. But could there be other ways of linking word and Spirit, perhaps creating new possibilities for inter-Christian and inter-religious relationships? How about a pneumatological theology of basic and loving relationality, of hospitality, for which Christology and pneumatology are not competitive but complementary ways?

No one owns the winds of the Spirit. The Spirit works in different ways at different times, perhaps simultaneously. There are boundaries—conformity to the witness of Christlikeness—love, patience, generosity, grace, forgiveness, and reconciliation, a passion for justice, peace, and those in greatest need. Community is important, and may include non-believing community. Where there is suffering there may be especially the presence of the Spirit. A triumphalist community is unlikely to hear the voice of the Spirit. The Spirit may speak through the crucified peoples of God's creation.[4]

Recent Reflection—Expansion Exponential

There has been an enormous burst of recent reflection on Spirit, and I want here at least to indicate its scope. Barth famously affirmed that the Holy Spirit is "the most intimate friend of a proper human understanding of man."[5] Rahner put it like this: "The essential nature of genuine experience of the Spirit does not consist of particular objects of experience found in human awareness but occurs rather when a man experiences

---

4. I'm grateful to Simeon Zahl for reflection on Spirit in relation to suffering. Cf. *Pneumatology and Theology of the Cross in the Preaching of Christoph Friedrich Blumhardt: The Holy Spirit between Wittenberg and Azusa Street.*

5. Barth, *Kirchliche Dogmatik* 4/4, 31.

the radical re-ordering of his transcendent nature in knowledge and freedom towards the immediate reality of God through God's self-communication in grace."[6] Beyond the classical tradition, Pentecostal Christians have developed a fast-growing tradition around Spirit which captures the imagination of hundreds of millions.

My friend Geoffrey Lampe, one of the founders and earliest Presidents of SST, was struggling towards "realistic theology," notably in *God as Spirit*.[7] Stressing the unity of creation and redemption, he had problems with "the restriction of the term 'Spirit' to the 'Holy Spirit' as the third person of the Trinity." This has come about through the hypostatisation of the concepts of Wisdom and Logos, their appropriation to Christology, and the emergence of the model of Logos, God the Son, personified as the pre-existent heavenly Jesus Christ, as the classical expression of the significance of Jesus. He summed up his position:

> I believe in the divinity of our Lord and Saviour Jesus Christ, in the sense that the one God, the Creator and Saviour Spirit, revealed himself and acted decisively for us in Jesus. I believe in the Divinity of the Holy Spirit, in the sense that the same one God, the Creator and Saviour Spirit, is here and now not far from every one of us; for in him we live and move and we have our being, in us, if we consent to know and trust him, he will create the Christlike harvest: love, joy, peace, patience, kindness, goodness, fidelity, gentleness and self-control.[8]

For John Webster,[9] Lampe's "Spirit" is virtually co-terminous between God and man, and so the church may not regard itself as the exclusive location of God's Spirit; rather, it is the focal point of God's personal presence to all creation. This pneumatology is too generalized, and fails to state how the Spirit is Christologically identified in the New Testament. Charlie Moule commented that "Lampe had no intention of abandoning the essentials of Christian faith and practice, of which he was a shining and inspiring example." Tim Gorringe[10] suggested that Spirit language will not do what Logos language can do for us. For Rowan Williams,[11]

---

6. Rahner, *Theological Investigations*, XVI, 27.
7. Lampe, *God as Spirit*, 228.
8. Ibid., 228.
9. Webster, "The Identity of the Holy Spirit," 4–7.
10. Gorringe, *Discerning Spirit: A Theology of Revelation*, 42ff.
11. Williams, *On Christian Theology*, 109.

Lampe tends to reduce Word to Spirit, while Barth tends to reduce Spirit to Word. Looking at the historicity of Spirit, Williams sees the Spirit as transforming, not just communicating, creating Christlikeness where suffering and promise meet. Characteristically he brings together Luther's *crux probat omnia* with Lossky's assembly of redeemed human persons.

Alii alia sentiunt. For myself, I still regard Lampe as a highly significant and prescient thinker in this field. Different traditions bring different insights. Peter Hodgson associates the work of the Spirit with the emancipatory theologies.[12] Amos Yong[13] stresses the fallibility of all appeals to the Spirit. He cites Elizabeth Johnson[14] on the Spirit as relational and feminine. Father, Son, and Spirit are three realities, and within this Spirit is a field of force. Theology has triadic structures and a hermeneutic of trialectic. Anselm Min offers the most specific integration of the work of the Spirit, with the task of building solidarity with the oppressed, especially the most economically impoverished on the planet. *The Solidarity of Others in a Divided World: A Postmodern Theology after Postmodernism*[15] is a dedicated theology of the Holy Spirit. In *After the Spirit*, Eugene Rogers[16] reminds us of the vibrant tradition of Spirit in the life and worship of the Eastern churches.

For James Alison[17] Spirit brings in the outsiders. The Holy Spirit "makes available to us a wholly benign secular createdness." Furthermore, "[t]he Holy Spirit is there to empower us to put up with the hatred which is how the collapsing sacred is held together, and it is by our standing up that the new creation will be brought into being through us." The Other is importantly also The Same, and so inextricably locked in a kind of solidarity, Graham Adams[18] finds solidarity in respect for otherness—Jesus as The Shaken One. In his paper at SST last year, Stuart Weir[19] linked human agency to eschatological completion through a pneumatological reading.

Michael Welker's collection, *The Work of the Spirit: Pneumatology and Pentecostalism*,[20] provides a wide spread of proposals. John

12. Hodgson, *Winds of the Spirit*.
13. Yong, *Spirit, Word and Community*.
14. Johnson, *Women, Earth and Creator Spirit*, 58ff.
15. Min, *The Solidarity of Others in a Divided World*.
16. Rogers, *After the Spirit*.
17. Alison, *On Being Liked*, 11.
18. Adams, *Christ and the Other*.
19. Weir, unpublished SST paper, 2011.
20. Welker, *The Work of the Spirit: Pneumatology and Pentecostalism*.

Polkinghorne, linking Spirit to current cosmological research, suggests that we should not expect always to *see* the Spirit in action in creation: "If it is indeed the cloudiness of intrinsically unpredictable process that affords the causal space within which pattern-forming influences of these kinds can be active, then the Spirit's interaction with cosmic process could indeed properly be described as the working of the *deus absconditus*."[21] In David Jensen's collection,[22] *The Lord and Giver of Life*, Roger Haight sees Spirit as not just enabling but provoking from within the Christian tradition inter-religious engagement, avoiding competitive theologies: "[t]he Spirit of God pervades human history. But in the Christian dispensation and from a Christian perspective, by definition, Jesus Christ becomes the open norm for discerning the Spirit truly. . . . The point that is driven home then, is not a grudgingly tolerant view of the religions, but the vision of God's relation to history revealed in Jesus Christ that validates the autonomous saving character of other religions." John Cobb understands the Spirit as a guard against assault on human dignity, often in the name of faith, in areas of gender and sexuality on the one hand, and through delusions of empire on the other.[23] From my perspective, one of the most fascinating pieces is an essay by Amos Yong, "Guests, Hosts, and the Holy Ghost."[24] Yong focuses on hospitality as key to engagement: Christians are always guests, as Jesus was always a guest, and will respect their hosts, while offering their own distinctive gifts. He offers a pneumatological theology of hospitality. Like Min, Yong is mindful of the role of the Spirit in the public square, in movements for liberation and alleviation of poverty.

With Prejudice—Hospitable Spirit

Taking up these themes we might say that in the economy of creation and reconciliation, Word and Spirit are active in the interstices of world and church at every level, a gracious presence recognized by faith. The form of Christ in the world is also the form of Spirit in the world. The church is church when it listens for the real world and the world is

---

21. Ibid., 178.

22. Jensen, ed., *The Lord and Giver of Life*. Cf. Haight, "The Holy Spirit and the Religions," in ibid., 65, 68.

23. Cobb, "The Holy Spirit and the Present Age," in ibid., 147–62.

24. Yong, "Guests, Hosts and the Holy Ghost," in ibid., 71–86.

real world when it listens for the true church. There is then no rivalry of faiths and philosophies, but only the ongoing task of achieving true complementarity in God.

As Father, Son, and Spirit, God relates ceaselessly to herself in non-competitive activity. The triune God gives herself to the church and the world: the cosmos and the *polis* are the wider horizon of God's gracious reconciling action. God is forever in an unconditionally loving, active relationality. The hallmarks of this action are, for Christians, the characteristics of Jesus as the Christ crucified and risen. For others, religious or non-religious, they are the corresponding signs of unconditional love, peace, and justice. In a sense this renders superfluous endless argument about the roles of particular persons of the Trinity, talk of Spirit helps us to imagine the constitutive relationality; however, as the Bible shows, invocation of Spirit can be toxic. Discernment is where the Christological factor comes in. In turn, thinking of Spirit helps us to understand the meaning of incarnation and of Jesus' divinity.

God is concerned not only for the religious but also for the non-religious. Many of the positive features of secular perspectives are derived from reflection on the tradition of the gospel of Jesus Christ. Through the form of Christ in the world, the religious are not the sole gate-keepers to access to the Spirit. Discarding the exclusive aspect from Barth's critique of religions, we can take the point that secular ideologies can be toxic, religious perspectives can be toxic, and Christologically framed perspectives can be equally toxic. The Spirit works now in the created order, but our perceptions of her action are partial, and our grasp of the implications through faith rather than sight, as hope and promise, understood as doxological affirmation. This does not, however, mean that we can postpone response in concrete action to the call to the hospitality of unconditional love, and trust that we may be given grace to discern its implications.

My suggestion would be that the Spirit is simultaneously the bond of love between the Father and the Son, on the one hand, and also the bond of love between the Father, the Son, and the whole created order, on the other. Spirit is not to be understood as an ethereal, vague transcendent entity hovering above the created order. Spirit is intimately related to body, it is manifested concretely and locally. The Spirit is not the sum of an infinite number of concrete instances. The presence of the Spirit is the tone that makes the music. But that would be inadequate. The Spirit is active in creating and enabling the possibilities of a reconciled creation through the structures of the cosmos, and, at a human level, through the structures of the human environment—culture, history, and language. This does not rule out singular, unique actions of the Spirit. But it understands these actions as embedded in that bond of love—that field of love, which is generated and sustained by the triune God.

The Spirit may be thought of as acting in, with, and under, and also without human action, guiding the cosmos towards fulfilment. Spirit has both theological and anthropological dimensions. St. Paul's Spirit interceding for us in prayer is a powerful symbol of the encompassing nature of the action of the Spirit, within yet encompassing humanity in the complexity of God. This intercession is one of the gifts of the Spirit to humanity, along with the gifts of love and patience. We pray for the presence of the Spirit in human affairs as a promise and warranted hope of eschatological fulfilment. The penultimate is not the ultimate, and the future of God's relationship with the reconciled order is likely to be infinitely more complex than we can imagine.

In *Hospitable God* I attempted to set out the basic elements of a comprehensive theology of hospitality.[25] We noticed Amos Yong's pleas for a pneumatological theology of hospitality. Here perhaps is the possibility of a fresh perspective on pneumatology. In medieval times the locus of the Spirit was centred on the church and the Christian tradition. At the Reformation the Spirit was related centrally to the Bible. Pietism brought appeal to the fruits of the Spirit in the heart. The Enlightenment construed this appeal to inner persuasion as a moral imperative, Schleiermacher and liberal theology linked the Spirit firmly to Christian experience of the presence of Christ. Orthodox Protestantism and Catholicism brought back the qualifiers of Bible and church, modified in the case of Barth to a Christological concentration. Pentecostalism exploded into charismatic reception of the gifts as prophetic and inspirational.

It would appear that after the crucial turn to Pietism, essentially a pre-Enlightenment Christian movement, the way was opened for an exponentially larger field of interpretation of Spirit than before. One might almost see this as a second Reformation. Where all kinds of things became possible, it was of course necessary to provide safeguards. This stimulated a return to the criteria of Bible and church, but within a radically changed landscape—a process which continues at speed, not least in the vast proliferation of Pentecostal churches. For the traditional mainline churches the Bible and the tradition of the church were to be read

---

25. Newlands and Smith, *Hospitable God*.

as reservoirs of authoritative Christian experience. For the charismatic communities this was also the case, but the readings were to be much more diversified. For all, however, the presence as such of multiple readings rendered the notion of ONE canonical construal less evidently tenable, explicitly or implicitly—exclusive readings required new statements of warrant. In this situation, alternative, fresh, and non-competitive readings become possible. We can neither reduce Spirit to Word nor Word to Spirit. It may become possible to speak of different orthodoxies with one thing in common—Hospitable Spirit—Spirit of Charity. Word, for Christian faith, is the Word incarnate, committed to the diverse and often struggling people of the world. The letter kills, but the Spirit gives life. It is perhaps in the ongoing tension of Word and Spirit that each generation must work out the shape of Christian engagement.

Part II: *Spirit in the Vertical City: Harmony and Disharmony—CHINA*

In the second half of this paper on the *City and the Spirit*, I want to connect the theological with the industrial and the global. The activity of the Spirit, the Spirit of God, creator and reconciler, is not confined to Christian contexts. The biggest cities in the world are in China. In recent years there has been a concentration in Western theology on dialogue in the Abrahamic tradition, and especially with Islam. Instead of a concentration which often focuses on an axis Christianity/Islam as contrasting cultures, it may be helpful to see both against a wider background of world cultures, to which both make important and non-competitive contributions. I'm a little concerned here about a possible drift towards a tyranny of the text. I want now to focus on Spirit in relation to East Asian religion and culture, notably in China. Like most of the five billion non-Chinese people on the planet, I know little of China. But it is always worth recalling that there are 1.6 billion people in China. The great majority of these (approximately 85 percent) would claim to have no religion, while a minority have commitments in Buddhism (7 percent), and the others to Daoism, Confucianism, and Christianity (approximately 2 percent each). Even minorities add up of course to considerable numbers.

To enter into a full scale discussion of inter-religious engagement with Chinese religions and cultures, a subject studied intensively in

China and beyond, is beyond my competence. What follows is not a contribution to this discipline but a suggestion that Christian theology may have potential to be a conversation partner, a resource in ways which only Chinese people themselves can determine, in an area where comparatively little engagement currently takes place.[26]

It is often noted that large numbers of modern Chinese people appear to have no sense of transcendence, and there is uncertainty about the status and role of ethical values. (This is not confined to China!) At the same time there has arisen awareness of a need for transcendent values, and a desire to link this contemporary quest with the long tradition of reflection on spirituality and transcendence in the history of Chinese culture. The question arises of what connections there might be between these values and the powerful residual influence of traditional folk religion in China. Here a strong sense of "multiple identities" is often a cultural reality.

Conversations

Dialogue between Western and Eastern religious thought has been developed in various ways, as in the "Boston Confucianism" of Robert Neville and his colleagues, and between John Cobb and process philosophers with Chinese philosophy. Cobb's belief that he has detected opportunities for bridge-building between central aspects of Chinese conceptuality and process thought has created ongoing conversation. It may be that aspects of Christian understanding of God as Holy Spirit may facilitate such conversation. I find process thought more useful as a tool among others for reflection than as a stand-alone framework. Somewhat as diverse approaches to the theology of the Holy Spirit in Christian tradition may lead to unforced consensus on the character of the Spirit as Holy Spirit, it may be worth reflecting whether a similar pattern might not lead to deeper engagement with Chinese religion and culture. The Spirit as the Spirit of the Third Church of the *Vertical City*, as in areas of modern China, may be a potential growth point of such dialogue.

I have tried to underline some paradoxes in this paper. On the one hand, appeal to the Spirit is a call to universal love and open relationality. Yet claims to be possessed, guided, or commanded by the Spirit have

---

26. See now Ford, "Flamenco, Tai Chi, and Six-Text Scriptural Reasoning" and symposia at the University of Aarhus and the Chinese University of Hong Kong.

been an excuse for the violation of human dignity on a small or massive scale throughout history. The doctrine of the Trinity is *par excellence* an affirmation that God is instantiated in loving relationality. Yet the Trinity has been the flashpoint for bitter division. Christianity is one dimension of that wider Abrahamic tradition, which has contributed enormously to human flourishing. Much interfaith dialogue has concentrated on working towards much needed mutual understanding and illumination. We know too that aspects of the whole Abrahamic tradition have been harmful to human flourishing, on a wide range of ethical issues, where reliance on "certainty" about God's law, and the need to enforce it, continue to create and perpetuate the injustice.

We must look beyond a pooling of traditional resources. One important source has been the European Enlightenment. Despite limitations it has contributed greatly to the protection of human dignity. The development of human rights, despite flaws and critics, has been one of the great achievements of the last two hundred years. I want to suggest that we may look to dialogue with Eastern religions, culture, and philosophy as a way of widening our horizons, and making more effective all our contributions to the human future. This is not an issue of the secular modifying the religious, but a plea for a wider equilibrium of a non-competitive nature.

It would be convenient if we could find a seamless transformation through the Spirit, an informal consensus of Abrahamic and Eastern religion, and culture with the benefits of secular reflection to temper the excesses of religious zeal. It would also be manifest nonsense. There is nothing in the violations of human rights and human dignity in Western culture in the twentieth century that cannot be comfortably matched in Eastern cultures. Pol Pot may stand as a convenient cipher. Not every Spirit, not every appeal to transcendence or immanence will do.

No magic wands. A Christian understanding of humanity as made for compassionate relationality has to reiterate the priorities of love, peace, and justice. These values continue to be subverted in the business of exploitation and discrimination. Candid engagement is only possible when suspicion and paranoia are absent. I suggest that a Christian understanding of the Spirit, deepened by the vision of the God of Jesus Christ, may still be a uniquely valuable contribution to engagement with our human future. The obstacles are obvious. There is a truth in the familiar saying that we can go global by going local. If we can't show how the love of God transforms our local ecclesial communities, we damage our credibility in the wider realm. Equally, we need to lift our eyes beyond the local to the global. This is not a call for more World Council of Churches (WCC) resolutions. It is a suggestion that theology still has a vital role to play in the providence of the transformative God.

Cultural and Political Contexts

I reflect on the role of the Spirit in public theology. After a short visit to China in 2011, I was curious to imagine how a Christian understanding of Spirit might contribute to the development of the public sphere in China. There is, of course, a huge amount of literature on religion and politics in China, much of it in Mandarin, which I do not read. I found a starting point in Duncan Hewitt's highly readable *Getting Rich First: Life in a Changing China*,[27] an accessible survey by a writer who lives with his Chinese wife in Shanghai, and in Zhibin Xie's *Religious Diversity and Public Religion in China*.[28]

Hewitt's focus is on the changing environment—construction and destruction, education and the media, aspiration and inequality, moral values, religion, and globalization—viewed through the power of specific examples. Zhibin Xie discusses the public status of religion in China, relating his analysis to the US debate on this topic. He looks at Rawls' and Audi's discussion of restraints on religion in political life, and Rawls' "wide view of public life," contrasting this with the pleas of Wolterstorff and others for religious moral involvement. He examines the relationship between religious freedom and religious expression, the value of pluralism, and the role of religion in public political culture in a democratic China. He concludes that religion needs a balance between freedom from state interference and ambitions for the direct exercise of political power, taking moral positions publicly but respecting other groups.

What of religion, and particularly Christianity? Clearly Western theology cannot aim to influence the development of spiritual values in China on our terms. It is perhaps unlikely that Christianity, even as it grows at an astonishing speed, will become more influential than the culture of one of the many ethnic minorities. Most urban professionals, academics, and politicians will still embrace a largely secular vision, construed in Chinese terms. For the foreseeable future, the church of

---

27. Hewitt, *Getting Rich First: Life in a Changing China*.
28. Zhibin Xie, *Religious Diversity and Public Religion in China*.

the intellectuals will remain a comparatively small group, and the main growth will be of the rural Christianity which blends traditional local culture with a strong conservative and millenarian faith. We may see in China some of the tensions now evident in relations between some African and some Western churches. Matters are not helped by memories of The Denunciations, a movement during the Cultural revolution where more liberal Christians sometimes concurred in and even initiated the denunciation of conservative Christians as unpatriotic.

This tension is epitomized in reactions to the work of Bishop K. Ting, (Ding Guangxun), probably the most prominent twentieth-century Chinese Christian leader. Ting sought, and demonstrated the pitfalls of, an Anglican *Via Media* in the tradition of *Lux Mundi*, aiming for a theology of evolution, with emphasis on "justification by love" based on the Cosmic Christ. It has been suggested by Jieren Li[29] that this model is now too "top down," and not appropriate to a world of post-globalization and a market economy. There are varieties of polity and practice between official churches and unofficial "house churches," and perhaps the embryonic so-called "Third Church" of urban professionals. There has been a strong growth of Pentecostalism, not least in the *True Jesus* church of Taiwan, and in groups with a strong eschatological or millennial emphasis. These conservative groups may actually be closer to the ethos of traditional Chinese local religion than more liberal trends. One of the most balanced assessments of these tensions is still the study by Hunter and Chan.[30]

In the last twenty years there has been a quest in China for a "socialist spiritual civilization," to replace the idealism of traditional Marxism. This has proved hard to define, and harder to promote, given the increasing awareness of diversity among the Chinese peoples. "One-size-fits-all" slogans are not persuasive. What can still be offered in fellowship to this complex civilization? Reflection on examples of a chastened but persistent faith may be of value. We have suffered in the past from creating authoritarian church structures and authoritarian theologies. Eastern religion, and particularly Buddhism, respects kenosis, humility, self-emptying, though of course it has often been just as authoritarian as Western theologies. Against the taint of cultural imperialism, Western and indeed Eastern, we need non-competitive structures and we need

---

29. Jieren Li, *In Search of the Via Media between Christ and Marx*.
30. Hunter and Chan, *Protestantism in Contemporary China*.

to listen. In relation to Confucian notions of *harmony* we may offer a vision of the Spirit of God which is centred on unconditional, relational love. No doubt such notions are already there—we can only offer to make common cause in their articulation. In such ways, we may hope perhaps to share the fruits of our own difficult learning process, while not prescribing how spirituality in China is to be moulded. These are naive suggestions for a conversation of daunting proportions. I shall be happy if I have succeeded in bringing the subject up a little higher on your Internet search list.

I come back to the city—in this case the *Vertical City*. From no skyscrapers in 1999, Shanghai now has almost 2000 skyscrapers, many of them immensely tall. People continue to migrate into cities from the countryside—now almost 60 percent of the population. If current trends continue, Christianity will play an increasing role in Chinese culture in the future—though the total is unlikely to go much beyond 5 percent. There are liberal Christians and also "cultural Christians," mainly university scholars who have come to Christianity through the academic study of religion. The majority in China, as in Africa, are likely to belong to deeply conservative churches. Historically there have been deeply rooted conflicts between the various groups—the potential problem of the double minority. Conservative Christians may be dominant in the churches, but perhaps far from the bulk of their fellow citizens, in terms of cultural, ethical, and political appreciation.

One thing which these groups have in common, is suspicion of cultural imperialism from outside. What may Western theology and church still offer? A powerful existing connection is with deeply conservative and economically well placed groups in the USA. But the transplantation of something like this would not be helpful for China. Even if thought successful, it would remain a force among the 5 percent minority, probably not conducive to encouraging engagement from the 95 percent majority of Chinese people. There is also a small but longstanding liberal Christian tradition, largely around the universities. The stage could be set for a parallel series of dialogues of the deaf.

Complexities

The potential for Christianity in China is great, but there are problems. Consider South Korea. Here there has been huge growth in Christianity, often linked to a perception of Western values and customs as creating material prosperity. This has led in Protestant circles to considerable inter-church conflict and often to an intolerance of other religions. The result is a decline in Christian profession. In China there is huge appetite for Western ideas among the young. If Christianity is assimilated on the same basis as Levi's, similar issues arise. The growth of a strongly conservative Christianity may lead to intolerance of other faiths, become a challenge to the government's declared aim of achieving social harmony, and eventually decline, as it has in Europe. There will be occasions when Christian defence of human dignity may clash with governmental policy. But a Chinese Christianity closely resembling, indeed perhaps embracing, "Tea Party" style politics would not be a step forward.

When we look at contemporary Christianity in Africa, where an increasing percentage of the world's Christians are to be found, the results have hardly been always positive. There has been reaction against colonialism, and the associated missionary enterprise. There have been outstanding examples of Christian and political leadership—Mandela and Tutu. Yet the record of nominally Christian populations in advancing democratic procedures and human rights has been very mixed. Strongly Christian states have been unable to check high levels of corruption, while human rights are often neglected and even minimal levels of charitable giving are not reached by comparatively wealthy states like Nigeria. While the genocide in Rwanda, with a more than 90 percent Christian population can be seen as a real exception, aggressive Christian actions in other states do not make for inter-religious harmony or social tolerance. Even South Africa, source of hope after the Truth and Reconciliation Commission, has deep residual problems. These uncomfortable facts—and we can certainly not hold up the UK as a shining example—cannot be avoided.

Facing this challenge it seems to me that a contribution which emphasizes the varieties of the forms of the Spirit of Jesus Christ in the world could be helpful in promoting engagement over a constantly changing landscape. Emphasis on areas of convergence between visions of the dynamic action of the Spirit might facilitate that coming together of evangelical, catholic, and progressive faith which is essential to discipleship—the opposite of a quasi-mystical amorphous amalgam. Bigotry and intolerance on the one hand, and a lack of commitment to the core of the gospel on the other, could perhaps be better seen by all of us for what they are. A Christian community so related, could make a sane contribution to development—a local development with potentially enormous global implications.

Effective conversation does not take place with eyes wide shut. This applies especially to polite academic exchanges and conferences which are truly important and yet sometimes laden with political ambiguity. The horrors that have sometimes accompanied the Western tradition are plain for all to see. In China, despite the real changes since the chaos of the Great Leap Forward and the Cultural Revolution, things happen that are hard to understand. For example, in June 2011, while Premier Wen Jiabao was in Europe discussing trade and human rights, President al-Bashir of Sudan, wanted by the ICC for alleged genocide, flew to China to meet President Hu Jintao and strengthen diplomatic ties. At the same time, the famous dissident artist Ai Weiwei was fined over £1 million for alleged financial irregularities and the Nobel Prizewinner Liu Xiabao, a supporter of Charter 08 calling for democratic reform, (see Human Rights In China website) was serving an eleven year prison sentence for "inciting subversion."[31] In 2013 problems are ongoing. On the other hand, Chinese delegates were involved in the drafting of the United Nations Declaration on Human Rights of 1948, which could be said to be eminently compatible with Confucian values, and in Confucian thought there is a long tradition on the importance of human dignity. The insight that human dignity involves identity as relationality and reciprocity could be seen as a particularly Asian contribution.[32]

Conclusion

I have not considered in any detail the existing religions and social philosophies of China. Here we find a long tradition of tolerance of variety. There is a surprising amount of discussion of Christianity in modern Chinese fiction. Confucian thought has been the most pervasive, but it has not usually been as aggressive as the Abrahamic religions have been. There has been hugely varied discussion of transcendence and immanence, of ethical values and ethical conduct. "It is always better to give than to receive" (Acts 20:35) has been perceived as an ironic comment on much ecumenical discussion. Simply to be self-giving may not be what is

---

31 *The Times*, June 29, 2011. For Liu Xiabao cf. HRIC website.

32. Berthrong, "Human Rights and Responsibilities," 199f., and Twiss, "Confucian Values and Human Rights," 283f.

needed. We should be prepared to receive, and just to make available, to be acted on by our conversation partners as and when they choose, what we may have to offer. That is what I have been attempting to do here.

The Spirit and the Vertical City. It seems to me that we can begin from the particularity and the inspiration of our own traditions, intellectual and spiritual. But we cannot stop there. We need to recognise the global dimensions of Christian service to humanity, more than we have often done: hence my concentration on China. We need to develop fresh expressions of dialogue, negotiating with difficult partners as necessary, bringing to the table what we have to offer, neither timidly nor dogmatically. For each of us this will involve different insights, trusting in the conversation to sift out the better proposals. We have much inclusivity to make up. We seek to express a vision with human dignity and social justice at its core, and we can never give up on this priority. The churches will always remain key pointers to the transcendent love of God, sometimes despite themselves. We have to go forward profoundly chastened, with chastened hope, and without drawing too many premature conclusions.

2

Faith after Faith—
Perplexed and Unperplexed

*Ferguson Lecture University
of Manchester, 2013*

Are you perplexed by faith? Tens of millions of your fellow human beings are not. They have faith, packaged in assured certainties about the reality and the shape of faith, or they do not have faith—it's no longer a useful topic of conversation. End of story. These are perfectly reasonable views to hold, and there is no need to regard them as inappropriate or even wicked. But there might be a way of understanding faith as embracing a transformative perplexity, which may be an option still worth considering. I don't mean just a complexification—often a synonym for fudge (although fudge at the right time can be nutritious). How this might work out I'd like to explore in this lecture. Most of my examples will be taken from Christianity, which I know best. Those of you who are more familiar with other faiths will hopefully find some interesting data to compare. This is, in many ways, a lecture on the blindingly obvious, which often seems to hide itself in plain sight.

Faith and Ambiguity

The last half century has seen endless demolition and reconstruction, in various shapes and forms, of the Christian faith. Exactly fifty years ago there appeared J. A. T. Robinson's *Honest to God* which was scathingly criticized on all sides but undoubtedly one of the most influential pieces of British theology in the twentieth century, and written by a very considerable scholar. This was all part of a "Death of God" discussion which took in very different writers from Dietrich Bonhoeffer to Tom Altizer. In twenty-first-century Britain, a new debate about the existence of God erupted, somewhat to the surprise of most people, who had thought that evolution had moved on from this topic.

In the background there looms a disastrous decline in church attendance in Britain and in much of Europe generally, in no way disguised by valiant attempts at reinterpretation—believing without belonging doesn't greatly help the diocesan coffers—and a pretence to business as usual. The core of the religious establishment seemed as impregnable as ever, but the waters were already lapping close to the foundations. *Kirchendaemmerung*[1] easily follows *Goetterdaemmerung*. This had, of course, all happened in the early church and been overcome, but history does not always repeat itself so conveniently.

There were a number of different strands to the new debate, and it was at least gratifying that this suggested more than indifference. Most prominent was the Richard Dawkins approach—frontal assault. This could easily be dismissed as simply another form of fundamentalism—one simplistic certainty against another. But despite the learned rebuttals, there were basic questions to be answered. Bluntly put, what was the empirical evidence for the existence of God? The theological arguments were certainly coherent, but did they correspond to any sort of empirical reality? Well of course not, in the nature of the case. But was this special pleading, and did not faith's appeal encompass historicity and the reality of the created order? Then there was the Christopher Hitchens approach, arguing that the banal realities of evil and suffering, sometimes random and sometimes actually created by religion, constituted an insurmountable barrier to the presence of a loving God. This tack was followed by A. C. Grayling and others.

Defending Faith

What could be said for the defence? Philosophers of religion were able to underline the unsophisticated nature of much of this argument, demonstrating to their own satisfaction at least, that the God of the critics

---

1. Graf, *Kirchendaemmerung*.

was not the God whom they worshipped. She was a much more complex and in some ways a residually mysterious God. Philosophical theologians could argue that the structure of the universe was not incompatible with orthodox Christian belief, and indeed, could sometimes be seen as tending to confirm aspects of beliefs held on other grounds. Religion could be held to be generally good for a society, whether the existence of God could be proved or not. From the cave art of prehistoric Spain, to the cutting edge discoveries of contemporary neuroscience and cognitive theory of the mind, as well as the nature of dark matter and dark energy permeating everything, all kinds of unexpected things happened which stretched the imagination beyond the quotidian and demolished any ideas of a closed universe as the arbiter of our fate. It was somewhat striking that the paradigms discovered sometimes tended to reflect the ecclesial and even denominational preferences of their distinguished scientific supporters. Behind this stood, *inter alia*, the impressive financial resources of the Templeton Foundation, a *deus ex machina* willing to rescue the sparsely funded world of modern academia, with its emphasis on business models and the generation of capital reserves. None of this cultural baggage detracted from the weight of the actual arguments, and the need to assess all the data in a judicious manner.

There were other forms of defence of faith. Different and original was Francis Spufford, whose focus was not on empirical evidence but on the sense of the presence of God as a powerful reality in his day-to-day consciousness. Granted that this presence might not meet some sorts of standards of proof, it was a significant force in his daily life. From the point of view of the professional theologian, this left gaps to be filled, but it constituted an attractive and, for some, persuasive option.

Much of this debate has been succinctly analyzed by David Fergusson in his excellent Gifford Lectures. In *Faith and Its Critics*, Fergusson explores the strengths, weaknesses, opportunities, and threats of religion in ways which might well suggest that we are hard wired to believe in Fergusson, not to mention, believing in God.

Not many stones are left unturned. Fergusson explores different varieties of atheism. Arguments ranging from traditional natural theology to theories of multiverses are succinctly deployed: they lead into a discussion about the explanatory power of Darwinism. We are soon deep into the delights of the flagellum bacterium, intelligent design theory, Marx, Freud, and cognitive science—a miracle of miniaturization. There doesn't have to be a God, but we are encouraged to think that, if we have come to believe in God, perhaps in part on other grounds, this is certainly not unreasonable.

What about morality? The selfish gene may grow into the cooperative gene—the selfless gene. The Good Samaritan promises marginally more congenial company than the flagellum bacterium. What of moral concern? "What it suggests is that while evolutionary forces may have generated powers of empathy and moral reasoning in human societies, these then have a capacity for more independent reflection and assessment that is not bound by evolutionary drives."[2] Is religion bad for your health? Saints, martyrs, and terrorists? Fergusson is careful not to place Professor Dawkins explicitly within this taxonomy. Nasty things continue to happen under the guise of religion. Are religious moderates no more than chastened fanatics? It is true that Al-Qaeda continues to attract young people, but there are counter-examples.

What about the title deeds of religion—sacred texts that become texts of terror? Fundamentalism is bad for your health. The interpretation of Scripture is never fixed or settled. Dialogue, interfaith reading, conversation is already happening. There is a sympathetic analysis of contemporary developments in Islam. Conclusion: "Far from being an egregious act of unreason in the face of contrary evidence, a commitment seems an unavoidable feature of our human condition." End of an alternative story.

Times change and we change. A lot has happened since 2008—we're now onto iPhone5 (I'm not being paid for this advertisement by Apple, by the way). Cultures shift. We live in a world in which there is daily waste and disaster on an unimaginable scale, though it can just about be imagined in fragments in the debris of individual shattered lives. Here too there are traces of huge compassion, usually invisible to us who are external observers.

Faith after faith. Let me try to underline the massive impact of changes in the last century, which have turned the world upside down a few times, and which have affected theology and church much more decisively than we often imagine. Everything has changed. Some things, we may reflect, have remained the same. But the frame in which they are set has shifted sharply. We can see this in struggles everywhere, in global politics and economics, in communication, and in lifestyle. The arts strikingly reflected the turmoil of the twentieth century, in sculpture

---

2. Fergusson, *Faith and its Critics*, 108.

Henry Moore and Barbara Hepworth, in painting Lucien Freud and Pablo Picasso, and in music. In Manchester we think at once of the New Music Group, Harrison Birtwhistle, Peter Maxwell Davies, and Alexander Goehr. It is significant too that Sandy Goehr was to turn to the Japanese Noh Theatre for inspiration. Culture, like politics, went global. You could Skype people in Japan in an instant. If there could be no poetry after the Holocaust, could there be theology? Theology too exploded into the radical and the reactionary, with everything in between. Churches could save the appearances, but there was tectonic shift underneath. You could still dream of Little Gidding, but the view outside your window would more likely be of high rise towers, and your dream might suddenly switch to high rise towers imploding.

A Cumulative Case, Reconsidered

I come back to my first category of perplexities. It's often assumed that we must choose between the paths of fideism or rationalism. This is not a sensible dichotomy. Faith in God can't be proved by reason. But it can be shown to be consonant with reason, not against reason. Arguments from various perspectives can be deployed in constructing a cumulative case. Here from my perspective is a place for the role of tradition. I still think the traditional combination of arguments from *notitia, assensus,* and *fiducia*—information, assent, and trust, remain as appropriate now as they have always done.

Information. Christian faith has always had its mystical aspect, its awareness of the hiddenness of God. But it has always been based on the testimony of what the Old Testament scholar Gerhard Von Rad long ago called the double choir of those who came before and those who came after. It has involved an assent to this tradition which is different from assent to the data in a train timetable or whatever. This is an assent which may have life-changing consequences, sometimes totally dramatic, sometimes understated. And then trust, *fiducia*, sometimes rendered as *fiducia promissionis*, trust not in something, I know not what, but in the promise of the presence of God which the gospel declares.

How this is imagined and assimilated depends on the historical circumstances in which faith is received. In some traditions Christian faith has been strikingly illuminated by reflection on the centrality of incarnation, new birth, new creation, a new social order. In others, the catalyst has been the cross, the suffering of God, the cost of sin, and the cost of discipleship. Each of these icons of spiritual meditation has been important to faith, and each has been in danger of turning from icon to idol. There are risks in all theological ideas and in all spirituality, and that is part of the struggle of faith.

A further facet of faith is often seen in the notion of obedience. In reflection on obedience, countless good acts have taken place, and countless bad acts too. Obedience, it has been said, is the subtlest form of temptation. Obedience to God, we may say, is different from obedience to human agents. Yet obedience is one of the icons most easily turned into idols—what we find convenient to imagine as obedience may just be an exercise in self-delusion or in coercion of others. It is also, however, a notion which we find hard to honour in a contemporary culture which greatly prizes freedom. Yet faith involves a call to discipleship, to following in the way of Jesus, reflecting the unconditional love of God. Faith is a current in human existence which constantly eludes stereotyping.

St. Paul may not have got everything right about faith. He laid huge stress on faith. But he recognized definitively that faith without hope, and faith without love, is ultimately sterile. If I were to think of one book about faith, which scarcely mentions the word faith at all, but in my own view is one of the most accessible recent fruits of a life of faith, it would be Archbishop Desmond Tutu's *God Has a Dream*. Tutu was not infallible, but perhaps that belongs to the fragility of goodness, and that too is part of the mystery of faith.

The traditional appeal to reason, revelation, and experience has been around for a long time and it remains as sensible as it has always done. Such a complex strand of faith is always going to look very different from the models demolished by hostile critics. History too, in its contingency and capacity for multiple and contested interpretation, is an important component of Christian faith: necessary but not sufficient. Revelation, knowledge, however incomplete of things that we could not have discovered for ourselves, is key. Of course, all of this comes through cultural traditions, the tradition of the gospel as interpreted and lived out in different times and at different places. This makes the nature of faith itself essentially contested in some areas, though exhibiting also a core of basic structuring elements. None of this is remotely new, yet its formative consequences for the shape of faith are routinely ignored in contemporary debate.

As far as correlation with science is concerned, a Christian understanding of creation entails that there has to be a close correlation between scientific and theological understandings of the natural world. "The world" used to refer almost exclusively to the planet we inhabit, and that remains our chief concern as human beings. But we must now see it in the context of an unimaginable number of universes moving apart at an ever accelerating pace to infinity, perhaps including parallel universes constructed in ways which we can scarcely imagine. This raises hugely challenging issues about how we can imagine divine action in relation to us as human beings. St. Thomas never had to worry about a quantum vacuum! Yet the ground rules of traditional constructive argument about primary and secondary action may still help us to see *what* might be possible, even when we can't see *how* things may be possible. The work of cosmologists and neurologists have at least helped to clarify what we don't know, and produced suggestions about what may be conceivable. It remains important not to go beyond what can honestly be claimed.

Ethical Perplexities

At the end of the day, whether it's true or not, is religion good for you? Perhaps it depends where you are. If you are open to the notion of faith, a cautious, low key, and still modestly confident apologia might just help to tip the balance for you. Some might have wished for a more extended, perhaps more constructive account of faith. But this is a case where less is probably effectively more.

So far we have been thinking of logical, metaphysical, and scientific arguments about faith. There is however, another stream of issues that are at least as important. When we are absolutely certain of the details of the truth of faith, then those who disagree easily become enemies of the truth, and must be dealt with as such. We come to the ethical perplexities about faith. Untold violence has been perpetrated in the name of religion—and indeed of atheism. It is true of course that much violence has been used against Christians, and that as much violence has been unleashed by non-Christians, not least in the last hundred years. But that does not solve the faith-dissolving character of Christian violence. The early Christians were sometimes merciless in their treatments of heretics, as were the medievals, and indeed Christian groups in every age. Contemporary citizens are aware of continuing discrimination against minority groups, more subtle yet no less damning. Tangible discrimination against racial minorities, disabled people, sometimes older people or single people, and most absurdly of all against women, is not so far away, and is, in part, at least perceived to have the churches' blessing. Jimmy Carter, former President of the United States, has recently written movingly about his decision to leave the Southern Baptist Convention after six decades of active commitment, because of continuing discrimination against women. Only in cloud-cuckooland could we have a Church of England without women bishops in 2013. In 2012, Manchester celebrated the centenary of perhaps the most famous member of its University staff, Alan Turing. Today, Turing would most probably have joined the Bishops in the House of Lords. It was not like that half a century ago. The churches still have a long way to go on sexuality, and their obsessions, not unlike their obsession with witches, have littered the landscape with random casualties on all sides.

There are issues too in medical ethics which tax the powers of the most highly qualified professional experts. Churches often blithely pronounce anathemas which may ruin the quality of life in times of greatest need for compassion, whether at the beginning or the end of life. As has often been said in irony, but with a certain truth, one might think that the churches' continued life in these circumstances is itself a ground for belief in the existence of God.

I paint a dark picture. But if I did not believe that the perplexities can be addressed, and that faith can still be, despite all, a precious gift of God, I would not be giving this lecture. We can learn a great deal from the professionals in theology and church. But perhaps today, we can also absorb the message most effectively with the help of those whom we have traditionally discounted.

We turn again to the serious ethical perplexities. Here I look for help from the ethical specializations, from medical ethics, environmental ethics, political ethics, and legal ethics. To refuse the substantial research which is already there would be arrogant, foolish, both. But I also look to contributions from the constituencies which have traditionally be marginalized, disenfranchised, constantly discussed, and disposed without having a real voice in decisions. There is no doubt that Christian faith owes a great deal to white male thinkers who have often envisaged God almost exclusively in their own image. In this they were simply unable to jump out of their cultural skins, as we all are. Today, our cultural traditions have now the possibility of making us a little less exclusive. To bring different voices into the conversation is not simply to substitute one monopoly for another. It is to try to harness resources to which we have long been blind.

A chorus of pleas that the emancipatory disciplines have long passed their sell-by dates has a kernel of truth, but it is more often a rearguard defence of exclusivity in the name of postmodernity. To some extent, the liberative impulse has succeeded only in telling us about itself, redressing the balance, rather than telling us about God and about faith. Women have been able to grow in faith, often exemplary faith, under the ministry of men, for two thousand years. Yet more recently women have undoubtedly provided new avenues for imagining the God of human beings which have enhanced the bounds of our imagination, and therefore the potential of our response in faith. I think of Elizabeth Schuessler Fiorenza, Martha Nussbaum, Catherine Keller, and many others. Black theologians help to modify and go beyond the limits of existing spiritual imagination and engagement. The names that spring most immediately to mind are Martin Luther King, and Desmond Tutu. Gay theologians include Mark Jordan, James Alison, Jeffrey John. The same applies to advocacy for disabled people and the mentally challenged—Nancy Eiseland. God is not simply the perfect totally abled athlete. There is a need too for substantive contributions from people who do not themselves personally self-identify with these constituencies. Entering the solidarity of others is a litmus test.

The Role of Experience, Individual, Communal, Vulnerable

Where does all this lead us? Have we been hunting for the ghost in the machine, the proverbial will o'the wisp? We have seen that there can be a constructive appeal to reason as a guide to an important dimension of faith. St. Paul's appeal to a reason for the hope that is in us remains as valid as ever. Few of us would consider an invitation to blind credulity worth contemplating. We noted that an appeal to revelation need not be an appeal to a theological fundamentalism. Fundamentalists, we may think, are not perplexed enough. Christian faith claims that through revelation we may come to a knowledge, not complete but sufficiently reliable, of things that we could not have discovered for ourselves. This comes through the multiplex strands of the tradition of the gospel, the resource of written word, oral communication, sacramental worship, and *experience* of life in community that flows as a cultural tradition through the centuries. Christians understand this tradition as a tradition with a difference. Through this tradition there is experience of what is called grace, the presence of the Spirit of God in human life. Divine presence is not confined to this tradition, but through this tradition it is understood by Christians to mediate the presence of a Trinitarian God. Nothing here is new, but it may remind us of the multifaceted dimensions of an understanding of God, which is not always recognizable in contemporary discussion.

Experience. Experience always has a subjective aspect and can be challenged. The experience of faith is the ground of a decision and an ability to trust. This is often, though not always, a struggle which repeats itself. It's part of our everyday experience of our world. It may be understood not as experience of experience, but experience of God. The content of faith's perception of God is imagined as not fully conceivable, based on the tradition of the gospel in all its dimensions over three millennia, and understood within the sphere of all our human knowledge of human religion and human development. It is a vision of creation and reconciliation, centred upon God incarnate in Jesus Christ and present though the Holy Spirit. This is the shape of Christian faith, and because it is a dynamic process, it is often said that it matters more that God has faith in us than that we have faith in God. Such faith should reflect the nature of God as unconditional love, catholic and evangelical, inclusive and generous, though of course it often falls short.

The exploration of faith as experienced has been much criticized in modern theology. Karl Barth stressed that theology was about the sovereignty of God and not our faith—though of course he also came back frequently to speak of faith—this was not always noticed. The centrality of faith was stressed by Friedrich Schleiermacher, notably in his hugely influential *The Christian Faith*. This is often seen by Neo-orthodoxy, Radical Orthodoxy, and other conservative theologies as the *fons et origo* of a liberal theology which fatally compromises apostolic truth for the sake of cultural assimilation. This, of course, can and did on occasion happen. But over-reaction has its own dangers, as the recent eclipse of the theology of Vatican II and of theologians inspired by it, notably Karl Rahner and Eduard Schillebeeckx, has eloquently demonstrated. Despite the critics, faith that emphasizes hiddenness and struggle, from the medieval mystics to Luther, and to the "modest" theology of contemporary writing, will doubtless remain a vital strand of Christian spirituality.

It sometimes surprises me that in all the talk in recent debate about the existence of God there is usually little mention of faith. Faith need not mean fideism. But faith is faith in God, and the concept of God without the dimension of personal engagement is a very limited concept. Schleiermacher wrote of the centrality of a sense of dependence in God. This was famously mocked by Hegel, and Hegel's critique has become almost axiomatic in recent theology. Yet the affirmation that "[a]ll my hope on God is founded" is basic to Christian life and worship. Faith as trust in God is basic to the theology of Karl Barth, despite his strong advocacy of the objective rather than the subjective dimension of revelation. It is in the Lutheran tradition that reflection on faith as key, on justification by faith as "der Angefochtene Glaube," the faith that has to be struggled for, continues to be most eloquently expressed. In Anglo-Saxon theology we have been acutely aware of the dangers of an appeal to faith. Yet faith remains absolutely central to talk of God and a living belief in a living God.

There is a particularly striking picture of faith in Rudolf Bultmann's seminal commentary on the Fourth Gospel, in his treatment of the parable of the vine and its branches in chapter 15. He stresses that faith is not something that we do for God, but is a resource that God enables us to have. As the branches of the vine draw life from their attachment to the stem, so our life of faith flows from God's reaching out to us.[3] Appeal to faith is sometimes construed as invocation of a warm feeling of subjective well-being, often precisely absent in times of deep stress. There can be a sense not of the presence, but of the absence of God. This too is part of the complexity of faith, which has objective as well as subjective elements. Faith is not faith in some vacuous blank, but in the triune God.

Faith has a vital personal dimension. A God with whom we can have no relationship is not of great interest. But faith need not be entirely individualistic. Faith is faith with others in community. It comes from a tradition and invites into relationality. Christian faith specifically direct us to hospitable engagement with those who are at the point of greatest need.

---

3. Bultmann, *Das Evangelium des Johannes*, 412.

Culture and Conversation

We come to faith among the currents of broad cultural traditions. This is another notion which makes the theologians nervous. Is that all there is? Not if faith is faith in the God of Jesus Christ. Is the notion of inculturation the first step to towards dilution and corruption? Frequently it has been. But the abuse need not take away the proper use, and the notion of faith as sustained and enriched by a deep cultural tradition can help us to see more of the dynamic of faithful formation and practice.

Here is a cultural tradition in which we are invited to participate. We may choose to understand this tradition and its places of worship as a sort of background wallpaper which we occasionally visit because we find the atmosphere, the buildings, the music, and the liturgy meaningful. We may become much more intensively committed to a life of discipleship in prayer and service. Perhaps we should be careful not to prescribe too much, always to know what is best for people. The God of unconditional love who is central to faith is generous and inclusive: all are welcome.

All these elements, of faith, presence, and cultural tradition, are linked, in Christian understanding, with the Holy Spirit. The Spirit creates and sustains faith in a transcendent God. And in being the Spirit of the incarnate Christ, the Spirit guides us to engagement with the structures of the created order and human society. This has been particularly emphasized in liberation theologies. Faith is best seen in its own light and its own context. Apart from this, it ceases to be to be interesting, except to professional sociologists of religion.

Faith is best seen in its own light. It is faith in the God of Jesus Christ, the God of the Qur'an, the God of other faiths. But faith calls us, as David Kelsey has strikingly put it, to an eccentric existence, or perhaps we could say, to an exocentric existence. We are called out of the world to be called back into the world. When we cease to be there for others, and especially with suffering others, we subvert the essence of faith. This is why constant negativity in judgemental church pronouncements is such a disaster.

If I have faith to move mountains but have not love. . . . The problem of *odium theologicum* was well known as an unfortunate by-product of polemics in the past. But it remains a toxic and often unacknowledged accompaniment of much faith and theology. Why so? Faith involves trust and commitment. In some parts of the world at least, and for some time, we have been able to avoid wars of religion and even the openly vituperative polemic of the past. We are now angelic in our theological perspectives, at least in academia. Well perhaps not quite. There are still countless opportunities for constructive change in the nature of much theological dialogue, not least at home. We might consider that intellectual tribalism and rivalry, though not to be recommended, preserves important freedoms of speech in the academic world. Yet when these group perspectives are linked to power, influence, career progression, and financial resources, we are moving very far away from the mainsprings of faith in a loving God.

In dialogue involving the central structural elements of faith we need to retain the courage of our convictions, to work through rational argument and to commend this through advocacy and persuasion. All too often this is tangled up with a less than legitimate exercise of power. When conversations come to include coercion, faith has been betrayed. How to achieve an effective non-competitive form of dialogue which still allows for conviction and the establishment, of the best available solutions, remains a challenge. A first step perhaps lies in the full recognition of the provisionality of all our perspectives. We see through a glass darkly.

Dialogue Contributions

Dialogue needs some substantive proposals to dialogue about. Dialogue about dialogue gets you nowhere. I'd like to go back to some basic elements of Christian faith—not as framing the dialogue but as *one* starting point. In the Bible we see images of faith involving the three elements of assent and trust on the basis of information. This is not a faith in an empty void, it involves rational reflection, and it includes commitment. These elements may build up slowly or quickly, and may be imagined in many different ways. At different times and places, different elements have been stressed. Within these elements the content of the information in its historical and doctrinal substance has been a constant variable in public worship and community sentiment, and has been mirrored in our individual consciousness. Faith, it is said, is caught rather than taught. But it is more than the Kierkegaardian leap of some Protestant devotion. All of these factors have appeared, between a blind devotion, and a purely rational calculation.

Beyond the three elements I have mentioned lie other factors which help to shape faith—the focal points of word and sacrament, the practice of prayer. None are infallible. The cult of the Word and the cult of the Sacrament can be subverted by institutions. There is such a thing as bad faith, inauthentic belief and practice. We have to try to minimize the negative and to maximise the positive dimensions of faith. Faith is not fanaticism, and it is not a purely casual calculation either. Faith has consequences.

Is there a faith instinct built in, perhaps hard wired into the human brain? If so, does this stem from the action of God in creating humanity in her image, thus with aninalienable human dignity? Christians believe that we are creatures of the loving action of God in creation. Do we need faith in God in order to be moral? We do not. Does faith always lead to moral actions, to social justice, to generosity and hospitality? History shows us that it does not. The pursuit of freedom and justice is an immensely valuable quest by itself. If that is all that is available to us, that is still crucially important to human flourishing.

Why then consider faith? Not because it may fill some perceived gap in our lives—though it may do this too—but because it is just there, a possibility which may become an actuality. There is a story, not the only story in town about God but the Christian story, built up through human experience over millennia, the story of a God who has created the universe and has created humanity for a loving relationship with himself. This carries an invitation, neither self-evidently conclusive nor totally vacuous. When this invitation has been perceived and acknowledged, perhaps over a long period of time, the experience has often been thought of as a gift, the gift of faith. It may be imagined as something out there which has always been there and makes a difference to our understanding of ourselves and our fellow human beings. *Fecisti enim nos ad te, et cor nostrum est inquietum donec requiescat in te,* as they say in the outer suburbs of Manchester.

As faith seeks further understanding from reflecting on its own tradition in the light of contemporary experience, this has come to be seen as the gift of the Holy Spirit, a consequence of the coming of God into human history.

Faith has consequences for our actions, because the tradition of the gospel points us to core values—characterizing love, justice, and generosity in the context of the events concerning Jesus as the instantiation of God. The result will not necessarily trump other sorts of moral consideration, but faith will hope to add a deeply significant dimension to human reflection. History suggests that it can and often does make hugely valuable contributions to both individual and communal welfare.

Should we strive to respect faith in God in its many different manifestations around the world? Yes we should. But is everything done in the name of faith to be respected? Clearly this is where agreement may break down. Looking at the history of Europe, faith which leads to coercion cannot be respected and has to be actively opposed. The deaths in the name of faith of countless Muslims in the Balkan wars of the late twentieth century was clearly a prime example of bad faith and a wake up call to complacency. Examples from different religions could easily be multiplied.

Even in less clear cut instances, there will always be scope for discussion about the implications of faith. We struggle to find the best understanding that we can achieve, and this may develop in different ways throughout our lives.

Sometimes faith fails: it seems finally impossible to have faith in God. There are just too many negatives. There is no sense of the presence of God, only of absence. At these times, it has been helpful to reflect again that what matters is not that we believe in God, but that God believes in us. Reflection on the substantive content of faith, the Christian narrative of the life, death and resurrection of Jesus Christ, memories of word and sacrament, consciousness of the faith of a long tradition of Christian devotion, have served to sustain faith through darkness. To such experience the blackest periods of the last century bear much profound testimony, a light that may seem to go out completely, but has always come back. That is in itself a solid ground of faith. Sadly, faith does not always come back. But for many of us, the shared testimony of many has been enough to light our way through the shadows. On this note of chastened confidence, rather than triumphant assertion, I'm going to stop.

3

Luther's Ghost—
Ein gluehender Backofen voller Liebe

From Theology in Conversation, Festschrift for Daniel Migliore.

I

IN THE DECADE OF student revolution, Dan Migliore, Darrell Guder, and I were all studying theology in Germany, the land of Martin Luther. We did not know each other. We were of course, and obviously remain, archetypal revolutionaries. We have since had long association with Reformed theology. But what of Luther, whom I guess we all read surreptitiously from time to time? In this essay I want to look briefly at the role of Luther—or rather, a kaleidoscopic variety of Luthers—in Reformed theology. The reason lies in a simple truth: Luther is often excoriated but ever present as a sort of "hidden hand" in Reformed thought from Calvin to Barth and beyond.

It might seem that this is an odd topic for a Scottish theologian. After all, Luther did not get off to a particularly promising start in the Scottish Reformation. On the morning of February 29th 1528, a meeting of top Scottish theologians decided—it being too damp for golf—to condemn Patrick Hamilton, our first genuinely Lutheran theologian, to be burned that afternoon. Sadly they had overlooked the fact that no suitable store of combustible material had been arranged. Still, they were able to burn him a little at noon before taking lunch, a little more before adjourning for a Starbucks in the afternoon, and finish the day with a celebratory fellowship barbecue just after six o'clock in the evening.[1]

Deus vivifacit occidendo, as Luther puts it. As is well known, Hamilton's fate inspired others to take an interest in Luther: "Patrick's Places" has generated a vast scholarly literature on justification from Hamilton to McCormack, not to mention Contarini to Küng. Not least of these eminent Luther scholars in Scotland was the impressively learned Alexander Alesius, who was happily to escape both the fire and the local climate to end his days in a chair of theology in Leipzig.[2] England too had its martyrs. In my old college, Trinity Hall, Cambridge, Thomas Bilney demanded "to go up to Jerusalem" so importunately that the local bishop eventually burned him in 1531 on grounds of pastoral necessity.

We might illustrate the complexity of the Reformation debate on justification, to which we shall have to return again and again, by noting that Gerhard Ebeling—well-known straw man of modern Reformed polemic as a Lutheran, neo-Kantian, modernist, Enlightenment liberal—once suggested that a crucial difference between Lutheran and Catholic thought was that the former stressed Word and faith, where the latter stressed Sacrament and love.[3] Yet Luther too stressed the centrality of the divine love—God as *a glowing oven full of love*.[4] He could be heard when provoked to utter comments to the effect that *hoc est corpus meum*. *Fides*, *spes* and *caritas* have been central to all respectable theology from St. Paul to Luther to Barth—*Gott ist der Liebender in der Freiheit*. I shall suggest here that a concentration on one aspect of the gospel as the essence of the faith is always suspect, but that an all-embracing conceptual benevolence can become too diffuse to be illuminating.

But what of Luther as the ghost, constant guest, ghostis/hostis, at the Reformed feast? It was after all a ghost of sorts, a Teufel's *Gespenst*, that first brought Luther into the monastery. "Ueberall hat hier 'Gespenst' den ganz allgemeinen Sinn von 'Tauschung, Vorspieglung,' ohne das dabei an

---

1. Iain Torrance notes (*DSCHT*, 390–91) that "he was roasted rather than simply burned alive."

2. Cf. 'Alesius', NEW DNB, I, 640–45, by Gotthelf Wiedermann. J. T. McNeill in ARG, 55 (1964) 161–91, and A. S. F. Pearson in RSCHS 10 (1949) 57–87.

3. It is a pity that Ebeling's magisterial three-volume *Dogmatics of Christian Faith*, which focuses on experience, the experience of the presence of God in prayer, has never appeared in English. I have tried to summarize the main elements in *God in Christian Perspective*, 21–23, 229–31, 342–43, 392.

4. Sermon of 15 March 1522

etwas Bildhaftes gedacht wird," said Karl Holl—another ghost haunting Reformed corridors.[5] It is this mysterious, diaphanous—dare I say ubiquitous—aspect of the Lutheran legacy which sails through the Reformed tradition, always to be treated warily and not to be trifled with.

Surely without Luther there is no Calvin. And there were, of course, many precursors to the Reformation. Luther was himself faintly scandalized to think of himself bracketed with Huss. Most figures, however, were victims of the doctrine of the unripe time. Reform movements require scholarship and time for "reception." They also need a prophetic figure—and that figure for the Reformation was Luther, who combined public witness with profound theology: "Er hat von Grund aus d.h. vom Gottesbegriff aus neu gebaut."[6]

Calvin's turn to Reform did not begin with Luther, but his reading of Luther gave depth and urgency to his theological development. From Luther's exegesis of the Bible, Calvin developed his own understanding of the heart of the gospel, especially as expressed by Paul. He learned that the Christian life is a life of participation in God through union with Christ. Repentance happens through participation in Christ, through which the laws of God and nature are interpreted. "With repentance and justification we participate in the 'perfect gentleness' which is God's most complete accommodation to our humanity."[7] We shall return to the nature of participation below.

Embodiment has become a catchword of much postmodern theology. Luther was clear that faith had to be incarnated in the ordinariness of life and in flesh and blood. We all know that Calvin, on the other hand, laid a distinctive stress on the role of the Spirit. Yet Calvin was always concerned to avoid the spiritualization of the gospel. God's presence is a hidden presence, but it is always a *true* presence. The word as preached and the right administration of the sacraments brings Christ as presence into the community. As with Luther, worship is central to Christian life.

We should acknowledge here that, as in all else, there is always a possibility in embodiment of turning the gospel into its opposite. The death of Hamilton, Luther on the widest assortment of marginalized groups, Calvin on Servetus, and the embodiment of the divine law in theocracy each testify to this fact. Equally, the appeal to the Spirit as justification,

---

5. Holl, *Gesammelte Aufsaetze* I, 15, n1.
6. Ibid., 2.
7. M. S. Johnson, "Calvin's Ethical Legacy," 83.

such as in John Knox's "We have the Spirit and you do not," and to the Trinity (see Thomas Aikenhead, executed in Scotland, who serves a salutary reminder to all M.Div. students) will not guarantee discipleship. But the abuse does not take away the proper use. Or, as Luther put it: *Nulla enim heresies unquam fuit, quae non etiam vera aliqua dixerit. Ideo vera non sunt neganda propter falsa.*[8] And indeed despite the evident *falsa*, Luther could understand the *humilitas fidei* and envisage Christian freedom as being Christ to one another.

Among the Reformed, Brian Gerrish has reflected over the years on Calvin's relationship to Luther. In "John Calvin on Luther," he notes that, "[t]he casual reader of the Institutes, who is not skilled in identifying unacknowledged debts or anonymous opponents, could certainly be pardoned for concluding that Calvin had never heard of Luther."[9] He also notes that, "[o]n the other hand, a glance at the first edition of the Calvin's *Institutes*, already published in 1936, is sufficient to prove that he was deeply indebted to Luther, and this, no doubt, promised better things."[10] The most important sources are his correspondence and the "minor theological treatises." "We may say, then, that Calvin's churchmanship and evangelicalism prevented him from being narrowly confessional. Nevertheless, the plain fact is that his affection for Luther was occasioned by the generosity of Luther himself."[11] "In the treatise against Pighius, Calvin sums up his opinion of Luther in a single sentence. We regard him as a remarkable apostle of Christ, through whose work and ministry, most of all, the purity of the gospel has been restored in our time."[12]

In "The Pathfinder—Calvin's Image of Luther," Gerrish noted that Luther and Calvin never met, and that Calvin's understanding of Luther may have been hampered by his lack of German, concluding that, "[f]or all his devotion to Luther, Calvin never appeals to his ideas as though they were final and definite. Luther for him was not an oracle but a pathfinder—a pioneer, in whose footsteps we follow and whose trail has to be pushed on further."[13] Later, he mentions Calvin's own distinction, concerning his relation to Luther—that is, the distinction between being an

---

8. WA XIV 694, 30, cited by Holl, *Gesammelte Aufsaetze* I, 415, n2.
9. Gerrish, "Interpreters of Luther," 67.
10. Ibid., 71.
11. Ibid., 69.
12. Ibid., 79.
13. Gerrish, "The Pathfinder—Calvin's Image of Luther," 27ff.

ape and being a disciple—and suggests that there is an important distinction between continuity as repetition and continuity as development as a "Reformed habit of mind."[14]

It would take too long and involve a descent into a catalogue of often tedious cases for us to explore the long historical dialogue between Luther and the Reformed tradition, although some mention, however, is allowable. It is, of course, true that much seventeenth-century theological literature is preoccupied with confessional polemic between Lutherans and Reformed. Every area of doctrine could be and was to be exhausted to provide ammunition for a triumphalist celebration of the virtues of one confession over against the other. We need only recall the complex dances of the theologians over theories of *kenosis* from the sixteenth to the nineteenth century and beyond: my *krypsis* is better than your *kenosis* and my *genus apotelesmaticum* simply encapsulates the truth of the universe. Nothing here was to be less sophisticated than medieval arguments over varieties of the doctrine of impanation and the like. But at the same time, the Reformed Confessions—notably the Heidelberg Catechism—are built up in dialogue with Lutheran documents, and the *Confessio Augustana* is respected in Reformed communities. Communities living side by side inevitably influenced one another in subtle ways, and there were to be a series of church unions from the nineteenth century on. These were perhaps more influenced by Enlightenment notions of tolerance than by Reformation principles, although tolerance is also a theological virtue. Church music influenced by Luther's hymns, quintessentially in the magnificent work of Johann Sebastian Bach, has kept Luther fresh in cultural memory.

The reading of Luther himself was a seminal part of theological education, at least on the European continent, and it continues to be so. The presence of Lutheran faculties and Lutheran churches from Finland to Germany ensures a constant flow of new interpretations of Luther, both as historical studies and as systematic theology. Reception of Luther through different cultural frameworks continues to generate both creativity and controversy. Schleiermacher was more influenced perhaps by Calvin than by Luther, but Luther was of course important to him. Looking at more modern German interpretation, we see the Luther of Theodosius Harnack transformed through the influence of Albrecht Ritschl, and transformed again into the strongly community-orientated Luther

14. Gerrish, in *The Legacy of Calvin*, ed. D. Foxgrover, 158ff.

of Karl Holl. For Holl, Luther is the key to the gift of the German spirit to humanity, an antidote to American and Anglo-Saxon empiricism. For Hirsch, Luther is the stepping stone to a National socialist polity. For Althaus, he is key to a revitalizing of the church as church. For Ebeling, Luther was the source of an existential interpretation of the gospel in a hermeneutical framework appropriate for a theology of religionless Christianity. For Ernst Wolf, Luther could be read in conjunction with Barth as the basis for a theology of resistance against the cultural imperialism of National Socialism. For many, Luther provided in the end of the day a kind of ultimate spiritual refuge from, and a bastion of resistance, to the complexities, dangers and uncertainties of the contemporary intellectual flux. With this appreciation there was at least sometimes awareness there were many Luthers, and that the master himself was *simul justus et peccator*, by no means the source of an infallible organic unity of truth.

In the Scandinavian countries, in America, and to a lesser extent in other parts of the world, interpretation continues as an ever-evolving area of scholarship. It would be misleading to see Reformed interaction to Luther as a reaction to a fixed corpus of thinking. There is a good discussion of this wide legacy in the *Cambridge Companion to Luther*,[15] including a fine survey of Luther's ecumenical significance from Guenter Gassmann, who highlights Thomas Carlyle's view of Luther as a prophet of intellectual freedom.

In England, it seems that Luther was very little read til Coleridge and others brought a kind of brief mini-Renaissance at the beginning of the nineteenth century. Luther was important to Hooker, arguably the keeper of the theological title deeds of the Church of England, but interest in the twentieth century was largely stimulated by the Methodist Gordon Rupp and the Reformed Brian Gerrish. The situation in Scotland was perhaps slightly better—certainly from 1880 in the work of T. M. Lindsay, James Mackinnon, and others, brought Luther to light in new ways. More recently, the rise of Barth scholarship has again placed Luther in the margins, and he is seen perhaps more as a stormy figure of European church history than as a source of theological renewal.

In America the influence and dynamism of immigrant Lutheran communities in the nineteenth century was reflected in the new Lutheran Scholarship led by Walther, Schaff, and Krauth, and in twentieth-century scholars from Wilhelm Pauck to Robert Jenson. Luther has been

---

15. McKim (ed.), *Cambridge Companion to Luther*, 289.

of interest, too, to American Catholic theologians—one of the best recent essays on the hiddenness of God in Luther is David Tracy's lecture, "Form and Fragment: The Recovery of the Hidden and Incomprehensible God."[16]

II

What of the great Reformed icon of modern theology, Karl Barth himself? Barth is famously on record as having said that Luther is an inspiring figure, but Calvin is a far better teacher. A mythology has grown up of Lutheran gloom, of the pessimism of the North German plain. The contrast between the law and the gospel smacks of dualism, practically Gnosticism, political quietism, Scotist dualism and potentially the whole raft of Old Testament plagues. Calmer reflection, however, seems to suggest something rather different. I want to examine the Luther legacy in some more detail.

When does Barth first mention the name of Luther? Enthusiasts for numbers might note that in Romans, and even in *Church Dogmatics* I/1 and I/2, there are more mentions of Luther than of Calvin. Indeed, Luther played an important role in the great Barthian revolution. Barth is often seen as the great Christocentric theologian, but Luther, too, was always Christocentric: *Wo nit Christus ist, da ist finsterniss, es scheyene wie gross und hell es ymer mag.*[17]

In *The Theology of the Reformed Confessions* Barth tells us that he was not in *Romans* consciously confessional theologian. "It was not for me a matter of significance that I was Reformed. I was not a confessional Reformed Christian."[18] Only with the move to a Reformed chair did he begin to develop a more Reformed stance. In the lectures, he notes the dangers of a creeping Lutheranisation of Reformed communities. As it happens, he sees other dangers too:

> We come now to the Scots Confession of 1560. Here another spirit, which is radical and aggressive, is blowing. It closes with the words, "Arise, O Lord, and let thine enemies be confounded." Bristly John Knox and his friends are speaking here.[19]

---

16. Tracy, "Form and Fragment: The Recovery of the Hidden and Incomprehensible God."
17. WA X, I., I., 528.21, quoted in Wolf, *Peregrinatio*, 68, n160.
18. Barth, *Theology of the Reformed Confessions*, viii.
19. Ibid., 127.

As the lectures develop Barth settles into the task of creating a consciously Reformed theology. His strictures remain more of Lutheranism than of Luther. (There is an excellent comprehensive account of Barth's Reformed development in John Webster's *Barth and the Reformed Confessions*.)[20] But in the Göttingen Dogmatics, we hear very little of Luther himself.

In the *Church Dogmatics*, Luther returns much more frequently—the index to *CD* I/1, for example, offers sixty-one citations. Luther can be quoted appreciatively when appropriate, but he can also be firmly criticized. Barth is now much more sure of his own Reformed position, and consequently much less inhibited about Luther. If Luther is to be criticized, it is to be for real and not imaginary mistakes. Typical is this comment found *CD* I/2:

> It would be a sorry delusion to think that in this matter, because of his well-known and pointed doctrine about the law and the gospel, and because of the tone of belittlement with which in this connection the name of Moses in particular is incidentally mentioned by him, Luther is bound to look in a different direction from Calvin.[21]

There is to be no scoring of cheap points.

When we turn to Barth's correspondence, we find that in 1967 he can quote Luther approvingly to a Japanese scholar in Göttingen, criticize him firmly a month or two later in a letter to a Zurich pastor, Max Schoch, and then compare Hans Küng to him as a good example of courage in a letter to Küng. In his later years, deeply interested in Vatican II, Barth seemed to have more interest in Catholic than in Lutheran theology.

Barth's relationships with Luther, Lutherans, and even Liberals, were of course complex. He saw good theology and bad theology in Luther. He was suspicious of "the Lutherans" but many of his close friends were Lutheran: Ernst Wolf, Helmut Gollwitzer, and Eberhard Jüngel. He broke with the Liberals, but kept up an affectionate correspondence with Martin Rade until Rade's death in 1940.[22] Rade was dismissed for criticizing National Socialism in November 1933. In a letter to Pastor Max Schoch on June 9th, 1967, Barth wrote:

---

20. Webster, "Barth and the Reformed Confessions."
21. Barth, *Church Dogmatics* I/2, 76.
22. Schwoebel, ed., *Karl Barth-Martin Rade: Ein Briefwechsel*.

Luther's *Romans* was one of the books I read and had ready to hand at Safenwil in 1916–1918. But even then I had some mistrust of the man which became stronger during my fifteen years at German universities—the German soul is by nature Lutheran—and here at Basel when I held a seminar on Luther and the fanatics. Calvin is not my man at every point, but he was and is the superior teacher.[23]

III

One of the central issues in Christian systematic theology (indeed for some theologians *the* central issue) is of course the doctrine of justification by faith.

This *locus classicus* continues to be the subject of impassioned debate in the twenty-first century. How does the Reformed tradition relate to the tradition of Luther in this area? Once again we note at the outset that there are many different Lutheran interpretations, and many different Reformed interpretations, of justification.

The doctrine of justification by faith can be related to many different areas of the biblical narrative, but it derives most immediately from Paul, whose sources stretch back into the Hebrew Bible and beyond. It is decidedly inconvenient for contemporary dogmatics that the interpretation of Paul among biblical scholars has undergone seismic shifts in recent years. Indeed, some scholars believe that Paul would have found the "received" doctrine of justification by faith unrecognizable.[24] In Protestant doctrine, sinners are saved by the atoning death of Christ, through which God is enabled (roughly!) to impute to us the righteousness which belonged to Christ alone, thereby achieving our salvation. Instead, in the more recent formulations, God is enacting the new creation by transforming all created relationships, encompassing the Gentiles and conquering the powers of the universe.

How is justification to be construed today? This issue remains as keenly debated today as it ever was. For example, Bruce McCormack sees justification as an attempt to say what is essentially human as part of a "covenant ontology."[25] Through justification we are granted participation

---

23. Barth, *Letters, 1961–68.* 255.
24. Harink, *Paul among the Postliberals.*
25. In the standard Reformed account of justification, as Bruce McCormack puts

in true humanity which is at the same time true participation in God. This is a regenerative process, a judicial act with transformative consequences. The faith and obedience by means of which my humanity conformed to the humanity of Jesus Christ is the effect of the divine transformation given in justification of the ungodly At its heart, forensicism is deeply ontological.[26]

As such, justification has consequences beyond the individual; it has consequences for the individual in *community*. McCormack preserves the link with judgement while opening up the social dimensions of the act. This move approaches the wider significance given to justification by Paul Lehmann—another Princeton theologian—for whom "the reality of justification transfigures the nature of the boundary between the Christian community and the world." Thus justification becomes a gateway to liberation theology, the kind of liberation theology which Dan Migliore has himself envisaged, without losing the theological heart of the matter.[27] In justification, we participate truly in the person and work of Jesus Christ, as Christ is really present in us and to us. Yet, as McCormack stresses, we remain fully human, utterly dependent on the grace of God. We are not deified.

Eberhard Jüngel has written an impressively precise study of justification. This stresses against Tuomo Mannermaa, the distinguished Finnish theologian who has daringly connected justification and participation to orthodox understandings of *theosis*, the forensic dimension of justification. Jüngel shares with Ebeling an existential understanding of personal righteousness through grace alone, defends a highly traditional and ultra-conservative doctrine of total depravity, and combines this with a strictly exclusive Christology.[28] Little is said here about issues of sin

---

it, "[t]he just judge acts justly in that he forgives those whom he 'clothes' with Christ's righteousness. Clothed with Christ's righteousness, they are already in Him what they are only gradually being made in themselves, the 'new humanity,'" McCormack, "Iustitia Aliena," 171. Justification must always be for us a *justitia aliena*. 189. In the seminar in the winter semester of 1966 on *de divina revelation*, Barth asked whether we should choose Christ or his benefits. Ever seeking the *via media* I diffidently suggested *Christus cum beneficiis suis indutus*. The great man would have none of it—but he still welcomed my wife and I to his sadly incomplete Schleiermacher seminar in the spring semester of 1968.

26. McCormack, "What's at Stake in the Current Debate over Justification?" 81ff., esp.115.

27. Migliore, *Called to Freedom*.

28. Jüngel, *Rechtfertigung, Dogmatisch*, RGG 4.7 111–18. Cf. Sauter, *Rechtfertigung*.

and evil, exploitation and discrimination, and the connection between justification and justice in the real world, apart from making a sensible distinction between God's justice and ours. Jüngel's approach reminds us of the importance of Migliore's concern for engagement.

Dan Migliore has highlighted the nature of Christian participation in Christ in his seminal article, "*Participatio Christi:* The Central Theme of Barth's Doctrine of Sanctification": "Christian life is a *participatio Christi* in the active, agential, ethical sense of free and glad participation in the service of Jesus Christ and his work of reconciliation."[29]

The idea of participation is meticulously unfolded in relation to Barth by Paul Nimmo in *Being and Action*,[30] from which I have learned much on this issue. In a reflection on being as action, Dr. Nimmo detects an ontic dimension in Barth's view of participation. All individuals participate in Jesus Christ through divine election, but there is also for the Christian a response in action to the passive participation in Jesus Christ. This ethical participation occurs only as a gift of the grace of God, being realized only as an event, and always related to Christian community. Here is participation without divinization, but with genuine humanization. Such an interpretation is essentially consonant with the thought expressed in Karl Barth's Wolf Festschrift essay, *Extra nos-pro nobis-in nobis*, in which he addresses the question, *Wie kann, was er extra nos war und tat, in nobis Ereignis werden?*

The understanding of the center of Lutheran-Reformed discussion is not unconnected to the urgent need for effective delivery of doctrinal affirmations within public theology. Despite often voiced reservations about modernization of the pure essence of the doctrine in Luther, justification is related to grace and simultaneously to justice. Whatever else, the luxury of permanent suites in a dogmatic Wartburg was not what Luther intended. Justification has consequences for this world as well as the next: "[t]he churches need to understand that human rights work is an expression of the churches' public theology."[31]

TRE 28, 282–367.
    29. Migliore, "*Participatio Christi,*" 291.
    30. Nimmo, *Being in Action*, 171ff.
    31. Lutheran World Federation documentation, 51/2004, 51.

IV

Justification is related to justice, but justice distinctively related to transcendence and to reconciliation. How can we find new points of entry to transcendence in the twenty-first century? Here we must turn to modern focal points in Christian doctrines of God—existence and being, relationality and the image of God, otherness and gift, divine action and human response, universality and particularity, grace and history—and make a provisional assessment of the new directions which might be taken.

We have noted a potential tension between one Lutheran interpretation (in this case Mannermaa's Finish interpretation) and one Reformed interpretation (Jüngel), as tension between the forensic and the theotic. Since Mannermaa there have been interesting attempts to re-imagine grace as gift from a number of quarters including the Finnish Lutheran tradition. Gifts have many dimensions, from expressing deep affection to facilitating defence contracts. I want to suggest briefly here a construal of justification as the gift of the divine hospitality.

Hospitality in talking about God suggests a language of being and sharing. We can trace notions of the hospitable God in the pre-modern era, in the modernism of Schleiermacher, and in postmodernity. Much has been said of hospitality in relation to God in the tradition of French philosophy arising largely out of the work of Jacques Derrida, who reflected famously on the theme of "impossible hospitality." To be hospitable, it is first necessary that one must have the *power* to host. One also must have some control, for otherwise, one cannot be host. There is a need to abandon all claims to property or ownership, if one does, then one cannot be a host. Christian theology might reflect that only God can do this. Derrida in *De l'Hospitalitie* considers hospitality and hostility, the other and the stranger, from Plato and Herodotus to Oedipus and Antigone and the issue of fratricide. He invokes Klossowski and Kant on the laws of hospitality. There is an inevitable hostility/hospitality dialectic. One must be prepared to accept the truly strange and uncomfortable. So, this remains always an impossible possibility:

> Hospitality is culture itself and not simply one ethic among others. Insofar as it has to do with the *ethos*, that is, the residence, one's at home, the familiar place of dwelling, as much as the manner of being there, the manner in which we relate to ourselves and to others, to others as our own or as foreigners, *ethics*

is hospitality; ethics is entirely coextensive with the experience of hospitality, whichever way one expands or limits that.[32]

In a seminar at the University of Sussex, Derrida discussed friendship, democracy, and hospitality. Hospitality involves unconditionality:

> But of course this unconditionality is a frightening thing, it's scary. When I speak of hospitality I have in mind the necessity not to simply assimilate the Other, but that's an *aporia*. Hospitality, and hospitality is a very general name for all our relations to the Other, has to be re-invented at every second, it is something without a pre-given rule. We have to negotiate also, that's a complicated unconscious operation, to negotiate the hospitality within ourselves.... If you are at war with yourself you may be allergic to the Other, that's what complicates the issue.[33]

Kant's idea of hospitality, described by Derrida as "cosmopolitics," has laws and limits. For Derrida, unconditional hospitality asks no question of the stranger, there is no legal, political or moral obligation, it is "rendered," "given prior to all knowledge of the subject."[34]

Unconditional hospitality "produces itself as impossible" and can "only be possible on condition of its impossibility."[35] There is an *aporia* between the law of hospitality and the laws of hospitality!), between a law or a politics of hospitality and an ethics of hospitality is necessary to do the impossible. If there is hospitality, the impossible must be done.[36]

Christian theology might reflect that hospitality is not only a feature of God's eternal dance of love, but is radiantly manifested in the out-working of that life in the creation, redemption and completion of humanity, and the entire cosmos. It is often a judgement on our inhospitality. We might reflect that this is somewhat akin to Niebuhr's notion of the relevance of an impossible ideal, or the vision of eschatological hope.

The consciously postmodern theologian Jim Olthuis,[37] asking "What of Derrida?" comments that "Derrida remains on the threshold." Derrida points illuminatingly to relationality. Olthuis's response is this:

---

32. Derrida, *On Cosmopolitanism and Forgiveness*, 16–17.
33. www.hydry.umn.edu/derrida/pol+fr.html.
34. Derrida and Dufourmantelle, *On Hospitality*, 27, quoted by Paula Keating, *The Conditioning of the Unconditioned*, 3/1.
35. Derrida, *Adieu to Emmanuel Levinas*, 19–20.
36. Derrida, *Of Hospitality*, 14.
37. Olthuis, "Crossing the Threshold," 34.

> "I am loved, therefore I am." ... [t]he gift of love is also the gift *for* love. The gift is simultaneously a call.[38]

The *Gelassenheit* of love eschews control:

> I want to suggest an ethics of mutuality in which self-sacrifice is seen not as the heart of ethics, but as an emergency compromise ethic because of the breakdown of mutuality.[39]

Caputo adds that "[c]reation must be a risk for God, a venture into the outside in which God makes Godself vulnerable. Otherwise creation is simply a divine display of power, a laser show of lights and explosive cosmic events."[40] Richard Kearney, in the same volume, adds this gloss:

> Everyone makes their choice, but the God of love and justice is the only God I'm interested in. I'm not interested in the God of evil and sadism. I'm just not interested in these Gnostic (or neo-Gnostic) notions that see the dark side of God—destruction and holocaust—as an indispensable counterpart of the good side. Such theories or theodicies can justify *anything*.[41]

How far can we go with postmodernity? David Klemm, in a Glasgow paper, raises some sharp questions about the "posts," and searches for a new Christian theological humanism:

> Deconstructive theology thinks not of the transcendent other but traces of the other—infinitely deferring that of which the trace is a trace. Consequently, in much postmodern theology, theological language loses its subject matter and is indistinguishable from any other utterance. It becomes the theological equivalent of Duchamp's readymades.
>
> For postmodern theology, nothing is holy—or, I should say, not even nothing is holy. Post-liberal theology, by contrast, denies the experience of the holy as a universal human capacity in order to protect the special status of its own particular position. ... For different reasons, neither form of post-theology can affirm authentic humanism. (In post-liberalism) Theology once again inscribes exclusivism on to its own body of thought.
>
> Theological humanism is both an outlook on being in the world and a practical orientation to life's problems. ...

---

38. Ibid.
39. Ibid., 36.
40. Caputo, "Olthuis's Risk," 50.
41. Kearney, "Philosophizing the Gift," 68.

> Theological humanism wants to affirm and appropriate the positive contributions of both postmodern and post-liberal theologies, while negating and transcending their deficiencies. On the one hand, it has the task of reconstructing religious traditions in order to challenge them to realise their own most humane expressions. On the other hand, theological humanism has the task of developing theological interpretations of significant expressions in any domain of culture.[42]

Jim Olthuis voices similar theological reservations about aspects of postmodernism when he asks, "Is the postmodern not postmodern enough?" but moves in a more conservative direction:

> In the world of being-as-power, suffering has no legitimate place.[43]

> Indeed, I suspect the postmodern self will be shown to be as mythical as its predecessor, another adapted, false self. There is still room for an agent self that is not absolute, with no claims to self-authorisation and full presence, but a gifted/called self, gifted with agency and called to co-agency by an *Other*.[44]

There are however constructive construals of the postmodern which are germane to this enquiry. Outstanding is Calvin Schrag's *God as Otherwise than Being*. "The grammar of 'gift' has become virtually a household topic in certain contemporary philosophical and theological circles."[45] In seeking precision in talk of being, he discusses "superessential essence" and hyperessentiality:

> The not-being of this and that is not the assertion of an absence. It is rather a serendipitous effort to point to the superabundance or surplus of the divine majesty. . . . Whereas the denials within deconstruction "defer" all determinations of being in its positivity as presence, negative theology continues to reside in the hollow of a metaphysics of theism.[46]

---

42. Klemm, "Theology at the End of Art," n.p.
43. Olthius, "Crossing the Threshold," 26.
44. Ibid., 28.
45. Schrag, *God as Otherwise Than Being*, xv.
46. Ibid., 11, 12.

He adduces another Princeton theologian, Wentzel Van Huyssteen,[47] who speaks of coming "to the point where we can celebrate the truth behind truth, the God behind God, and the religious behind religion."[48] Schrag widens the discussion to consider the work of Marion, who reflects Derrida and the much earlier work of Marcel Mauss. Marion exemplifies the danger of ecclesiastical idolatry in Catholicism and in Protestantism:

> The truth of the sacraments and its tenuous connection with an elusive presence remains one of the more enigmatic truths of institutionalised religion. . . . And it is here we have much to learn from Levinas, specifically from his accentuation of the disclosure of the Deity in the face and call of the neighbour and the stranger, the afflicted and the suffering, in which there is a beckoning to a responsibility that points beyond the multiple responsibilities in the economy of civil society.[49]

Derrida's principal point in *Given Time* is that in the insertion of a gift into a network of exchange relations, one cannot dispossess without first possessing:

> With the instantiation of the gift as love, external to the economies of distribution and exchange, reward and recompense, we have an occasion to refigure and revise the metaphysical concept of transcendence, which has been such a bane for classical theism. . . . Insofar as the gift exceeds even the domain of the ethical, the transcendence at issue cannot be construed as a moment within the ethical itself a move that was made in certain expressions of nineteenth—and early—twentieth-century liberal theology, which sought to reduce religion to morality. . . . An infinite God who is found in the depths of the finite soul is no longer God, and the self that seeks to constitute itself as infinite loses itself as finite self. . . . The gift is transcendent.[50]

Schrag speaks of the asymmetry that always travels with the gift, "the grammar of asymmetrical reciprocity," and goes on to explore the ethics of charity in the (very Reformed) village of Le Chambon in World War II. Justice and democracy also become asymmetrical.[51]

---

47. Ibid., 43ff.
48. Van Huyssteen, *Essays in Postfoundational Theology*, 279.
49. Schrag, *God as Otherwise Than Being*, 92, 99.
50. Derrida, *Given Time*, 111, 112, 113.
51. Schrag, *God as Otherwise Than Being*, 142.

In the context of hospitality it is worth reflecting on the very similar preoccupation with gift in Marion and others. Marion in *The Idol and the Distance* (1977) explores the saturated phenomenon. This becomes a mysterious and undefined cipher, somewhat perhaps like—like Moby Dick, or Barth's Word of God? The icon can become an idol for theologians, and nothing is exempt. Biblical metaphors appear to be normative for Marion and the relation of all this to engagement remains unclear.

Marion, in answer to Mauss, suggests that "Gift can be just pure givenness."[52] For Marion, there is the actuality of pure givenness (contra Derrida). Robyn Horner stresses that, "[f]or the Marion of *God Without Being*, God gives Godself in a gift of love that can be recognised but not appropriated."[53]

The question remains: how to unpack the gift and use it? Parcels are useless as such. Is this only a form of Neoplatonism repackaged? We might speculate. For Marion, no historical criticism of the New Testament is needed. All is achieved by intuition. Here there seems to be theology without a cross? Where is this world? *Gelassenheit* may be too comfortable. In Christian theology, we might reflect, Christomorphic action happens through history and politics, and not just through vision. One might recall Jürgen Moltmann's early criticism of the epiphany of the eternal present. Rather, hospitality concretizes a specific gift, unpacking the package. There would appear not to be much instantiated incarnation in Marion—or priority for the marginalized. One might reflect that we may not be able to give without self-interest, but God *qua* God can—this is part of the divine/human asymmetry.

Does the icon of gift obscure as much as it reveals? Paul Lakeland as said of Marion:

> His fundamental theology is only a natural theology, in other words, and he must retire into revelation to spell out the austere phenomenological concept of contentless giving. . . . Christ the icon of God is *not* transparent at all, but deeply and ineradicably coloured by historical circumstance and profoundly reflective of the tragedy of being human in a nonanthropocentric universe.[54]

To return to the Reformed tradition of Luther and Calvin, the gift is examined in a rather different dimension by the Finnish Lutheran

---

52. Marion, *The Idol and the Distance*, 115.

53. Horner, *J-L Marion: An Introduction*, 101.

54. Lakeland, *Postmodernity*, 95, 109.

theologian, Risto Saarinen, who has also written on Luther and justification.[55] Here is an ecumenical theology of giving. Ecumenism is often explained in terms of an "exchange of gifts." (Cf. the notion of Reception in *Lumen gentium*.) That there are problems with gifts, from Mauss to Bourdieu are abundantly clear.[56] "No free gifts" is a slogan of anthropologists, but at the same time it is a challenge to theology.[57] Saarinen, too, quotes Derrida.[58] One should make the effort of thinking "the transcendent illusion of the gift" and Marion on givenness:

> Somewhat like Karl Barth or Hans Urs von Balthasar, Marion is opting for a consistent theology of revelation, in which revelation gives God without the alienating Cartesian category of objective being.[59]

He finds some help in the work of John Milbank. For Milbank, a gift without being cannot be a gift of anything.[60] What is needed is "precisely an ontology of the gift." Is there here a real reciprocity? There are clues in Luther on God's gift in Christ. This leads to reflection on forgiveness and negative giving (Milbank),[61] forgetting sacrifice and thanksgiving (Girard),[62] and Luther on spiritual sacrifice.

When you are forgiven, you receive positive gifts of God.[63] Ecumenical giving means sharing reciprocity.

What does this postmodern talk of gift amount to? Not necessarily a great deal. As we have already suggested, much depends on whether the gift can be unwrapped and used, in practice, old and new. Hospitality means unwrapping and distributing the gift. Being and other than being—all have metaphorical elements and have value—but none is a magic formula. Unwrapping the gift: faith, engagement and human rights. In thinking of a hospitable God, all the basic structuring elements of the Christian understanding of God should be represented fully. But this need not be a comprehensive study of all aspects of the classical doctrine

---

55. Saarinen, *God and the Gift*.
56. Ibid., 17ff.
57. Ibid., 18.
58. Derrida, *Given Time*, 24.
59. Saarinen, *God and the Gift*, 27.
60. Ibid., 30.
61. Ibid., 59ff.
62. Ibid., 89ff.
63. Ibid., 125.

of God. It is a focussed a meditation on hospitality and God. Hospitality, in recent thinking, can be seen especially though not exclusively through the emancipatory theologies. The Hospitable Christ in twentieth-century hospitality has been seen notably through the friendship motif. The hospitality and friendship motif can be seen though the contemporary novel in its emancipatory themes. The Hospitable God is the source and goal of emancipatory theology—expressed through being/active love/creation/redemption. Hospitable faith attempts to express faith afresh in reviewing our image of God. Belief in God usually derives as much from the Christian tradition, the events concerning Jesus, as from contemplating the question of what it is for there to be a God. The Inhospitable God should be rejected firmly; this is a lesson from emancipatory theology's critique of traditional church views. We may find it best to begin from the tradition of human faith in force, presence, absence, rather than from God as being. Faith arises from grace through the Word of God. Beginning from God as hospitable may have a practical cost—hiding enemies of the state poses risks. It may be desirable to begin from community rather than confession. "What holds the Christian community together is not a common theology but a common faith."

Above all, with the hospitable God it is the tone which determines the music. Desmond Tutu says this.[64]

> Ubuntu. A person with ubuntu is welcoming, hospitable, warm and generous, willing to share. Such people are open and available to others, willing to be vulnerable, affirming of others, do not feel threatened that others are able and good, for they have a proper self-assurance that comes from knowing that they belong in a greater whole.

God only has us.

Part V

Not every sort of hospitality will express the distinctiveness of the Christian Gospel. What would it mean to think of Jesus Christ as the incarnate hospitality of God?

I return to Luther. In March 1522, Luther left the security of the Wartburg and returned to Wittenberg, where he delivered his eight famous "Invokavit" sermons. This is from the seventh:

64. Tutu, *God has a Dream*, 26.

> We shall now speak of the fruit of this sacrament, which is love; that is, that we should treat our neighbor even as God has treated us. Now we have received from God naught but love and favor, for Christ has pledged and given us His righteousness and everything that He has, has poured out upon us all His treasures, which no man can measure and no angel can understand or fathom, for God is a glowing furnace of love, reaching even from the earth to the heavens.
>
> Love, I say, is a fruit of this sacrament. But I do not yet perceive it among you here in Wittenberg, although there is much preaching of love and you ought to practice it above all other things. This is the principal thing, and alone is seemly in a Christian. But no one shows eagerness for this, and you want to do all sorts of unnecessary things, which are of no account. If you do not want to show yourselves Christians by your love, then leave the other things undone, too, for St. Paul says in 1 Corinthians, "If I speak with the tongues of men and of angels, and have not love, I am as sounding brass or a tinkling cymbal." (1 Corinthians 13:1) This is a terrible saying of Paul. And further: "And though, I have the gift of prophecy, and understand all mysteries of God, and all knowledge; and though I have all faith, so that I could remove mountains, and have not love, I am nothing."[65]

The Lutheran tradition, like the Reformed tradition, has been and doubtless will be developed in all sorts of directions, in conservative and in progressive frameworks. I want to suggest that what matters is not the genetic pedigree—theologies are not quite like racehorses—but the service to the gospel today which the huge variety in the tradition can still encourage. We do not have to go back quite as far as 1522 to find a comprehensive vision of the unconditional love of God and the Christian response in love:

> God *is* self-expending, other-affirming, community-building love. The exchange of love that constitutes the eternal life of God is expressed outwardly in the history of costly love that liberates and reconciles.[66]

> That God's life can be described in the light of the gospel with the beautiful metaphors of Trinitarian hospitality and the dance of Trinitarian love has far reaching implications. . . . If the triune God is understood as a continuing history of victorious and

---

65. Translation: www.godrules.net/library/luther/NEW1luther_b8.htm.
66. Migliore, *Faith Seeking Understanding*, 63.

> compassionate love, it follows that we must not, like so much of the tradition, think of the Trinity primarily in retrospect... We must also think of the Trinity prospectively, looking forward to the glorious completion of the history of divine love.[67]

> Like faith, Christian love is an act of freedom. It is the free practice of self-limitation and regard for the other. It is the willingness to assist others, especially those others called enemies, and to take the first step in promoting justice, mutuality and friendship.[68]

This profound and irenic vision recalls the tradition of Alesius, whom we met at the beginning of this paper, rather than Knox. One of the most learned of the early Reformers, Alesius devoted considerable effort to identifying the best in Protestant and Catholic traditions and to seeking reconciliation rather than polemic. It is not always the most strident theologians who are the wisest, and who contribute most to a mature and thoughtful Christianity.

Dan Migliore calls on us not to look backwards but to look forwards. I have taken a brief look at the Lutheran ghost in the Reformed tradition and suggested there may be scope for more reciprocal appreciation in the future, not uncritical but not unmindful. In 2006 the executive committees of the World Alliance of Reformed Churches and the World Lutheran Federation met together for the first time. In 2013, they hope to have a joint ecumenical Assembly. *Quid Athenis cum Jerusalem? Quid Wittenberg cum Geneva?* However that may be, it is a pleasure and an honour to write an essay for a distinguished, wise, and faithful servant of the Reformed tradition, the Reverend Professor Daniel Migliore.

---

67. Ibid., 70–71.
68. Ibid., 137.

4

Humane Spirit—
Towards a Liberal Theology of Resistance and Respect

From Religious Pluralism in the Modern World, Festschrift for John Hick's 90th birthday

I

JOHN HICK HAS MADE ground-breaking contributions to many areas of theology and religious studies. Much attention has deservedly been given to his work in interfaith studies. Here I shall reflect on the some aspects of the liberal tradition in Christian theology, a tradition in which John's work continues to be important, a tradition currently out of fashion, but in my view vital for the future of Christian faith and community, for interfaith engagement, and for engagement with a wider society.

Faith comes in many forms. Its diversity is also its continuing strength. Currents of faith stream through cultures and civilizations. They are dammed and disappear underground. Often they reappear in unlikely guises. There are many sorts of faith—here we shall be concerned with Christian faith, and the specific contributions that liberal Christian faith has made, is making, and will make to the future of the churches and society.

There are a number of recent studies on the future of liberal Christianity. Sensibly they note the decline of liberal theology and liberal congregations, and the difficulties of effective renewal. This paper would not be possible without a considerable debt, conscious and unconscious, to existing work. Surveying the roadblocks, we might try to suggest new routes through which liberal Christian presence may continue to make sustained contributions to the understanding and the service of the Gospel and humanity. Our paradigm case is Christianity, but an inclusive faith is always open to learn from engagement with people of other faiths, and none.

This paper is designed to reflect upon the substantial and complex reality of liberal Christian presence in the past and in the present, and to encourage its development through new currents of engagement in the future. The attempt to produce a "pure" liberal presence inevitably constitutes a rather attenuated expression of Christian faith. Liberal presence permeates Christian life, and is hugely influential even in unlikely places—readers who doubt this need only look at Augustine through the eyes of Eric Gregory. Our task here is to trace this powerful current and to suggest new ways of harnessing its continuing energy in the future.

As is well known, John Hick studied philosophy as a fairly conservative evangelical Christian, gradually developed more liberal perspectives, and became increasingly concerned with interfaith issues. In the theology of religions he has been a pioneer—indeed, it is ironic that many of his most severe critics in that area would probably not receive the attention that they currently enjoy without his earlier initiatives. His engagement with issues and people outside the churches has not been limited to intellectual issues—social issues and human rights have been in the centre of his concern at least since his arrival in Birmingham. He has been in every sense an immensely humane scholar, a characteristic not least exemplified in his constantly irenic responses to his often extremely abrasive critics. Though Hick has developed his own distinctive positions in theology, he has never made exclusive claims for his work. The much excoriated *The Myth of God Incarnate*, for example, reflects perspectives which differ and in some areas disagree with each other. In the serious search for truth, dialogue and argument are encouraged.

II

How can we benefit from the insights which the work of Hick and other liberal scholars have given us, and take this legacy forward? First we may recall the context in which the marginalizing of liberal theology has occurred—reaction against "the Enlightenment," and "Enlightenment rationality." This critique is in itself in large measure a product of the critical rationality of the Enlightenment, a multi-faceted phenomenon which clearly had its limitations, explored by the Romantic movement, by Karl Barth, the radical orthodox tradition, and similar movements. Alasdair Macintyre, Stanley Hauerwas, Richard Neuhaus, and John Milbank have been central to this reaction to Enlightenment. Hans Urs von Balthasar and Josef Ratzinger have once again become influential authorities, along with appeal to Augustine, Aquinas, Calvin, and Barth. Academic theology has been paralleled by movements in the churches. In the Roman Catholic Church, the progress of Vatican II has been systematically dismantled. In Orthodox churches, there has been a solid reaction, e.g. in the WCC, against Western liberalism. In the Anglican Communion, the Covenant process, supported strongly by the senior clergy, breathes a very different spirit from that of the bishops of the previous era—Runcie, Montefiore, Jenkins, Robinson, and others. In American Protestant circles, conservative evangelicals have powerful influence, intellectual and economic, at home and abroad—not least in Africa.

There are reasons for this reaction to Enlightenment. The world has moved on since the eighteenth century. Defects in Enlightenment thought have been identified. The validity of alternative visions had been recognized. We shall not attempt a comprehensive response to this critique here, though we shall have occasion to examine some specific issues. In any event, a liberal perspective such as I espouse attempts to learn from criticism as well as from commendation. The major thrust of this book is a constructive exploration and development of liberal theology over a very broad field. I am concerned to demonstrate that the liberal project is not vulnerable to sophisticated demolition based on any narrow focus of study. It is a project with widely spread roots, and, as such, it can safely withstand serendipitous attack from narrow standpoints.

Given the strong position of anti-Enlightenment theologies in prestigious university departments, it might seem that liberal theology is obviously moribund, and that is the end of a conversation. However, as has been forcefully pointed out, notably by Gary Dorrien and Philip Clayton in the United States, there is a great deal of imaginative and creative liberal theology in America today—in the work of the successors of Cobb and Hick, Hodgson, Tracy, and others. I want to draw equal attention here, in no particular order, to a previous generation of phenomenally gifted liberal scholars, for example Lietzmann, von Soden and von Campenhausen, Ebeling and Käsemann in Germany, Ronald

Gregor Smith and the Baillies in Scotland, Lampe and the Cambridge theologians of the Sixties, the Christian Realists in the United States, and Rahner, Schillebeeckx, and Tracy in the Catholic world. Here is a galaxy of people who were both devout Christians and immensely erudite scholars, each with distinctive perspectives, yet each committed to a humane, liberal Christian vision. This is the broad base on which each generation of liberal Christians stands, from which it continues to draw inspiration and to move ahead. This was no narrow liberalism. These scholars were able to draw on writers who espoused different positions. Their interests overlapped with those of writers who straddled different schools of thought—Bonhoeffer is a classic case. They listened, they argued, and they did not neglect the spiritual and pastoral dimensions of their faith. When one compares the professional achievement and expertise of this array of great scholars from different academic and church traditions with the currently fashionable despisers of Enlightenment, it is hard to conclude that liberal theology has been refuted.

Citation of authority is never enough. The wisdom of the past may simply have been rendered obsolete—though oddly enough, theologians who ignore much of the past two hundred years of academic scholarship are often those who stress most vigorously the importance of tradition. It seems that authentic tradition stops with Aquinas, or at least with Calvin. It is as though the Holy Spirit took early retirement around 1300 AD, and certainly would never be associated with any thought which might have been influenced by the *proton pseudos* of all modern thought, Immanuel Kant.

III

Liberal Christianity is often portrayed as a rather shallow form of theology and spirituality pursued by a fringe collection of theological amateurs. I turn to just a couple of particular examples of the strength of the liberal tradition, beginning with my first graduate supervisor, Hans Freiherr von Campenhausen.[1] Born in 1903 on the family estate in East Prussia, he was banished to Siberia in 1919, escaped to Marburg when his father was shot by the Bolsheviks, and became a student of von Soden, von Schubert, and Lietzmann. Refusing to join the Nazi party he was disqualified from a number of chair appointments in the 1930s, joined

---

1. Slenczka, ed., *Die "Murren" des Hans Freiherr von Campenhausen.*

the Confessing Church in 1935, spent the war as a lance-corporal in Czechoslovakia, and was elected Rector of the University of Heidelberg in 1947. I was his student in 1966-68. Campenhausen was and remained a devout Lutheran, and preached regularly in the University Church, the Peterskirche. He wrote books on Ambrose of Milan, on martyrdom in the early church (a topic not without resonance in the Germany of the 1930s), on ecclesial power and spiritual authority in the early church, on the formation of the Christian Bible, on the historical evidence for the resurrection of Jesus Christ, on the church fathers, on humour and theological jokes—he regarded cheerfulness as a true Christian virtue—and on countless topics in early church thought. Demanding but unfailingly kind and hospitable to his students, Campenhausen was one of the last examples of that great scholarly tradition which knew the patristic writings intimately in their original languages and within the thick culture of the ancient Mediterranean world. Entirely absorbed in Enlightenment critical procedures, he was also steeped in the theology and spirituality of Martin Luther.

In England I detect a very similar perspective in the work of Geoffrey Lampe, a senior colleague in Cambridge till his tragic early death in 1980.[2] Lampe had a curiously similar shadow cast over him by war. In 1914 his German father returned from Brighton to Germany and was killed in the war. Lampe was educated in Devon and Oxford, won an Military Cross in the 1939-45 war, and became a professor in Birmingham (a predecessor of John Hick and a Pro-Vice Chancellor) and in Cambridge. Also a distinguished patristic scholar, he edited the definitive Patristic Greek Lexicon, wrote on baptism in the early church, on the Holy Spirit and on the church, and spent much time as a Cambridge University representative on the General Synod of the Church of England, during which he campaigned tirelessly for the ordination of women. Lampe was a large man with an equally large spirit, tolerant to a fault and immensely generous. Cambridge at that time was fortunate to have a number of impressive liberal Christian scholars. Maurice Wiles, Hugh Montefiore, John Robinson, Arthur Peacocke, Don Cupitt, and John Hick contributed greatly to the theological discussion. Impressive too, but scarcely acknowledged, was Norman Pittenger, an American transplanted to Cambridge, and the author of numerous solid liberal works

---

2. Moule, ed., *G. W. H. Lampe, A Memoir by Friends*.

on Christology and other central doctrinal themes. Pittenger wrote in support of gay Christians long before it became respectable to do so.

IV

In contrast with the above, here is a classic example of the tensions involved in debate about liberal Christian faith—attitudes to human rights. Liberal perspectives in theology and politics have frequently been attacked in modern thought, famously by Pius IX and John Henry Newman. Human rights has become for many people in the last decades a central concept for ethical reflection. The churches have maintained a seriously ambivalent attitude to human rights, in theory and in practice. On the other hand, where the language, culture, and enactment of human rights have been absent, oppression and even atrocity flourish. The adoption of democratic procedures, which might be expected to encourage human rights action, has not always done so—conservative majorities in church and society have sometimes overturned progress already made. It is good to recall that John Hick was a very active supporter of action against racial discrimination during his tenure of the Birmingham Chair and in Claremont.

In recent years I have written extensively on human rights, in one project together with another Claremont scholar, Richard Amesbury,[3] and on hospitality as a path to extending human rights into a thick culture. Human rights have of course been much criticized, most recently by Samuel Moyn,[4] who has argued that rights are a cultural concept of very recent origin, and will soon be succeeded by other cultural paradigms. Hospitality was famously critiqued by Derrida as impossible to actualize. I am still persuaded of the crucial relevance of an impossible ideal, provided that it can be embedded in specific and particular locations. In this there is encouragement in Amartya Sen's recent reflection on human rights and global imperatives,[5] where he defends both the continuing seminal importance of human rights and the need to instantiate them in particular cultures. Conversations in various parts of the world suggest that churches are often still highly suspicious of the work of human rights

---

3. Amesbury and Newlands, *Faith and Human Rights*; Newlands. *Christ and Human Rights*; Newlands and A. Smith, *Hospitable God- the Transformative Dream*.

4. Moyn, *The Last Utopia: Human Rights in History*.

5. Sen, *The Idea of Justice*.

commissions. This often reflects sensitivities about their own structures of power and control, not least on issues of gender and sexuality.

It is a strength of progressive traditions that they welcome reasoned critique and conversation. In his challenging essay, *Against Human Rights,* John Milbank[6] argues robustly against liberal notions of human rights. In doing so, he seeks to refute various arguments recently advanced by Jennifer Herdt and Nicholas Wolterstorff about subjective rights. He argues that subjective rights were not central to medieval notions of *ius*. They could be alienated and reconciled with authoritarian control of society, both in medieval and in Enlightenment polities. Where they were of value, the value is derivative from Christian theological notions and will not exist without the Christian context. Much more promising is a development of Plato's concept of right order. We may readily agree that all notions of rights could be and were exploited in feudal society, and also by the absolute monarchs of the eighteenth century. Jonathan Israel in particular has underlined the limited nature of what he terms "the moderate Enlightenment." We may also agree that liberal traditions were not the exclusive source of movement on rights issues in the last three hundred years. Yet to privilege a highly exclusive interpretation of Christianity, while eschewing all interaction with a secular society, and failing to recognise the constructive aspects of secularization, can hardly be seen as a step forward. To deny the significant positive role of liberal Christian faith on the basis of an argument from a very narrow area of interpretation of medieval praxis is, at best, a doubtful strategy.

John Milbank sharpens his case by maintaining of Wolterstorff on justice that, "[r]eally he is involved in a common Christian-American doublethink."[7] The argument is developed with a polemical assessment of the Franciscan theological tradition, from Bonaventure, through Scotus, to Ockham. "This led them into fantastic depths of double hypocrisy."[8] The stakes are doubled throughout. Liberalism is the deeply flawed progeny of a deeply flawed nominalism. "A utilitarian 'do-gooding' is an eventual upshot of the Franciscan approach."[9] We are therefore forced to seek for "an alternative modernity."

---

6. Milbank, *Against Human Rights*.
7. Ibid., 24.
8. Ibid., 29.
9. Ibid., 38.

How are we to assess this brilliant piece of characteristic radical orthodox writing? It is of the essence of liberal theology that it should be open to challenge and be subject to reassessment and change. Liberalism values tradition, but it values it as a tradition of disruption as well as continuity. Liberal thought is certainly indebted to Enlightenment—Schleiermacher is the archetypal, liberal Christian—and is therefore committed to a critical assessment of the Enlightenment's failures.

Liberal Christian faith is built on much more than particular philosophical trends. It is built on a broad band of appropriation of revelation, reason, and experience stretching back to the early church. It is built on the interpretation of Scripture, on critical rationality, on the experience, shared by millions of Christians through the ages, of the presence of God in Jesus Christ through the action of the Holy Spirit within Christian community. It is ecumenical and emancipatory. Liberal Christian faith is grounded in trust that God is equally near to every generation, in times of flourishing and of suffering. God has indeed not opted for early retirement around 1300 AD, and we expect to revise our understanding of God as we are led to deeper understanding in the future. That is why faith's commitments are both serious in their engagement and yet provisional in their formulation. Some certainties must await the eschaton.

V

Liberal faith need not be unexciting. It will be expressed differently in different religions.[10] In a Christian context, it may be liberal evangelical, liberal catholic, or somewhere between these in its liturgical expression. Far from being dryly rational, it may be conceived as a theology of the Spirit. It will express humility but will also express confidence. In the context of a Christian theology, it will be Christomorphic, a theology of resistance which opposes firmly whatever is not Christlike. It will be a theology of respect, which values the dignity of all human beings equally. It will be a theology of risk, which engages with serious issues in solidarity and identification.

Liberal faith is committed to the church, as a centre of worship and pastoral care. But it does not confuse the church with the kingdom of God, and is aware of the shortcomings of the church throughout the ages. It has no brief for ecclesial triumphalism, and for prejudice confused with

---

10. Siddiqui, ed., *Islam*, and Siddiqui, "Between God's Mercy and God's law."

obedience to God. Liberal faith is committed to dialogue and engagement with people of other religious faiths or none. It is always open to learn, but not to abandon the contribution which it brings to the dialogue. It can assimilate neither with atheism on the one hand nor religious fundamentalism on the other. It remains committed to historical and philosophical enquiry, and cannot revert to premodern perspectives. This does not mean that it cannot learn from other perspectives, notably non-Western perspectives. It serves as a community of inspiration and support to fellow liberal Christians, and is there as dialogue with specific contributions to bring to the table. Humanism is a term from a valuable tradition of faith. I prefer to speak of humane Christianity, the fruit of a humane spirit which brings faith to the service of a wider humanity, a spirit which depends on the existing presence of the Spirit of God. This liberal spirit may be seen one of the currents of the spirit of Christlikeness which flow through human history and are the bearers of surprise and resurrection, the source of unlimited energy and unlimited love.

I have mentioned non-Western perspectives. The Abrahamic tradition is important, and, particularly since 9/11, there has been a concerted effort in Europe and the United States to focus on a dialogue between Christianity and Islam, and to a lesser extent with Judaism. But it must be borne in mind that much of the world's population has no contact with the Abrahamic traditions, which can also be regarded as the product of a particular cultural development in a limited geographical environment. Hundreds of millions of people, equally valuable human beings in the sight of God, are steeped in traditions of Eastern religions. And there are many millions who have simply no belief in any transcendent source of being. Despite appearances, there may be more atheists in the East than in the West.

These are highly general notions. Most of the time liberal Christians are there to play their part in local community, and, where possible, in global solidarity, with individual people: a modest witness to the incarnate love of God delivered into human hands. And they bring this faith into their social and professional lives, without labels or manifestos, as an integral part of their understanding of discipleship.

A note of caution. Liberal Christianity has clearly not always been effective. This has, on occasion, occurred because of inherent limitations, sometimes arrogance, triumphalism and a variety of fundamentalism among liberal Christians themselves. It has also been the case that illiberal views have prevailed, the winners have written the master narrative, and the truly "Left Behind" have sunk into voiceless anonymity. Years later, many of the injustices have been rectified, not without a sense of satisfaction. Yet we should not forget the innumerable human beings whose lives have been wrecked while institutions have gone down blind alleys or waited for a process of "discernment" to take place. Sometimes the "left behind" have developed the diplomatic agility and the toughness required to resist conformity and to influence Christian thought and action. But in Christian community, toughness should not be the necessary criterion for respect and affirmation. Liberalism may have its difficulties: its absence often makes space for tolerance of the intolerable.

Hospitable Spirit, Holy Spirit. In the face of the rise of conservative thought and practice in the twenty-first century, and the huge media attention which such views often generate, it is sometimes good to remind ourselves of the immense richness of liberal perspectives, an encouragement to renaissance and reconstruction and of the obstacles to this. Here is a cascade of concepts which may remind us that progressive thinking in theology, in the academy, and in the world religions is not quite dead and that it resurfaces, often in unexpected forms.

Though among the churches ecumenical effort has almost vanished in recent decades, the vision of unforced consensus and mutual recognition is still there, an aspiration for a future implementation. Despite continuing intolerance, notions of constructive rather than destructive conflict have been established and will not go away. In theology, concepts which have led churches to turn in upon themselves, over against others, are, at least on occasion, open to reasoned argument. The development of new themes—the multiple identities of God, theological humanism, and the taking up older notions such as the form of Christ in the world, signal a continuing liberal theology of resistance and respect. Compassion and flexibility, rather than control and the competitive exercise of power, are persistent themes in theology.

The turn to art and film, literature and music, long banished to the sidelines of theology, and the development of comparative theology, can be seen as enlarging rather than diluting fidelity to long standing traditions. Warhol, Cage, Updike may point to creative interruption in the traditions, alongside Augustine, Aquinas, and Calvin. Anxious as they were to make their contributions to contemporary communities, the latter might well have turned to *YouTube*, *Facebook*, and *Twitter*, had these been available to them. The post-foundational and the meta-modern alert us to the less than obvious. The religious and the secular are not always in complete antithesis, in a conceptuality which can match fluidity, liquid concepts, and structures with rigour and precision. So often striving for a pure religious vision falls into an unreflective framework of deeply secular culture. Postcolonial reflection has re-imagined the practice of hospitality without being patronising, while learning that the reverse of the colonial is not always sufficient for substantial development. Good theology is continuing conversation rather than imposition. A thick culture of hospitality intensifying may begin to replace confrontation, in a medium where conflict is often endemic. Typical of the rethinking of traditional tensions is Richard Kearney, with his notion of Anatheism: "The sacramental moment of anatheism is when finally the hyphen is restored between the sacred and the secular."[11]

I make no apology for this long list. Deeply conservative religion is highly vocal, not only in the United States, where it is difficult to imagine the huge influence of such books as the *Left Behind* series, but in Africa and in Asia. In this context, it is important to foster religious inclusion, and varieties of religious inclusion. Inclusion and pluralism may not always be exclusive alternatives. This is a task which will require the efforts of more than the theological professionals alone. It is still unfortunately worth commenting that the progressive is not inevitably the antithesis of the evangelical. The impressive development of evangelical programmes on social justice issues is a reminder of the significant role of this movement. Despite the difficulties, real and apparent, it is manifestly odd to be enthusiastic about dialogue with exotic religions while avoiding engagement nearer home.

For Christianity, there is a huge challenge and opportunity for progressive Christian influence through professions other than theology. Liberal Christian lawyers can speak authoritatively about the potential for Christian influence on legal issues, etc. Medical ethics develops a complexity which has come with increasingly complex medicine, and is another area, vital to maximizing human capability, where religious input may be important, and where a liberal contribution is crucial. Christian education, seriously developed in the USA, often remains critically weak in the UK—faith does not mature simply through osmosis. At the same time, this only underlines the need to foster faith and action through liberal Christian preaching and worship—an increasingly vulnerable gap—the need for liberal theology and spirituality to encourage faith.

11. Kearney, *Anatheism*, 153.

Progressive spirituality need not be an exercise in reductionism. Faith does not flourish by gathering around the aspidistra to utter vacuous platitudes. Much professional theology is increasingly specialised and opaque to non-specialists. One avenue for such interaction might be a nexus of Church, Academy and Human Rights. Such a project, a Humanitarian Theology persisting with the relevance of an impossible ideal, might be one way of taking forward the progressive religious culture into the future.

In the writings of a white Western Christian it is unsurprising that liberal thought should reflect its cultural context. But it should be stressed that the liberal notes of compassion and understanding which faith inspires need not always be expressed in a Western context. In the lives and actions of non-Western Christians there are important lessons to be learned from the absence of Eurocentric and North American preoccupations, not least around the Pacific Ocean.[12] But it is not for this writer to presume to speak for progressive Christians who can speak eloquently for themselves. However we envisage the development of liberal theology, it is always essential to find fresh ways of continuing to remain aware, and draw strength from, the sense that the God of compassion and unconditional love is the source and goal of our lives. Human life is, as David Kelsey[13] has strikingly put it, an eccentric existence, centred in God the incarnation of humane spirit, the source of all hospitality and humane action.

This brings me back to the life and work of John Hick at 90. John would be the last person to want liberal Christians to be minor clones of himself. Yet he has been an inspiring, unfailingly generous, and modest example to liberal faith for many people of different faiths and none. More, we cannot ask: *multos felices annos*.

---

12. Pearson, ed. *Faith in a Hyphen: Cross-cultural Theologies Down Under*.
13. Kelsey, *Eccentric Existence: A Theological Anthropology*.

5

Christianity and Culture—
WARC at the Millennium

From Crossroad Discourses between Christianity and Culture, Festschrift for Hendrik Vroom

Professor Dr. Hendrik Vroom has been a committed and faithful churchman, making numerous significant contributions to Christian faith and practice. But he has at the same time been very open to the relationship between Christianity and contemporary culture—seeing these as entirely and essentially complementary activities. We can trace this reciprocity through the work of WARC (World Alliance of Reformed Churches, now World Communion of Reformed Churches) in the modern era. Henk is above all a listener. He does not tell people what to think. He responds to them at the point where they are. This was made very clear in his considered view on the nature of dialogue—an ideal stance for a participant in ecumenical engagement:

> Dialogue does not involve an exchange of ideas while avoiding critical questions. Rather, dialogue concerns truth and includes analyses, questions, answers, objections, judgements. A critical dialogue consists of four things: (1) examination of that which others actually believe; (2) articulation of one's own belief; (3) readiness to learn from one another: this concerns those aspects of the critique that are true and continue to obtain;

(4) open discussion on mutual criticism with respect to the conceptions and practices of belief.[1]

In 1982 the WARC General Council met in Ottawa, voted Apartheid an *articulus stantis aut cadentis ecclesiae*, and elected Allan Boesak as President. WARC was conscious of its worldwide responsibilities. But it was also aware of the need to develop a distinctive identity and presence in Europe. The Europe Committee met in Vienna, Austria 1987, in Lisbon, Portugal 1988, in Feketic, Voyvodina, Yugoslavia 1990, in Cambridge, England 1991, in Uzgorod, Carpatho-Ukraine 1992, in Athens, Greece 1993, in Kosice, Slovakia 1994, in Edinburgh, Scotland 1995, in Geneva Switzerland 1996, and in Prague, Czech Republic, 1997. Professor Vroom was at most of these meetings and made very substantial contributions, both on an intellectual and on a human level, helping the committee to bond together and to make progress through tough questions—for which I was not alone in being deeply grateful. It paralleled other regional committees, which met and exchanged ideas and representatives. At Seoul in 1989 the question: "Whom do you say that I am?" was pursued in great depth, with biblical study, theological reflection and engagement with local churches, including Minjung communities. It was recognized that the goals of mission and unity went together as part of the same gospel imperative. The great theme of *Justice, Peace and the Integrity of Creation*, coming originally from the North American churches, was developed in a new theology of covenant. There was reflection on a new proposal for a common testimony of faith in the Reformed churches. Creation led on the one hand to study of human rights as the rights of nature, and, on the other, to a new urgency in the search for justice, reflected in a WARC consultation in South Africa in 1993. WARC pursued a series of parallel dialogues with other churches, notably the Roman Catholic and Orthodox churches, but also Adventist–Reformed and African Independent–Reformed dialogue. It considered the challenge of new emerging ecclesiologies—e.g., in a consultation in Kampen in 1993.

Culture and Justice

In 1995, the themes of *Hope and Renewal in Times of Change* were central to the meeting of the European Area Council in Edinburgh. The Church of Scotland has always been much involved in WARC, notably in

---

1. Vroom, *No Other Gods*, 5.

recent years through the participation of Stuart Louden, Bill Shaw, Hugh Davidson, and Calum Miller. Here Henk Vroom spoke powerfully and progressively on the topic: "Reformed Identity is Reformed Interpretation of Christian Life":

> In this dynamic process of the understanding and re-interpretation of the Gospel in different historical, social and cultural circumstances, the expressions of the Reformed heritage will vary. I will give an important example of such a shift in recent history, the integration of equality between women and men in the understanding of Christian faith. . . . In this re-interpretation we have an example in the configuration of a shift in basic insights. Most women and men no longer perceive women as lower than males and as their helpers, nor do they think that such a societal ordering is evident. . . . Another insight has come into the foreground, equality. Now that insight has become central in the appropriation of Scripture. (48–49.)

This meeting was an important precursor of the General Council at Debrecen in 1997. The Europe Committee had already acquaintance with the Hungarian-speaking Reformed community through a meeting in Northern Ukraine. Here was an opportunity to deepen these bonds and also to engage in a truly global conversation once again. *Break the Chains of Injustice,* was the challenging theme. Once again as in Seoul there were important contributions from the Dutch churches, this time from Pieter Holtrop and Henk Vroom. Under the three central themes of *Reformed Faith and the Search for Unity, Justice for All Creation,* and *Partnership in God's Mission,* the central issues facing Christian life in contemporary society were addressed.

It would be unwise to overlook the fact that Debrecen was not without its tensions, some more constructive than others. There was some discussion on human sexuality, limited because it became rather heated, anticipating many of the geographical divisions which have affected the Anglican Communion in recent years. This limitation, among others, led to tangible frustration among the youth delegates, who felt that assurances of equal participation were not always delivered. (There had been an important European Youth Consultation in Belec in the Czech Republic in August 1996.) Here the official record (236) of the Public Issues Committee Report records diplomatically:

> Due to lack of time, the General Council was unable to deal with the following items.

Sexual orientation. Violence and discrimination are among the injustices committed in many of our societies endured by gay and lesbian people. Because of the deep differences of opinion surrounding this topic, consensus among member churches will require a period of open dialogue and careful consideration.

Though the majority of Reformed churches have yet to face this issue squarely, it should be mentioned that the Dutch churches have been among the most inclusive. Here was, and still is, the elephant in the room, or at least a litmus test, if not a case of *status confessionis*, for the churches. In the UK, the author was glad to be associated with the founding of *Affirmation Scotland*, a support group for gay and lesbian Christians. Other topics left over at Debrecen included "comfort women," child prostitution and aboriginal children in Australia. Again the tone and culture of the meeting is itself significant. It is good to note that this last issue was finally constructively addressed by the Canadian and Australian churches in 2008. I return to cultural analysis of Debrecen. The 23rd General Council of WARC met in Debrecen, Hungary from 8th to 9th August 1997. Each day there was a period of worship, Bible Study, and then plenary sessions of the council dealing with administrative matters. The reports were put together over the first week by sections, and subsections, of the conference meeting in committee. There were three main subjects of business. I was the Recorder for Section I, *Reformed Faith and the Search for Unity*. We produced a report including a series of recommendations for action, addressed to the Member Churches. The shape of Sections II, *Justice for all Creation*, and III, *Partnership in God's Mission*, were similar. There was also a report by a Policy Committee, on a variety of issues including the conditional re-admission to WARC of the Dutch Reformed Church of South Africa (approved) and a Public Issues Committee, with recommendations on subjects from human rights in Indonesia, to injustice in relation to gypsies in Hungary and Dalits in India. There was also a Message Committee, which drew up a series of recommendations which we finally signed, as the Declaration of Debrecen—in which, among millions of other things, we pledged ourselves to a simple lifestyle.

The other main formal item was the election of a new World Executive Committee, which, as at Seoul, created lively and at times heated debate. The new Committee consists of a larger contingent from the South, reflecting a shift in the number of delegates from Northern countries. There was a reasonable—but perhaps not large enough—representation of women. The other main category, youth, was nominally present, but in fact no one under 21 (29 before the next council) was elected. The youth were understandably unhappy that the actual representation failed to match the ringing affirmations of youth which had preceded the elections. "We are disappointed by the hollow words of our leaders." It was promised that four youth consultants would be named.

The Council ended with approval of a vast series of recommendations, covering the entire planetary system it seemed, approved for action or study, to break the chains of injustice. This has to be set against the perspective of a much reduced budget for the future. To match aspirations to resources will be a great challenge, as they say, to the new Executive. The issues debated often reflected the traditional liberal/conservative divides, the nations in the South sometimes reflecting cultural preferences originally taught by, and now heavily revised by, the North, notably on issues such as the ordination of women and sexual orientation. Breaking the chains of injustice could mean different things in different cultures. All in all, the chance to listen with respect to many different voices, seeking to articulate the Gospel *within radically different cultures* was a stimulating experience. It was also a timely reminder of how easy it is to get carried away with our own rhetoric.

Here we have more emphasis on confessionality. Beyond this we have more stress on Life and Work issues than on Faith and Order Issues. These are clearly always related, but the emphasis varies in different cultures at different times. Reflecting further on the Debrecen theme, it seems to me that one useful way of thinking about justice and injustice as a particular Reformed concern is to focus on the idea of generosity. This leads me to concentrate on the contribution of Christian faith to public issues, and especially to human rights. Generosity suggests going beyond the bounds of what is strictly required in giving. Generosity is what you embody towards the stranger in your midst tonight. Generosity includes acceptance, friendship, hospitality—the gifts of the Spirit of Christlikeness.

Generosity by example. How is faith in Jesus Christ is to be expressed in Reformed discipleship? The character of God is the character of Jesus Christ, who is with those who are in prison, who are ill, who are mentally handicapped. How is the Reformed community actively to respond to those who are in prison in Europe today? How is it to respond, e.g., to the quality of health care, to matters of taxation and social structures? How are we to respond to the issue of sexual orientation, divisive at Debrecen, Lambeth, and elsewhere?

Generosity takes place in community, and is demonstrated in stories of community. When we look at the Bible, we see stories of a lack of generosity in community, in the treatment of Philistine neighbors, in the bitter tensions between Jews and Christians. There are narratives too of generosity, in communal hospitality, in the parables of Jesus, in the sermon on the Mount. A generous community will always be an open community. It will be open to continuing change. It will believe that the human future is not simply the freezing of present structures as they are. It will reflect the overflow of divine generosity. For creation itself is God's first act of generosity, and reconciliation is the ultimate unconditional squandering of God's love for the new creation.

One of the things that theological professionals need to be constantly reminded is that actions speak louder than words, and that the Word by which we are called to live is often most effective as a silent word, a word of active hospitality, encompassing people with generous friendship. In that way, welcoming and friendly congregations can make hugely more effective contributions than writers on the subject can make.

Effective Dialogue and Embodiment

Effective dialogue needs embodiment. In all these issues of "Life and Work," subjects the relation of theology to culture, local, ecclesial, political, constantly arises. If we look for a moment at a third recent ecumenical and confessional occasion, the progress of the Lambeth Conference of the Anglican Communion in London in July 2008, we see that very similar debates to those at Debrecen took place on similar issues. Again there were divisions, often between North and South hemispheres, often between more conservative and more liberal understandings of the Bible. These differences involved theology. They also involved the coming into disagreement of different cultures. Behind much of the debate lay different attitudes to the critical interpretation of the Bible.

At this point we may recall some comments made in the *Gospel and Cultures* report at Debrecen. The *Gospel and Cultures* subsection derived the authority for its work from the statement of the 22nd General Council, which said: "[f]or us the gospel speaks in many tongues . . . there is no 'flesh' that is not nourished by a culture. No 'word' can be heard that is not the language of a culture."

The subsection developed several issues, of which these are two:

> Cultures Before Christianity: We <u>recommend</u> that the churches, both locally and regionally, incorporate the cultural values of each region. For example, such cultural values as expressed in music, dance or movement, dress, colour, language, and symbolism distinctive to each culture, are important for use in worship and other church practices. This recovery of regional culture in the life of the church should be done in light of a comprehensive, not narrow, reading of the Bible. Moreover, such recovery should be done with the understanding that not all cultural values and practices are acceptable to the spirituality and ethical values inspired by the gospel, retaining the integrity of both the culture and the gospel.
>
> Pluralism of Cultures: We <u>recommend</u> that WARC work with the churches to help them: discern how the gospel is embedded in each culture; identify the changing influence of the gospel or culture; study how the sacraments relate to culture including the aspect of human and ecological relationships; and scrutinize cultures ethically and spiritually.

Culture and the diversity of cultures are God-given but not every part of culture is given by God. Therefore we must begin the study of culture with respect for culture and people. The gospel is embedded in each culture and also critical of that culture. There are spiritual impulses within each culture. We seek to discern those impulses, recognizing that Christianity is not solely concerned with spiritual or religious impulses. Culture is changing, which means that the interaction of gospel and culture is dynamic. For instance, the church should not exclude from the means of grace people who live in a culture of polygamy because that culture is changing and is able to be influenced by the gospel. Study is needed into how the sacraments, baptism, and communion, relate to culture, including the aspect of human and ecological relationships. Sometimes cultural practices or questions reveal the gospel to the church, For example, women within and outside the church have asked how church practices are true to the spirit of Christ. We must subject all culture, including Western cultures, to scrutiny.

The last sentence is crucial: not all inculturation is authentically Christian. The incarnation of God in Christ sets a particular paradigm for Christians throughout time and culture, calling each of our communities to embody the Christian witness in ways which are specific to our own contexts.

Culture and Power

Given that we have such complex interactions between gospel and culture within our own Reformed confession, it is even more important to pay attention to the relationship between theology and culture in ecumenical dialogue. Here there is the possibility of further conflict, as different theological concepts are related to different cultural environments. Some of these differences go through the confessional differences, so that we may share more common cultural assumptions with people of another denomination than with our own denomination. On other issues the confessional bond proved to be more significant than the cultural bond. It becomes all the more important *to devise strategies for constructive conflict and common engagement with each other*. It may be necessary to create multicultural theological approaches to cultural variety, as the old cultural universalities of *ubique, semper et ab omnibus* disappear. At the same time, cultural variety must be consonant with a common human enterprise as part of our understanding of God's creation. Separatism and exclusiveness are not ultimate values in such a vision, though they may have some penultimate justification. Social and political factors are involved throughout.

Adoption of new ecclesial instruments may have a variety of perhaps unanticipated effects, which may be helpful in moving Christian communities forward in the future. On the other hand, they may have the effect of *inhibiting* forward-looking development. The coming of the Orthodox Churches into the WCC was, in many ways, a great step forward. But in other ways, it may have acted as a brake on progressive theology and practice. The Councils and Synods of the Catholic Church take place almost without the witness and distinctive contribution of women. It is hard to imagine enthusiasm in the Reformed tradition for such a development, and it is hard to think that decisions taken in an exclusively male environment are likely to produce ways forward into the future. Decisions based on pre-critical approaches to the interpretation of the Bible, from whatever tradition, are unlikely to commend themselves in all areas of the church.

There is a difficult but crucial dimension of ecumenical dialogue to be negotiated always between critical and pre-critical approaches to texts, traditions, and institutions. We have to recognise that the critical perspectives held by one dialogue partner may be seen rather as mere cultural conditioning by another. Yet if we are not to have complete relativity, and therefore no significant communication, it is necessary to search for common ground. Texts and traditions have power to liberate or to oppress.

We noted pre-critical attitudes to Scripture. What constitutes pre-critical attitudes to tradition? It is striking that in the details of the Porvoo arrangements, though clergy in the Lutheran Scandinavian Churches ordained by bishops are to be afforded reciprocal facilities in the Church of England, this does not apply to a small group of non-episcopally ordained clergy. All clergy are "recognized," but recognition does not automatically lead to interchangeability. If, as seems likely, this practice continues with the new Anglican-Methodist discussion, it is hard to see Porvoo as a breakthrough on the crucial episcopal/ non-episcopal front. It remains significant that the Meissen agreement with the German Lutheran churches, though agreeing mutual recognition, did not provide for interchange of eucharistic ministry.

Once more, the nature of *the relationship between international church bodies and local churches* becomes an issue. There is need for local subsidiarity, to respect local circumstances. But how far may this go? The Dutch Reformed Church of South Africa was suspended from WARC for practising and supporting apartheid. This was considered a matter of *status confessionis*. But who is to decide how far *status confessionis* extends? An Orthodox or Roman Catholic synod might well, on the basis of tradition, consider a gathering which includes ordained women, lay clerical, or episcopal, to be incapable of decisions binding on all Christian people. A conservative evangelical gathering, basing itself on the authority of Scripture alone, might agree.

The whole question of *authority and democratization* in the church arises here. The church may not be a democracy. But is some kind of democratic ethos necessary for justice to be maintained in the church? Or is this only a Western preoccupation? Are Western notions of justice and human rights negotiable, and if not, how is dialogue to take place? There is an excellent essay on these issues by John A Coleman, "Not Democracy but Democratisation." For Coleman, the Roman Catholic Church may be seen as "a hierarchical communion instituted by the will of Christ and governed by norms of collegiality, subsidiarity, and justice as participation." Better vehicles must constantly be found for promoting these central values. He adds, "[a]bsent democratisation, churches suffer a crisis of legitimation."[2]

It becomes clear that there are *no simple solutions* to issues of ecumenicity and confessionality. It is necessary to go forward slowly, and to build trust and confidence through working together. Where dialogue partners act in ways which undermine trust, there are real setbacks. The centre remains the gospel of Jesus Christ, the incarnation of the creative, responsive loving God. But the working out of incarnation into culture will be interpreted differently at different times. This is when the Pauline virtues of charity, patience, hope, and long-suffering are much required. But perhaps that is how it ought to be.

Culture and Text—Solitaria Scriptura?

Crucial to these decisions from a Reformed perspective, but also, as was seen at Lambeth 2008, from other Christian perspectives, is *the role of the Bible*. Here again, dialogue at world level may assist dialogue at local level, and vice versa. Scripture has always been at the centre of Christian faith, and will always be there. The authority of Scripture is deeply embedded in the life of the Church of Scotland. This is extensively reflected in all its constitutional documents. Without the Scriptures we should know little of the character of God as self-giving, creative, responsive love, shown in the events concerning Jesus Christ. What we have tried to do here is to reflect on the *interpretation* of Scripture: how can church members be helped to reflect on this ancient and diverse collection of books, in ways that speak to their need at the end of two millennia of Christian faith? The Bible plays a key role in the construction of Christian doctrine, and its role in helping to shape doctrinal decisions has always presented the church with the challenge of how to read it rightly. We don't expect now to produce a definitive statement for all time, but we hope that this study may help to inform debate on our other studies over the next few years, and also contribute to the use of the Bible today within our church.

Within the churches, the Bible has been interpreted and used in many ways at different times. Distinctive groups have had particular interpretations. In the life of communities, the Bible has had consequences

---

2. Coleman "Not Demoncracy but Democratization," 226.

for the use of power, authority, and influence. It is important to learn to respect difference and to listen to the stranger, not least when the stranger is God. This is vital. We want to encourage the church to be ever more sensitive to the challenges raised by diverse and sometimes unfamiliar voices. The Scriptures should be at least as accessible to people in our time as in former times. As we struggle in the next century for love, justice, and full humanity, we want to see the Bible as a central resource. God who has brought redemption to humanity through Jesus Christ encourages us to fight against powers of evil and domination, and to strive to participate in that liberation which is based in the freedom of the children of God.

Interpreting the Bible will not in itself solve all the problems facing us in the present. We agree that we are called to lives of justice, mercy, and humility. We believe that the life of Jesus Christ shows us the basic form of humanity. We believe that his death and torture on the cross, has fundamental implications for human rights. We believe that through his resurrection there is, and will be, transformation in the cosmos. But we have to be able to translate this into practice, to realize it, to actualize it, and to build freedom for transformation into all our structures. This is what the gospel demands of us—not in theory, not some time in the dim and distant future, but right now. Through the living Spirit, the Bible becomes transformative. God's good news is communicated throughout the world. The word of life is broken for us; here is the healing presence of the divine love.

Re-examining ecumenicity and confessionality, it seems to me that discernment and wisdom in reading the Bible may be at the centre of progress in an ecumenical development, which is unequivocally based upon justice, peace, and the love of God in Jesus Christ. As such, it will be crucial also for the local dynamic tension between ecumenism and confessionality demonstrated in documents of the SCIFU (Scottish Churches Initiative for Unity) type. It is clear that mere organizational unity is not worth the huge effort which must be spent to achieve it. Beyond this, it is increasingly true that "Life and Work" orientated projects are of greater existential interest to many Christians today, especially the younger generation, than "Faith and Order" issues. In Europe, the youth has already in large measure voted with its feet. We cannot expect to challenge the next generation on the strength of what are perceived to be boring and disengaged doctrines. *Only a unity that strengthens justice, peace, and the love of God for all humanity will deserve to catch the imagination of Christian people, and will have some chance of becoming an ecumenical reality.*

This is a slow process. But the realization of the COCU agreement in October 1998 demonstrated that with sufficient patience and faith unexpected things become possible.

Culture and Human Rights

Meanwhile the Alliance's publications came to reflect an increasing concentration on Human Rights in global discussion.[3] The original emphasis, in 1875, was on the protection of weak and vulnerable churches. This had expanded by 1879 to "persons and groups suffering from social, economic and political oppression" and to critique of social and economic structures producing inequity and suffering. 1880–81 brought attention to persecuted Armenians and native Americans, 1884 brought mention of indigenous churches, 1888 workers' rights and the need to bring political pressure on King Leopold on conditions in the Congo. Slavery, the plight of native Americans, and of persecuted denominations in Eastern Europe, were highlighted in the 1890s. The Alliance was critical of the First World War and held a "John Hus Day" of reconciliation in 1915. The 1920s brought critique of white domination in Africa and attention to Japanese atrocities against Koreans, and, in Europe, attention to poverty and women's rights. In 1933, with the growth of Nazism, the Alliance protested against "every form of slavery, oppression, exploitation and spoliation" and, at the same time, attacked the notion of "aggressive war." After the war there was an unusual and curious silence. Condemnation of racism came again at Frankfurt in 1964. This was soon to focus on the struggle against Apartheid in Reformed South Africa, culminating in the *status confessionis* declaration at Ottawa in 1982, and the suspension of two of the Dutch Reformed Church denominations in South Africa. Appropriately, a handbook on torture was produced at this time. In the later 1980s, there were to be appeals and interventions on human rights violations in Guatemala, Chile, Taiwan, the Philippines, Sudan, and Egypt.

Since 1989, there have been further declarations and campaigns on women's rights inside and outside the churches, on sanctuary and asylum, on conflicts in the Balkans and in the Middle East, and there is continuing interaction with other interested bodies. There have also

---

3. Cf. Falconer, Schaefer, and John "Theology and Human Rights." There is a good survey of WARC's human rights involvement up to 1989 by Jill Schaefer (www.warc.ch/dcw/rw928/02.html).

been declarations on environmental ethics and ecological rights. Human rights was increasingly a theme in the Europe Committee. For this stimulus, I was to be personally indebted in my *Christ and Human Rights*, 2006. All of this tension, constructive and less so, led up to the first General Council of the new millennium, the first in Africa, at Accra in Ghana in 2004. Again there was emphasis on mission, and on justice—above all and much more imperatively than before—on economic justice. The strategy benefitted from meetings of a South-south forum in Buenos Aires in 2003 and a South-north forum in London in 2004. The dangers of globalization to human dignity and sustainability, and the challenge of feminist thinking—already highlighted in Europe in 2005 by Henk Vroom, now came to the fore in Africa.

Ecumenism was now to be re-imagined, bringing in non-traditional perspectives. Africa was to make its own contribution to Reformed worship. The legacies of colonialism and the dangers of neo-liberalism were now to be addressed, along with the ambiguities of "Empire." The voices of the voiceless were also the voices of the Reformed.

Accra was to initiate WARC's *Covenanting for Justice in the Economy and the Earth* Project. The Accra Confession highlighted the connection between faith and economics:

> Speaking from our Reformed tradition and having read the signs of the times, the General Council of WARC affirms that global economic justice is essential to the integrity of our faith in God and our discipleship as Christians. We believe that the integrity of our faith is at stake if we remain silent or refuse to act in the face of the current system of neoliberal economic globalisation and therefore we confess before God and one another. (para 16)

The main themes of Reformed faith were not to be subordinated, however, to a current geo-political agenda. That was made clear in a remarkable September 2006 issue of Reformed World, in which leading theologians wrote profoundly of "the grace which shapes their lives"—I think especially of the words of Nicholas Wolterstorff:

> And there's more to being human than being at that point in the cosmos where God's goodness is meant to find its answer in gratitude. To be human is also this: to be at that point in the cosmos where the yield of God's love is suffering.[4]

---

4. Wolterstorff, *The Grace that Shaped my Life*, 263.

Questions of the nature of justice and of righteousness continued to come to the fore. This concern was to be deepened further in the context of the celebration of the 200th anniversary of the abolition of the slave trade on British ships, in 2007.

As Setri Nyomi, General Secretary, put it memorably in his Letter from Accra:

> At the Elmina Castle, the Dutch merchants, soldiers and the Governor lived on the upper level, while the slaves were held in captivity one level below. We entered a room used as a church, with words from Psalm 132 hanging above the door ("For the Lord has chosen Zion . . ."). And we imagined Reformed Christians worshipping their God while directly below them, right under their feet, those being sold into slavery languished in the chains and horror of those dungeons. For more than two centuries in that place this went on.[5]

It should be said that the Netherlands had no monopoly on slavery. Britain benefitted at least as much, if not considerably more!

As WARC looks forward to celebrating the 500th anniversary of the birth of John Calvin in 2009, and on to the formation of the World Communion of Reformed Churches in 2010—getting used to the new acronym WCRC—it often finds the authentic voice of the Reformed tradition in different cultural contexts:

> In the factor of being human, we are all human together, no hierarchies, no pyramids, but a round table, the only imagery that befits the Akan saying that all human beings are the children of God and the biblical affirmation that all human beings are made in the image of God.[6]

As Henk Vroom has put it so perceptively himself:

> Because people are vulnerable and there are contradictory lines running through the soul and many voices are heard in the council-room of our internal conversation, it must be an extraordinary merciful and loving God who has given every person inherent dignity and finds every person as having dignity.[7]

---

5. Nyomi, "Life in Fullness for All," 6.
6. Oduyoye, "Talitha Qumi," 89.
7. Vroom, "The Dignity of 'I' and 'Me,'" 48.

This need for mutual understanding and forbearance has always been at the centre of Henk Vroom's life and work. What he has to say is as relevant to WARC as to all aspects of religion today:

> The religious questions and the deep experiences around the meaning of life will not fade away. Religions pass on deep motivations and therefore they can help but harm as well. Therefore, all religions need reciprocal critique and to learn to learn from the wisdom and perspectives of one another.[8]

The vision of a listening, hospitable church is one which WARC continues to honor and develop as it goes forward into the future. Meeting in Princeton Theological Seminary in June 2007, the heads of Reformed theological institutions concluded their strategy for wider international cooperation with this declaration:

> We are resolved that though working together, listening to one another and speaking out of different contexts, issues which are divisive elsewhere in the Christian world may for us become places of mutual understanding and strength.

It was a particular pleasure for me to contribute to this collection of essays for Professor Vroom, for I have benefited hugely from his generous friendship and wise counsel over the last twenty years. Sadly, Hendrik Vroom died in December, 2013.

---

8. Vroom, "Theology of Religions: Observations," 353.

6

Public Theology in Postfoundational Tradition

From The Evolution of Rationality, Festschrift for Wentzel van Huyssteen

THIS ESSAY EXPLORES THE relevance of Wentzel Van Huyssteen's work for public theology. It identifies three basic strands of a postfoundational public theology:

- a reasoned approach to open and engaged dialogue.
- a fresh hermeneutical retrieval of the classical Christian tradition.
- commitment to the expression of Christian commitment in rational engagement with major issues in social ethics.

Consideration of transformative engagement leads to a reconstrual of Christology as postfoundational Christology. Relating Christology to reconciliation, I reflect on aspects of postfoundational Christian engagement in South Africa, where a deeply unpromising situation has been transformed into an example of engagement through justice, mutuality, and reciprocity.

I then explore the turn towards science which has characterized much of Dr. Van Huyssteen's work, and indicates how this may be of value for the future of public theology, with special reference to the role of Christian theology in contributing to the effective enforcement of human rights.

The Postfoundational Turn

In his seminal study, *The Nature of Rationality*, Wentzel Van Huyssteen asks "whether any form of interdisciplinary rationality can be credibly achieved—an interdisciplinary rationality that might finally support the claims by at least some in the theological epistemic community for a public voice in our complex, contemporary culture" (3). He seeks to develop *a postfoundational notion of rationality* which will:

> first, fully acknowledge contextuality and the embeddedness of both theology and the sciences in the different domains of human culture;
>
> second, affirm the epistemically crucial role of interpreted experience and the way that tradition shapes the epistemic and non-epistemic values that inform our reflection about both God and our world;
>
> third, at the same time creatively point beyond the confines of the local community, group, or culture, toward plausible forms of transcommunal and interdisciplinary conversation. (8)

Accepting the demise of foundationalism, in explicit or implicit form, of the idea that there can be one overarching theory and structure of knowledge, and the advent of non-foundationalism, Van Huyssteen wants to avoid relativism, "where incommensurability may finally stifle all meaningful cross-disciplinary dialogue" (11). Knowing has experiential and hermeneutical dimensions, leading to a postfoundationalist fusion of hermeneutics and epistemology. Rationality balances "the way our beliefs are anchored in interpreted experience and the broader networks of belief in which our rationally compelling experiences are already embedded" (14). These networks include the "research traditions" in which communities are embedded. These ideas are then developed systematically in dialogue with other writers in the field, notably with Calvin Shrag's notion of "transversal rationality" and Susan Haack's concept of "foundherentism."

I have tried to re-imagine the movement beyond foundationalism and non-foundationalism in terms of the metamodern. The metaphor of the metamodern, as I would want to use it, signals postmodernity in an *inclusive* and transformative sense, rather than as a limiting and prescriptive mode. It underlines that the postmodern is in many respects very much part of the modern, and unthinkable without the modern, not only as its origin, but also as a continuing force. The metamodern acknowledges both the advantages and disadvantages of the traditional ontological categories of the European tradition. The metamodern underlines all that Bernstein and Berlin have had to say about engaged fallibilistic pluralism and agonistic liberalism. It is then not so much a category as a *signal*, indicating inclusivity and flexibility.[1]

Fundamentalism—Primary and Secondary

Wentzel van Huyssteen's recent acclaimed Edinburgh Gifford lectures reflected on the significance of paleoanthropology for religion and for Christian theology. He unfolded the complexity of cave painting as a window into transcendence, showing how a surge in the development of cognition in homo-sapiens led to an appreciation of divine mystery. He did not dwell on one of the other probably significant events of the period, the genocide likely performed upon the Neanderthals and other humanoid species by our illustrious ancestors. Perception of difference often appears to provoke in us feelings of unease, of fear, panic, and, just occasionally, of homicidal rage—quite possibly for the very good reason it provokes very similar feelings in the other, inviting the pre-emptive strike and, if we are unlucky, mutually assured destruction.

Not unreasonably, we who live in the twenty-first century still feel most at home with the people of our tribe, our country, our city, people with our accents and cultural habits. We feel safe when security is in the hands of those we know, at every level. Rule Britannia. Don't mess with Texas. We are all in so many ways, even when we have not yet committed Appleby and Marty to heart, happy fundamentalists. We may be recreational fundamentalists, conceptual or cultural fundamentalists, political, religious, or even economic fundamentalists. After all, there is no good reason why the likeminded should not congregate at the same country club, the same soccer game, and worship the same basketball team or other gods.

---

1. A valuable distinction is made by Cobb and Griffin between a postmodernism of construction, which seeks to relate the physical world to notions of Christian transformation, and a postmodernism of deconstruction, which tends to concentrate on individual self-understanding. Cf. too the excellent survey by Veldsman, "Revisiting the Implications of Contemporary Epistemological Models for the Understanding of Religious Experience," 288ff.

Unless. Unless our light-hearted tribal rituals lead to the serious devaluing of other people, their lifestyles, their traditions, their economic welfare, the values others cherish. Exclusion rather than embrace is the *proton pseudos*. Of course we are entirely justified in seeking grounds for believing that our beliefs and practices may be better for most human beings than others. We may be justified in preventing some people from enjoying their human rights—should a mad prime minister be discouraged from exercising the right to bear arms? But, on the whole, many of us at least have come to think that tolerance and mutual respect, conversation and engagement, are preferable to coercion and control.

What then is the problem with fundamentalism, religious or secular? If it is true that absolute power (or powerlessness) tends to corrupt absolutely, then it seems to be the case that often (though not always) fundamentalism tends to slide into discrimination. Religious fundamentalism tends to promote absolute discrimination. Faith turns into fanaticism. Robustly orthodox (not to say neo- or radical orthodox) theology may slide into a gentlemanly but still deeply exclusivist fundamentalism. Liberal theology may become reductionist fundamentalism, quietly discounting God in the cultural stock market. Biblical theology (or theology based on other sacred texts) may chain the inhabitants of the present in the shackles of cultures long since past their sell-by dates.

"The danger of fundamentalism is not only that it would make the Bible's authority dependent on an extrabiblical notion of general perfection or infallibility; but also, and far worse, that the belief in the authority of the Bible is (through one absolutized scriptural conception) made into an immunization technique to ensure that the Bible will henceforth speak only in terms of that conception or model. What is speaking is no longer the Bible but merely those abusing their conception of Scripture to make the Bible speak for them and their standpoint. The very soul of the Reformational heritage has rejected this from the outset."[2]

The same provisionality applies to all church confessions. Van Huyssteen's comment in 1989 is even more relevant in the present exponential growth of fundamentalisms.

Some religious fundamentalism is as harmless as other passions—for fast cars, tennis, and opera. Other varieties are deeply hostile to human rights and destructive of civilized community. The damage caused by extremist views is well known and well documented. Sadly, for every

---

2. Van Huyssteen, *Theology and the Justification of Faith*, 180.

published study of strong fundamentalism, ten thousand new fundamentalists, usually Christian or Islamic, appear to spring up daily. What I am particularly concerned with here is the phenomenon of a kind of secondary fundamentalism, which recognizes a *particula veri* in fundamentalist positions, and lends it a measure of academic and cultural respectability. In this genre, liberalism remains an essentially negative word, the extreme nature of fundamentalist claims is softened, and a strongly right wing ideology profits from tacit acquiescence. I want to suggest that the recent sharp rise in the Christian Right in churches and of Islamist fundamentalism in Muslim countries should serve as a definitive wake up call for a progressive Christian theology and spirituality. The successes, as well as the failures, of liberal values in church and state need to be articulated. These successes need to be built upon, not denied in self-generated embarrassment. The most likely alternative, described in graphic (perhaps slightly too graphic) terms in Philip Jenkins' *The Next Christendom* is not for many Christians a happy prospect. If it is to be avoided, action needs to be taken now.

How are we to cope with this wave of secondary fundamentalism? It cannot, in my view, be dealt with by adopting a supposedly neutral stance and striking a balance beyond liberalism and fundamentalism. I do not think a post-liberal tradition will do.

Sometimes a *via media* may offer a bridge for communication between different countries. But a bridge can also create one way traffic, and can be a springboard for hegemony. It is sometimes said that liberal theology has tried to be a bridge between faith and culture, but those who have tried it have often walked across to secular culture and never returned. It may also be the case that a bridge to dialogue with fundamentalism can sometimes act as a springboard for acculturation in another direction, in the case the strengthening of fundamentalist religion.

Is there then no way of facilitating constructive solutions to these dilemmas? It seems to me that a postfoundational theology may well have the resources to articulate a vision of faith which is both classically Christian and authentically progressive. This will not, however, be an easy task. It may be necessary to explore further the theoretical parameters of postfoundational thought, of foundherentism and kindred concepts. Beyond this a postfoundational theology solid enough to capture the imagination of contemporary Christians and to commend itself as a support of living faith, will need a grounding in spirituality, in social action, in ecclesiology, a dynamic interaction of both the mystical and the prophetic. This essay certainly falls short of any such specification. But even the theoretical equivalent of a call for papers may be worth uttering, if my reflections on the current dire state of affairs is in any way persuasive.

Do we need to be fundamentalists, or in some sense their fellow travellers, to maintain a viable and credible Christian faith in the twenty-first century? Or, to use a slightly different but similar question from Wentzel Van Huyssteen:

> Do we still have good reasons—and if so would they be epistemological, ethical or pragmatic—to remain convinced that the Christian message does indeed provide the most adequate interpretation and explanation of one's experience of God, of the world, and of one's self?[3]

This article merits closer scrutiny. Postmodern thought, he went on to reflect, rejects dominating global narratives of legitimation, and, as a result, embraces pluralism and diversity. But how do we distinguish between a wise celebration of diversity and a callous indifference to the welfare of any community but our own? Van Huyssteen looks to a "fallibilist, experimental epistemology" which shows itself not in flight from modernity, but in the constant interrogation of foundationalist assumptions. He engaged with Nancey Murphy's notion of the practice of communal discernment. How can we have faith without fideism? We cannot claim the authority of Bible or tradition, but we can seek to develop an adequate theory of experience, which we can share with scientific paradigms. How indeed can we justify transcommunal explanations conceptualizing conceptual experience in theistic terms in the first place? If not, fideism looms.

If reality is mostly encountered in language, then there are at least connections between theological and non-theological language. But some linguistic communications and recommendations are judged better and worse than others. Therefore there can be transcommunal, intersubjective criteria for theological language, developed through argument. When this conversation involves people outside as well as within the faith community, then theological discourse can claim to constitute knowledge that is on a par with the epistemic status of scientific knowledge.

Here, as I understand it, faith is again firmly grounded on the traditional trajectories of the interactions of *notitia*, *fiducia*, and *assensus*, while fundamentalism, even in a weak form, is avoided.

3. Van Huyssteen, "Is the Postmodern Always a Postfoundationalist Theology?" 2.

Between the Foundationalist and the Relative

The great concern which animates much foundationalist thought is the desire to avoid relativism at all costs. This is widely reflected in the writings and speeches of Pope Benedict XVI. A postfoundational approach aims to strike an intelligent balance between an essentialism which freezes all identities, in what Anthony Appiah has characterized as a Medusa stare, and a value-free perspective in which there are no viable truth conditions. This research strategy has obvious implications for tackling many of the issues which haunt contemporary American politics, and especially church politics—abortion, contraception, women's rights, and gay rights. It respects the realities of biology, tradition, and culture without being confined to replication of past practice. It leaves traditions open to future development. Because a postfoundational theology has a strong eschatological drive, it cannot be content to regard the conventions of the present, or the past, as the definitive manifestation of the divine will.

This perspective is supported by contemporary thinking in cognate philosophical research. In his excellent *Morality and Social Criticism*, Richard Amesbury sets out from Richard Rorty's proposal to replace objectivity by solidarity. He wants to replace human rights foundationalism by a human rights culture based on sentimental education. Amesbury objects that "his anti-authoritarianism—while ostensibly liberating—ironically renders Rorty incapable of seeing how it could be possible to dissent from the vast majority of one's peers without ceasing to be rational."[4] Rorty dislikes the idea of obligations. But "[i]t is difficult to see how Rorty can hope to continue to talk of 'a human rights culture' while abandoning talk of obligations that obtain irrespective of whether or not one's peers happen to hold one accountable to them."[5] People have felt obliged to rescue strangers in danger, people outside their own communities. Realism without Platonist foundationalism can be reserved as a basis for social action. Amesbury's approach fits well with this stress on the postfoundational.

How is critical rationality to be articulated in relation to the central structuring elements of theology? Realism without relativism characterizes Van Huyssteen's approach to the Bible, in his remarkable essay, *The Realism of the Text*. He speaks of the central metaphoric concepts of the

---

4. Amesbury, *Morality and Social Criticism*, 14.
5. Ibid., 16.

Christian tradition. The biblical text points not only to the past, but to an open future:

> The text itself, as a religious text, forms the source for a long chain of continuous metaphorical reference to God and for faith in redemption in Jesus Christ. This irreversible thrust towards the future is, again, what I in an epistemological sense have called *the realism of the text*.[6]

The centre of divine activity is seen to be located in redemption in Jesus Christ. Our experience of redemption balances the present, which may be emancipatory, against our obligations to faithfulness to the past. The text cannot be frozen in a fundamentalist grid. "The communication of the Biblical text is not complete until it has reached its final destination: the reception of the text by the reader."[7] The Bible has an authorised authority: "If the biblical texts refer to God, and if this reference ultimately refers to what we have metaphorically come to know and accept as redemption in Christ, then Jesus Christ alone authorises the Bible."[8]

Central to this metaphorology is inspiration: "And if the Spirit is in reality the creative, life-giving presence of God, then inspiration could never be attributed only to the text as a final product."[9] Rather, the community continues to be inspired in new ways in the present through the prompting of the Spirit.

Wentzel van Huyssteen's epistemology lays stress on the openness of the text. This sense of future promise is characteristic of his approach at every level. The postfoundational points to an eschatological openness in relation to Word and Sacrament. It preserves space for mystery at the heart of Christian experience, whether in liturgy or in the arts, as in Auden's poems or Bernstein's Mass. The spirit is the spirit of freedom. But not every spirit is the Spirit of God. In Christian faith, the Spirit is always the spirit of the crucified and risen Christ, the spirit of Christlikeness. God's presence is instantiated through the double helix of incarnation and inspiration.

I want in this paper to consider the impact of postfoundational theology on Christian thinking on human rights as a contextualized instantiation of redemption. In order to do this, it will be essential to

---

6. Van Huyssteen, *The Realism of the Text*, 187.
7. Ibid., 152.
8. Ibid., 154.
9. Ibid., 159.

reconsider the hinge of Christian engagement, the shape of a postfoundational Christology.

Tracing the Rainbow—A Christological Trajectory

Progressive Christology, contrary to some popular belief, need be in no sense a reductionist Christology. The eschatological element makes clear that all our theories are only pointers in the direction of the mystery of the divine love. The socio-historical dimension of faith, with its uncertainties and its cultural and temporal limitations, can be honestly affirmed. We do indeed participate in the life of God, but as pilgrims on the way to a mystery, a mystery which will reveal itself in all kinds of ways in the future. Christian truth is true, but it remains a suggestion, a pointer to the Christomorphic future.

Awareness of mystery is not a reason for indecisiveness. Faith remains decisively opposed to evil in all forms, to contempt for human rights and human life. Laws need to be enforceable, if rights are to be delivered. The Christomorphic shape of faith points to a *continuing invitation* to reflect on the mystery of God and of the human future in its various cultural dimensions. But the clearing away of injustice is an integral element of the Christian vision, not least where the vision has been clouded by human rights violations in the name of religion or by abusive ideological zeal. The trace of unconditional love gives a sharp refusal to the failure to respect individuals as precious to their Creator. An intercultural theology will *prioritize* the most defenceless.

It is through a conception of *divine action*, for Christian faith, through a sense of the *Christomorphic shape in history*, social, political, and personal, that an intercultural theology comes to speak most readily of God. In relation to human rights, in the experience of minority and marginalized peoples, issues of transcendence arise and are pointers for faith to God. We may not extrapolate from our preferred political patterns to the nature of God, to envisage a social democratic triumvirate to all eternity. Yet a God, whose nature and actions are less sensitive to the human condition than the best of human thought and action, can be neither respected nor worshipped by intelligent beings. For Christian faith, the Christomorphic paradigm is the icon of God's unconditional generosity. This generosity is God's nature. It is both self-subsisting and self-relating. How this is so, remains the divine mystery.

Creative transcendence points to God *from within* the mystery of suffering and reconciliation in the emancipatory quest. This does not mean that all creation necessarily points to God. Clearly not, for the theodicy problem, and especially omnipresence of luck, good and bad, and random evil, raises a question mark against all romanticism. The Christomorphic trace enables those who recognise it to cope with the created order and see it as not totally inconsistent with the divine love. Christian discernment is that faith is sometimes effective despite the appearance of things. Most of the time we can see only fragments, sometimes hardly a trace, of a Christomorphic element in the complexities of society. It is the Christian vision which "traces the rainbow through the rain" and may provide an antidote to indifference, lethargy, and despair. This is a *trace* which, from a Christian perspective, we may recognise in other religions and in humanist action, where we acknowledge the lineaments of the signature of the divine love. Such lineaments are, however, more likely to be found in concrete and coordinated instances of attention to grinding poverty than in sentimental reflection.

Christology FOR Human Rights

Christology relates to confession and context:

> In the present South African situation heresy is no longer an issue governed by a theory about the unity of Christ. The far more contextual question is the visible unity of the church, and specifically the question whether apartheid, as a political system, is essentially heretical because it discredits and negates salvation through Jesus Christ and thus directly jeopardizes the truth of Christianity.[10]

I want now to examine some aspects of the relationship between Christology and human rights, bearing in mind some of Van Huyssteen's methodological considerations. I do not intend to offer a Christology *of* human rights. More germane, in my view, is Christology *for* human rights. Direct one-to-one analogies with current issues as Christological moulds are always in jeopardy when they attempt to fit a given mould to a society which is always changing in many directions at once. Van Huyssteen saw the difficulty of simplistic solutions: "Because we as Christians rightly always ask the meaning of God's word for our situation, we

---

10. Van Huyssteen, *Theology and The Justification of God*, 191.

must be very careful to avoid a type of ethical fundamentalism, which always emerges as a form of naïve Biblicism."[11]

More helpful perhaps is the recognition that the relation between Christology and human rights will always be a dialectical one, in which the Spirit of God is constantly active from above and from below, and our task is to try to remain alert to its prompting.

Van Huyssteen has insisted that theology has a critical task both in relation to the central confessional affirmations of the church, and the social context in which the church is placed. It has to be rooted in context:

> A relational model founded on committed reflection must always lead back to involvement in the confessional and sociocritical praxis of the church. . . . A theology that defines its contextuality inter alia also as confessional can by no means separate confessional from theoretical language, nor can it depoliticize the theological task and thereby prevent the center of the Christian confession from speaking out directly on sociopolitical problems in our sociocultural context.[12]

Christology can never be as self-contained as we often find convenient. We are always thinking of the concrete instantiation of the love of the God who is, Christians believe, the Creator and Sustainer of all that is. We cannot impose a God concept on rights dialogue which is genuine dialogue, as a given foundation. But we can say that Christian communities and individuals who have worked out ways of living together on the basis of gradually agreed values, have drawn strength from the faith that at the root of all existence there is a power which is entirely non-coercive, and that this power is the power of unconditional love. At least in an informal sense, Christians will say with Jean-Luc Marion that before God is being, God is love. They will regard it as significant that human beings, to date the most complex known entities in the cosmos, are the field in which God has become incarnate in the shape of self-dispossessing love. It is as the shape of the mystery of ultimate reality that faith in God through Jesus Christ transforms hearts and minds and societies.

This does not mean that you have to believe in God to be able to access the Christian construal of ultimate reality as love in generous relationality. You may come from a humanist appreciation of social and ethical values without an appeal to transcendence. That distinctively

---

11. Van Huyssteen et al., *The Authority of the Bible*.
12. Van Huyssteen, *Theology and The Justification of God*, 169.

Christian tradition, which is centred on the self-abandonment of God, does not claim a monopoly on either visions of the common good or construals of God. You may come from another religious tradition, with its own rich resources for accessing and understanding transcendence and compassion. The Christian vision is offered as a contribution, along with other contributions, to the practical tasks of delivering human rights solutions at points of greatest urgency.

The Way, the Truth, and the Life?

In a postfoundational frame, what becomes of the traditional affirmation that God is the truth, and that Christ is the way, the truth, and the life? Christians in community believe that in God's purpose for humanity Jesus Christ plays an indispensable and decisive role. This is a pointer to mystery, a Christomorphic mystery. It seems to me that all Christians can affirm gladly and doxologically their participation in the life of the triune God in faith. The eschatological element makes clear that all our theories are only pointers in the direction of the mystery of the divine love. The socio-historical dimension of faith, with its uncertainties and its cultural and temporal limitations creates the other side of this theory of truth. We do indeed participate in the life of God, but as pilgrims on the way to a mystery, a mystery which will reveal itself in all kinds of ways in the future. Christian truth is true, but it remains a suggestion, a pointer to the Christomorphic future.

Christological Focal Points

None of the classical Christological perspectives, from the most conservative to the most radical, are likely to be as effective in co-ordinating human rights action as a consensus on what the basic Christian norms for human rights action should be. These norms flow from the continuing experience of the presence of Christ to Christian faith in community. The apprehension of the central structuring elements of faith is affected by local theological cultures and concepts. Individual people and communities should be free to contribute in their own ways, and no *single* approach should be understood as "the" authorised way, whether from the traditionally liberal or traditionally conservative wings of the churches. That is not an easy perspective to actualize.

Engaging in reciprocity with the human rights dialogue, we may say that there is in the understanding of Christ a considerable measure of agreement on the norms of Christology, on the central strands of what constitutes the character of the love of God through Christ, without agreement on the theory of how this can be so. At the same time, a Christian belief, still unfortunately widespread, that God coerces obedience to his will in ways which violate rights, individual and social, can be seen to be contrary to the central strands of the New Testament narratives and contrary to the faithful articulation of the gospel in history.

It seems clear that some Christologies have historically been entirely inadequate to support this faithful articulation, precisely because they have obscured the thrust of the gospel towards that concern for the marginalized in society which was central to the life of Jesus. Here the liberation and emancipatory theologies have performed a crucial service, and "non absolutist" Christologies have pointed the way to a conceptually open approach. At the same time, however, the Christian faith has classically drawn strength from an understanding of Jesus Christ as effective not only through his life, but also through his death. This has been seen as making a distinctive difference to the nature of the universe as God's creation, and through his resurrection as the first transformative product of that difference. This is why faith is quintessentially a trust in God against the appearance of things, often prepared to think and act *contra mundum*. It is important to recall that many Christian actions in support of the marginalized have been sustained through a faith in the efficacy of love through self-giving on the cross and a trust based on the resurrection of Christ.

God Instantiated

We are brought back to the classic but basic connection between atonement, incarnation, and inspiration. A Christology for human rights pays particular attention to the many dimensions of the continuing power of reconciliation in Christ. In the events concerning Jesus we see the instantiation of the person of God in a specific human being, identified with the loss of all human rights, without remainder. This cluster of events can be envisaged through different concepts, notably of incarnation and inspiration, each of which makes its own contribution to conceiving the mystery. It is possible to speak of a bifocal, or even a varifocal, Christology.

Incarnation, which itself may be conceived in different and sometimes overlapping ways, points to the reality of the involvement of God with human bodies. What happens to bodies is important to God, who has shared human embodiment in every range of experience. The consequences of incarnation include the creation of visible communities of Christian faith, who continue in communion with God through Word and Sacrament, response to proclamation and participation in Eucharist, in the tradition of the gospel. This tradition also embodies the ambiguities of the human, yet can still act as an outlet for the divine love. Incarnation simultaneously has a wider connotation, for it is a catalyst for the reconciliation of the whole created order. Where the church is outward facing as well as inward facing, there is a constructive relationship between incarnation and response. Where the church is purely inward facing, this relationship is diminished. Incarnation is concerned with all dimensions of human life, personal and social, and with the shape of the cosmos beyond the merely human. It is not a trump card, for it is always incarnation through humiliation.

Further dimensions of the archetypal divine instantiation are expressed by inspiration. Spirit is not in conflict with but complements embodiment. The consequences of resurrection are the presence within the created order of the Spirit of the risen Christ. Within Christian community the Spirit is always related to the focal areas of Word and Sacrament. How these are related has been the subject of endless sacramental controversy. What matters here is the intrinsic connection, and the central importance of both.

Two thousand years of Christianity has shown that the Spirit of Christlikeness is not confined to Christian community. The divine love has been experienced by Christians as active in other religions and in secular spheres, in individual lives, in social and political developments, sometimes from within the church and sometimes challenging the churches from outside. There is then a basic bond between the humiliated and exalted Christ and attention to human rights in all its dimensions. Christology is for human rights. Christian theology will understand action for human rights not as identical with, but certainly as caught up within, the much wider and more mysterious dynamic of the cosmic presence of the divine love. Because it claims this underlying ground it benefits from immersion in an inexhaustible vision, however unpromising the current outlook in any given area may become.

Where human agency produces outcomes in love and compassion, Christians may give thanks for Christomorphic traces of divine action, the spirit of Christlikeness, in the created order. This is the salvific outcome of the dynamic sequence of the life, death, and resurrection of Jesus Christ.

Inclusive Reconciliation

We are always vulnerable to forms of triumphalism. We cannot say of ourselves that because we are trying to respond in loving action to our understanding of the divine love we are automatically agents of divine action. This way madness lies. We can say only that we are hoping, in a provisional way and to the best of our ability, to follow in the way of Christian discipleship. We have seen only too plainly the disastrous consequences of Christian self-delusion and abuse of power in the past and in the present. But we may hope also to recognise in the actions of others the manifestation of the divine love and regard this as a huge encouragement for the future of God's purpose of love, peace, and justice.

For those who do not share Christian faith, Christian theology can offer the example of the life of Jesus as a significant pointer, along with other pointers, to the way towards a community of compassion and justice in society. Here is a human being whose life may be viewed as transformed and defined by constant concern for others in a less privileged position than himself, a concern which has individual but also social and political dimensions. In conversation with partners who do not share a religious perspective, Jesus the man can be seen as a humane example of self-dispossession and service. For conversation partners who share a religious perspective in other religions, Jesus may be seen as a major figure among others who opens up the nature of transcendence within a particular culture, but whose significance may be appreciated within other cultures in appropriate ways.

The history of Christian action is a history which calls for humility. How could we have got so much wrong so consistently often? Yet there are still outbursts of transparent goodness produced by the Christian gospel and shared with a wider humanity. This is what faith has understood as the fruits of the Spirit. Progress here will involve a comprehensive renunciation of traditions of cultural and religious superiority. On the one hand, it is important to distinguish Christian contributions from the Western or neocolonial packaging in which they have so often been offered. At the same time, it is desirable to acknowledge honestly the predominantly Western contribution of much Christian thinking. This should not be concealed. But equally, the real value of Western Christian thinking and action to the human future, need not be disparaged or underplayed. Despite its serious flaws and its only partial perspective, it is also a hugely valuable legacy to build upon.

An Enduring Vision

I have constantly stressed the need for sensitivity to alternative, perhaps non-Christian perspectives in seeking to make a Christian contribution to rights issues. There will be occasions in which it will be desirable to offer an explicitly Christian approach to justice and rights enforcement. But there will be other occasions on which the approach will be entirely implicit. This is not a matter of deviousness or hesitation. Loving action in society often takes place on an anonymous basis and is all the more effective for this anonymity. Action in the public square does not always preclude silent and unobtrusive engagement.

A Framework for Persistence

It may be that for every step towards effective human rights action there is an equal step towards violation. In this case, the solution will not be to give up, but to try harder. I suggest that a Christian contribution, specifically a contribution based on reflection upon Christ, can be continued on several different levels.

1. There is the level of relationality and solidarity, with the marginalized and the not so marginalized. Jesus the Christ is who he is and does what he does through his being as being through relationality. I begin with the not so marginalized. We have to recognise that different Christians will have different views of current flashpoints. Where there are deep differences, we have to struggle to maintain mutual respect and communication. Christians who may be deeply critical of one group of marginalized people may be hugely supportive of other groups. We cannot afford to waste resources on unnecessary quarrels. There may be reason to hope that separate support of different abused groups may lead in time to awareness of common grounds for affirmation and respect.

2. Privileging groups whose human rights are threatened. Christ is crucified outside the gate, outside the magic circle. Everyone feels marginalized in some ways at different times. It is both possible and necessary to make the imaginative leap into trying to look at issues from this position. Not all marginalization amounts to denial of human rights. But this is often the next step. It is incumbent on all Christians to do what they can to indicate solidarity. Where Jews, or Arabs, are persecuted, it may be important in some situations to stand in solidarity as an honorary Jew or Arab, and in other circumstances, as a clear outsider who is precisely, despite huge differences, standing in total solidarity with both. Whether solidarity is achieved by secret diplomacy or vocal public advocacy, or a combination of both, will depend on what is likely to be most effective in specific cases.

3. Inside or outside. One of the most important needs for those who are oppressed, by torture, hunger, racism or whatever, is to retain a sense of self-respect in the face of general vilification. Here the combined efforts of Christians both inside and outside the issue are required. Only women perhaps can fully understand the devastating effect of patriarchal attitudes in church and society over the last two thousand years, not helped by a uniformly patriarchal Christology. Yet men can take the trouble to immerse themselves in the issues and take steps to remove the barriers which they have themselves created.

It is true that human rights action is a high risk activity. It is true that Christians have supported human rights abuses with great tenacity. There is no quick fix. But as a community response, Christian action has had considerable success in mitigating the effects of slavery, racism, and many other abuses over a longer time-scale.

Christological perspectives may have both positive and negative value in contributing to human rights issue. Positively, reflection upon Christ has encouraged Christians to work by themselves and with others in addressing effectively many areas of human rights—individual liberty, torture, political rights such as the right to justice, and economic rights like the right to be free from hunger. It has been largely ineffective where scriptural tradition has had a strong influence in inhibiting rights—most notably in the areas of gender and sexuality. Here perhaps we have to look elsewhere for guidance. But Christianity has shown the capacity for change and development, e.g., in relation to such issues as slavery and race. We should not expect that today's status quo will be repeated in a hundred years from now. The Christian tradition has potential, in reflecting on the dynamic of relationality and respect for others expressed in the events concerning Jesus Christ, to have universal application, even in areas where it has largely failed. If it is able to face up critically to its failures it may have a future role in encouraging other traditions, religious and secular, to confront their weaknesses and make appropriate changes of attitude and action.

In this way human rights action may be seen as part of the consequences of the form of Christ in the world.

Postfoundational Transformation— Reconciliation and Forgiveness

Healing wounds requires reconciliation. Few countries have shown such an amazing example of the capacity for reconciliation and forgiveness as Wentzel Van Huyssteen's native South Africa.

Archbishop Tutu has said this: "I can testify that our own struggle for justice, peace and equity would have floundered badly had we not been inspired by our Christian faith and assured of the ultimate victory of goodness, compassion and truth against their ghastly counterparts."[13]

In the political realities of the contemporary world, these strands are present in different combinations. We have characterized the Christ of faith as the icon of the self-giving, outward facing love of God. In human relationships, individual and social, this translates into a catalytic capacity for reconciliation. Reconciliation recognizes damaged relationships, which are intrinsic to human rights violations, and facilitates restoration, restitution, and forgiveness. Reconciliation cannot be imposed from above. Its shape cannot be determined by one party to a complex issue. It requires patient preparation of the ground. It also requires an acknowledgement of fault. A Christian understanding of reconciliation will not necessarily always require an overtly "Christian" outcome. It will be understood as human reconciliation, worked at through faith in Christ and reflecting the divine love.

Tutu, in *No Future without Forgiveness,* gave an excellent description of the apartheid system itself: "The highest virtue in South Africa came

---

13. Witte and Van der Vyver, *Religious Human Rights in Global Perspectives,* xvi.

to be conformity, not bucking the system. The highest value was set on unquestioning loyalty to the dictates of the Broederbond. That is perhaps why people did not ask awkward questions."

He went on to look at the intractable problems of Rwanda: "Those who had turned against one another in this gory fashion had often lived amicably in the same villages and spoken the same language. They had frequently intermarried and most of them had espoused the same faith— most were Christian."

He concluded that: "Forgiving and being reconciled are not about pretending that things are other than they are."[14]

Forgiveness is not, in the first instance, the appropriate framework for those who have been the deniers of rights. Imagined transgressions on the part of the discriminated against have to be recognized as arising from the pressures of the situation in which they have been placed, and a new basis of partnership created. Yet here too there may be a significant role for forgiveness. The struggle for rights can produce victims, often unintended, on both sides. Here is an important role for forgiveness and reconciliation, as was seen in South Africa.

In *Between Vengeance and Forgiveness*, Martha Minow offered a profound reflection on the ambiguities of forgiveness, with particular reference to South Africa:

> So this book inevitably becomes a fractured meditation on the incompleteness and inescapable inadequacy of each possible response to collective atrocities. It is also a small effort to join in the resistance to forgetting. . . . The questions will outstrip any answers. As Ruby Plenty Chiefs once said, "Great evil has been done on earth by people who think they know all the answers."[15]

The language of forgiveness and reconciliation may be manipulated. Yet an awareness of forgiveness linked to compassion is a hugely valuable Christian contribution to the complex negotiation of the fruits of human rights in society. Forgiveness has often opened up the dimension of generosity, as a catalyst to move intractable issues forward.[16] The development of critical emancipatory theology provides some resources for comparative reappraisal of the history of marginal groups, and the

---

14. Tutu, *No Future without Forgiveness*, 217ff, 222, 258, 270
15. Minow, *Between Vengeance and Forgiveness*, 5, 8.
16. Cf. Alison, *Faith Beyond Resentment*.

impact of contemporary Christologies on their lives.[17] It raises, in acute form, the problem of undoing the past and of retrospective forgiveness and reconciliation—paradigmatically in the tragedies of anti-Semitism and the Palestinian crisis.

We have to try to see beyond the failures of the churches, past and present, to the continuing vulnerable love of God. George Ellis, another South African scholar, has written of the importance of kenotic actions in conflict situations, "[t]hey are appropriate when they have the potential to transform the nature of the situation to a higher level." They should not be able to be taken for granted by opponents, for then they could not be transformative.

In the same volume, Keith Ward writes:

> Jesus' life of healing the sick, forgiving the guilt-ridden, befriending social outcasts, and undermining hypocrisy, is a very good image of the compassionate and persuasive love of God. . . . In the moment of kenosis, God relates the divine being to creatures who have a proper autonomy and otherness, which it is the divine will not to infringe.[18]

There is a very definite cosmic vision implicit in a Christian view of creation as a cosmic and pleromal process.[19]

Reconciliation is not something which occurs spontaneously in complex conflicts, it requires action at various different levels, from the general to the minutely particular. It calls for a cumulative strategy which is neither distracted by detail nor marooned in romantic generality. How

---

17. Light is shed on the complexities of forgiveness in the volume edited by Helmick and Petersen, *Forgiveness and Reconciliation*. In the Preface, Desmond Tutu comments that, "We are made to tell the world that there are no outsiders" (xiii). Petersen stresses relationality, "[t]he terms of forgiveness are meant to bring us into relation with one another, not to drive us apart through self-justification or modes of insincerity" (17). Miroslav Volf seeks to preserve the link with justice, "[a] genuine embrace, an embrace that neither play-acts acceptance nor crushes the other, cannot take place until justice is attended to" (43). He further comments that, "[t]he step from the narrative of what God has done for humanity on the cross of Christ to the account of what human beings ought to do in relation to one another has often been left unmade in the history of Christianity" (47). Don Shriver reminds us of our own fallibility, "[w]e are all vulnerable to collaboration in the doing of great evil to our neighbours: If Christians bring any gifts to politics, this truth about us all ought to be one of them" (162).

18. Polkinghorne, ed., *The Work of Love*, 166.

19. Ibid., 166.

may we try to ensure that an effective strategy is not constantly derailed by uncertainty? We shall not do this by theology alone.

Recognizing God's Love—Christology and Human Rights in a Science-based Environment

A Christology for human rights can be articulated in a number of ways. If it is to enrich our understanding of the goals of human rights, then it should encapsulate the nature of the Christian understanding of the love of God, as we have sought to characterise this in an earlier chapter. It should illuminate the self-giving, self dispossessing nature of divine reality as a pattern for human relationships. The relationship of Christology to human rights can, and in principle needs to be, developed in many different fields—I want to say here something about science, which shapes so many of the conditions of possibility in our time, and to which Wentzel van Huyssteen has devoted much attention.

Much traditional discussion on theology and science has concentrated on the physical cosmos—still overshadowed perhaps by debates about creationism. I am going to concentrate on the dimension of the human. Christian theology argues that the fact of God has consequences for all human life. Christian theology is centred on Jesus Christ, as decisive for the welfare of humanity at every level—in individual and in social contexts. A Christomorphic vision of science and human rights is then more or less bound to argue and affirm the values of science in many forms, science as *Geisteswissenschaft* as much as *Naturwissenschaft*.

A Christomorphic vision of human rights and science will embrace Human Rights (HR) and the physical sciences, HR and economics, HR and life sciences, HR and law, HR and business studies, HR and politics, HR and culture, HR and literature, HR and music, HR and medicine, HR and life sciences, HR and history, HR, architecture, town planning, and engineering, and, if you will, HR and religion.

It may not be desirable to build all houses in a cruciform shape, as a sub-Barthian view of Christ and culture might suggest. But it is possible to build communities in ways which enhance or diminish humanity, and the possibility of exercising human capacities, in ways which are consonant with, or inconsistent with, the promise of Jesus Christ to bring life more abundant, life which is fair and just, into the world. And if the planning is not scientifically accurate, and the houses not soundly built, then none of this can happen, and the divine purpose is hindered, simply by ignorance, neglect, or greed. To fail to utilise the constructive dimension of science at every level is to neglect the fruits of creation.

If we do not have a scientific approach to the events concerning Jesus, not necessarily at the beginning but somewhere along the line, then all our speculation about the relation of indirect divine action to the motion of red-green anti-quarks will be seriously compromised. This happens, even in the most exalted circles.

If we are looking for a critically rational approach to Christian faith using experience in its various dimensions as an important factor, then the tradition of experience of Jesus, in his life, death and after his death, will be scientifically unavoidable. Here we have a figure who appears, in terms of reasonable probabilities rather than established empirical data, to have been committed to proclaiming and acting out a life of conditional love, coming from and privileging the marginalized areas of society. A perspective on science and religion which does not highlight this solidarity with the marginalized can scarcely claim to be scientific.

It may be said that this is an unscientific romantic holistic fallacy. You need to generate the resources in the first place in order to be able to spend millions on NMR scanners etc to improve the health of the poor. But unless there is some effective payback directly to the marginalized, then perhaps you can forget talk of a scientific *Christian* approach to theology and science. We can speak most tellingly of science and kenosis when there is a real outcome for those in whom involuntary kenosis is most starkly apparent.

Beyond the master paradigm of a life of unconditional love, there is death and resurrection. We are not God and we cannot pretend to be God. In human terms, the kenosis of kenosis tends to lead to complete powerlessness. Faith believes that God brings into being new, authentic existence out of non-being through self-dispossession.

History as part of the human sciences is also decisive for the tradition of common Christian experience. Of course all history is selective and reflects the times in which it is written. But if we do not strive for the best available historical perspectives, we necessarily delude ourselves about the nature of that common experience, in its good and in its bad expressions. This is especially relevant to Christianity and human rights. Part of the tradition of the gospel, reflecting early Christian experience, is the Bible. When we cease to reflect critically on this experience, the text becomes ossified, and we have incarnation into a text rather than a person.

This experience is fallible, reflecting what God said to people in the past and what people heard God to be saying. It may be revelatory and counter-revelatory by turns.

The tradition of the gospel goes beyond the interpretation of the biblical texts. It includes a history of prayer, worship, and Christian social action. It includes the sacraments of baptism and Eucharist, through which faith has understood God to be inviting human beings to participate in a mysterious relationship, a generous communion of hospitality. This too is part of the tradition of experience which is part of the warrant for the construction of the critical rationality of faith.

The tradition of the gospel is not simply a tradition of relationality. It is a tradition of relationality transformed. It points to reconciliation, justice, and liberation. As such, it suggests a critical rationality of human rights, in which the rational is not simply the intelligible but the just and fair. To be unjust and unfair is ultimately to be unscientific, if unconditional love is the ultimate ground and goal of the way things are. All else is a distortion, in the sight of God.

I return to the multi-faceted dimensions of a theological perspective on the human rights implications of science with a brief contextualisation what theology *could* potentially contribute.

The physical sciences. Theology suggests the use of the physical sciences for the enhancement of human society rather than its destruction—the peaceful rather than the military use of nuclear power, the use of geology and seismology to warn to coming tsunamis as well as to conduct blue skies research.

The life sciences. The production and use of drugs in ethically responsible ways rather than simply to make gigantic profits.

Economics and business studies. The deployment of the resources of global market capitalism to begin to meet the needs of the billions who are locked into poverty, with all its concomitant issues of healthcare, education, and plain starvation.

Law. The focussed deployment of legal resources at every level to support justice, and to combat the denial of justice.

Politics. The study of politics as a science which enables democratic participation, which does not muddy the waters of humanitarian efforts by hi-jacking these for political purposes, which promotes reconciliation and conflict resolution.

Culture. A scientific approach which recognizes the need for appropriate balances in different situations between pluralism, multiculturalism, identity politics and integration.

One common characteristic of unscientific thinking is its freezing of temporality. Historical perspectives are viewed ahistorically, provisionality is ruled out, and the present status quo is absolutizes. Here a research tradition of imagination may allow dialogue among a wider range of participants, from the voices of past civilizations to the voices, of course still contemporary but suggestive, of science fiction. But neither past nor present nor putative future is regarded as normative. We can neither be bound by the past, nor the present, nor can we hijack the future.

What is humane? We saw that human communication only became possible through the physical development of the faces of our simian ancestors. Let me go to the other end of imagination and consider the world of space fiction:

> Even as Fassin watched, another infant was thrown from one end of the giant blades, voiced a high and anguished shriek. This latest unfortunate missed the prop guards but hit a high-tension stay cable and was almost cut in half. A Dweller in a skiff dipped back into the slipstream, to draw level with the tiny, broken body. He stripped it of its welding kit and let the body go. It disappeared into the mist, falling like a torn leaf.
>
> Dwellers cheerfully admitted that they didn't care for their children. They didn't care for becoming female and getting pregnant, frankly, doing this only because it was expected, drew kudos and means one had in one sense fulfilled a duty. The idea of having to do more, of having to look after the brats afterwards *as well* was just laughable.[20]

The Christian understanding of the human is a fragile, potentially transient, and clearly precious contribution. If we are to defend human rights in a swiftly changing environment, we shall have to take account of theology and science, not only at the level of cosmological speculation but also at the level of human rights.

Here again is where the postfoundational emphasizes the contextual as the way in to the universal, the specific point of need as the clue to reconciliation undergirded by the divine love. I close with an application of postfoundationalism in a practical theological situation, the HIV/AIDS

---

20. Banks, *The Algebraist*, 246.

pandemic in Africa. Here Julian Muller and a team of graduate students has used Van Huyssteen's work to articulate a theology of solidarity:

> It is practical theology that is "HIV positive." In other words, it is a practical theology that is local and contextual, but it such a way that it identifies with the people in the context. It is not a system of theories, which is formulated and then imposed on a certain situation, but a story of understanding, which grows from a real situation. It is a story developing out of an interaction between researchers and a context. It is postfoundationalist theology. In other words it finds its identity in a balance and dialogue between theological tradition and the context.[21]

What could be more fitting than the application of a highly sophisticated and deeply illuminating conceptual framework to one of the most desperate problems for human rights and human salvation in Wentzel Van Huyssteen's native country?

---

21. Müller, "HIV/AIDS, Narrative Practical Theology and Postfoundationalism."

7

John Macquarrie in Scotland

From, In Search of Humanity and Deity:
Essays for John Macquarrie

JOHN MACQUARRIE, KNOWN TO his friends and family as Ian, was born in 1919 and brought up in Renfrew and then in Paisley, on the West Coast of Scotland. The West Coast often tends to be much more self-contained and "Scottish" than the East coast, and it come as no surprise that Professor Macquarrie, reflecting recently on "On Being a Theologian" laid stress on his roots in Renfrew. The West Coast tended, and still tends, to be more unselfconsciously religious than the East, and Macquarrie naturally grew up in a Presbyterian Sunday school context in the Church of Scotland. But already at the beginning of the "On Being a Theologian" reflections he sets down the marker of the Celtic tradition—back to Eriugena—as a kind of balance to the image of Presbyterian Renfrew. He notes that for Celtic Christians, "God was not a distant power in the heavens, but a presence that surrounded them. . . . The Celtic Christian lived every day in the communion of saints. They even accompanied him when he went out in his fishing boat."[1]

How far this thought is a theological rather than an historical reflection of early influences, will be for future research students comparing Macquarrie's with Augustine's Confessions to evaluate. He notes the residual Celtic influence on others from the West, notably John Baillie,

---

1. Macquarrie, *On Being a Theologian*, 8–9.

theologian of the sense of the presence of God. "Like Baillie too I thought of the mystery in terms of immanence rather than transcendence."[2]

From a successful academic progress through high school in Renfrew and at Paisley Grammar School (1934–36), he proceeded to the University of Glasgow. "My life seems to have been largely a series of fortunate accidents, for I had no ambitious plans about a career or where I would eventually end up."[3] Unlike the famous Scottish preacher James S. Stewart, he appears not to have spent his childhood playing at being a minister in his pulpit! In 1940 he graduated with a first class honors degree in Mental Philosophy, studying with the distinguished Scottish Hegelian philosopher A. C. Campbell of *Selfhood and Godhead* fame. "The one who really bowled me over was F. H. Bradley, whose *Principles of Logic* we had to study in considerable detail."[4]

In 1943 he graduated with a B.D. His reflections are strikingly reticent about Glasgow divinity—he won prizes and was bored.[5] "Dogmatic theology I had come to regard as little more than systematic superstition. Rudolf Otto's *The Idea of the Holy* and Dr Gossip's lectures on Buddhism were more appealing."[6] At the same time, he was being prepared for the ministry of the Church of Scotland—nothing much is said of this in his reflections. His old friend and fellow student Allan Galloway (later Professor of Divinity in Glasgow) recalls Ian as a student of philosophy and theology and a candidate for the ministry.

In 1943, at the end of his course, Macquarrie applied to the Royal Army Chaplains Department, and, in 1945, he became responsible for coordinating religious services for German prisoners of war in Egypt with the aid of a group of German pastors in captivity. Already he had learned some German, a skill which he was soon to develop much further. 1948

---

2. Macquarrie, *Theology, Church and Ministry*, 1, 2.

3. Macquarrie, *On Being a Theologian*, 12.

4. Macquarrie, *Theology, Church and Ministry*, 2.

5. As he put it in *Being and Truth*, "With this background, the three years that I spent in the formal study of theology were not the happiest in my life! . . . Dogmatic theology I had come to regard as little more than systematic superstition. Calvin and Barth (who was the big name at the time) I found especially insufferable. . . . At the end of the three years I was offered a scholarship to go to Cambridge do graduate studies at Westminster College. I politely declined, and for the next seven years I never opened a book of theology" (xii). In the *Theology Church and Ministry* version, he adds, "Theories of incarnation and atonement seemed to me a waste of time. If *The Myth of God Incarnate* had come out at that time, I should have swallowed it whole!"

6. Macquarrie, *Theology, Church and Ministry*, 2.

saw John inducted into the parish of St. Ninian's, Brechin, on the East coast of Scotland, and here he married Jenny Welsh, also from Renfrew, whom he had known for a number of years. The Professor of Divinity in Glasgow, John Riddell, suggested a part-time PhD, supervised by Ian Henderson.[7] This was to be the basis of his first book, *An Existentialist Theology*. Macquarrie's continuing interest in and interpretation of Rudolf Bultmann will be the subject of a separate contribution from David Fergusson, and we shall not cover it here. But Glasgow was to be a continuing source of Bultmann studies, from Ian Henderson to Ronald Gregor Smith and Iain Nicol, in contrast to the Barthian emphasis in Edinburgh. (In philosophy, Glasgow had a traditional interest in Hegel, from the Cairds to Campbell, and Edinburgh in Kant, from Pringle-Pattison to Nowell-Smith. The contrast was not entirely complete, however, since Henderson and Smith were Edinburgh graduates, pupils of John Baillie, and both had studied with Barth.) The external examiner for the PhD was to be Donald Baillie, and Bultmann wrote a *Gutachten* in commendation.

Bultmann proved to be a surer guide to faith than Bradley had been. "The idealist identifies the essence of Christianity with a high philosophy of the universe, but for Bultmann Christianity is a religion with a saving faith."[8] But there were better guides to come. Tillich was interesting. "But more important than Tillich was my discovery of Rahner, who at that time was untranslated and virtually unknown in Britain."[9] J. A. T. Robinson was also interesting. "But the reader can readily believe that 'death of God' and 'religionless Christianity' were movements which I felt had to be resisted at all costs."[10]

Meanwhile Macquarrie was summoned to a lectureship in systematic theology[11] in Glasgow, where the family lived for nine years (1953–62). In Glasgow Macquarrie was to start on the translation of *Being and Time*, give the Hastie Lectures on the philosophy of religion, which were

---

7. "His mind was both profound and acutely critical, and my theological pilgrimage owes more than I can express to his guidance and stimulation." Macquarrie, *Theology, Church and Ministry*, 3.

8. Ibid., 3.

9. Ibid., 4.

10 Ibid. There are few if any references to Ronald Gregor Smith in the reflections—yet students testify to a harmonious relationship with both Smith and Henderson—even after the two had famously fallen out.

11. "I no longer called it 'systematic superstition.'" Ibid.

to become *God-Talk,* and make a beginning with *Principles of Christian Theology* for Scribners of New York.

The early Sixties brought decisive change. In 1962 the Macquarries moved to New York, where John had been offered the Chair of Systematic Theology at Union Theological Seminary. (There had been an earlier suggestion of a Chair in Philosophical Theology in 1956, suggested to Union by John Baillie, as so often at that time the hidden hand in Scottish and American theological appointments.)

With this geographical move came the major ecclesiological move, to the Episcopal Church and ordination to the priesthood.[12] This is now material for other chapters. I recall, however, that when I was interviewed for the Chair of Divinity in Glasgow in 1985, John was one of the external assessors. He asked what I would do about churchmanship, since I was ordained in both the Reformed and the Anglican traditions. I said that I hoped to retain equally strong links with both. He replied that he regarded his Presbyterian years as a ministry completed.

Others have written here of John Macquarrie's later work in America and in Oxford. I confine myself here to noting the stress on the centrality of Christology—"if *The Myth of God Incarnate* did anything for me, it was to persuade me finally that we cannot speak of God apart from Jesus Christ."[13] This is interesting, especially in view of the strong critique of John's work often made—I think mistakenly—by his fellow Scot Donald Mackinnon. Prominent too was the stress on the need for dialogue with Rome—perhaps in part an antidote to West coast Protestantism, and perhaps too an indication of the strong affinity he felt for the work of Karl Rahner. Like Rahner, Macquarrie was concerned for theological anthropology, and like Rahner too, he stressed the importance of the religious dimension, in contrast to the secular theology which his successor, Ronald Gregor Smith, developed in Glasgow.

It is interesting that the Macquarries chose to retire to Oxford rather than back to Scotland, though they retain strong links with family and friends there. John graduated D.Litt. in Glasgow in 1964, received an honorary D.D. in 1969 (he now had the degrees M.A., B.D., PhD, D.Litt, D.D. from Glasgow) and gave Gifford Lectures, *In Search of Humanity* in St. Andrews in 1984. Invited to consider the see of Oban in the Scottish

---

12. "I should add, however, that in becoming an Anglican I did not feel that I was renouncing my past. Rather, I was taking it with me into something broader, richer, more fulfilling, more catholic." Ibid., 5.

13. Macquarrie, *On Being a Theologian,* 72.

Episcopal Church, he characteristically thought that others were better qualified than he—he would have made an interesting choice as Donald Mackinnon's bishop! Macquarrie was, and is very much, a cosmopolitan theologian, who draws inspiration from wells in many places. At the same time, it is pleasant to note his continuing interest in fellow Scots. There is a perceptive essay on John MacLeod Campbell, of whom it was famously said that he cast the first stone that cracked the ice of a rigid Calvinism. Macquarrie comments, "'Light' is one of the most frequently recurring words in Campbell's writing, but whether he deals adequately with darkness and death is open to question."[14] And of his old mentor Ian Henderson he writes, "He has left an example of integrity, tolerance and courage, that should be inspiring for theologians of the future, both in Scotland and beyond."[15] One might think that there is quite a lot of ice still to be cracked—but that would be another story.

The warm recollections of many of his former students, now at a distance of getting on for half a century, speak volumes for the place of John Macquarrie in Scotland. This is a time for gratitude and congratulation.

14. Macquarrie, *Thinking about God*, 177.
15. Ibid., 212.

8

John McIntyre and History

John McIntyre Day, New College, Edinburgh, 2007[1]

For those of us who had the privilege of being his students, Professor John McIntyre shed much light on the relationship between Christianity and history, and on many other things besides. I think of the light he shed as a rather like the light of a prism, which opened up the unexpected, and sometimes highlighted the strangeness of the familiar. You might not always notice the light. It was not that sort of light. It neither dazzled nor scorched. It was not the sort of light which blinded you and then lurched on to stab at some other random object. It was not that sort of light at all. The best way to illustrate this is to look at John's writing itself, and I want to introduce to you an essay which he offered for the Alec Cheyne Festschrift and which was not published there, because it did not quite fit in with the Scottish Church History theme of that volume.

Professor McIntyre always produced a handout. I continue the tradition, so here is one. I have included a few mistakes, as he did. I too will know who came to my lecture and who has stayed in bed and asked a friend to bring back the handout.

The Uses of History in Theology. John begins with an elegance and substantial tribute to Alex Cheyne, and then turns to the question of a "special relationship" between history and theology. Special relationships have a habit of imploding at inconvenient moments. But he immediately quotes Pannenberg—the more thoughtful Pannenberg—"History is the most comprehensive horizon of Christian theology." He opens up

1. Published first in *Theology in Scotland* XIV (2007) 19–32.

the subject of "the historical revolution, from Gatterer and Schlosser in Germany to Bury and Butterfield." (I'm aware of course that all New College students are still reading their Gatterer and Schlosser by day, and no doubt their Badiou and Agamben by night.) He traces the development of a new historiographical self-awareness. Collingwood—and indeed Gary Badcock, in his superb study of McIntyre, tells us that John nearly started an Oxford D.Phil. on the uses of history in Collingwood. Authorities, sources, and interpolations become issues. Science and history collide. Bultmann is a question but not an answer. Philosophers spin new global patterns out of the fragments. The problems of historical positivism remain.

John McIntyre narrows the focus to the biographical uses of history. The spectre of the historical Jesus—built on a highly selective view of history, stalks the nineteenth century and haunts us still. But deconstruction has to have some limits. "There has to be the 'historical' if we are make a process of 'dehistoricising' feasible at all." One response to the fragmentation was Cullmann—*The Essence of Christian Theology is Biblical History*. But this brings new difficulties. And John reiterates politely what he used to say in his lectures long ago: this *Heilsgeschichte* has more *Heil* than *Geschichte*.

We now come to "The Critical-destructive use of history." Here he puts his cards firmly on the table—face up. The logical structure of arguments about what could not possibly happen or be true is often unstable. Miracles can become too speedily unthinkable. The starting point of a Christology from below need not also become the finishing point. Destructive criticism is not enough.

Then we hit a note often heard in John's work. Too often the theologians rush to fall on their swords too soon. Kierkegaard embraced theological skepticism for the sake of pure faith. But this was a step too far. The minimal Christian core can't be salvaged by the subjective act of faith.

The denouement of this drama comes in the shape of Further Examples of the History connection in theology. If pure subjectivity won't get us there, artificial objectivity won't do either. I'm not going to go through the last section for you—there's a lot about hermeneutics.

It is fascinating to compare this essay with *The Christian Doctrine of History*, published forty years earlier in 1957, and based on lectures at Union Theological Seminary in 1953. In eight chapters history is related to doctrine, definition, necessity, providence, the incarnation (three chapters in all), freedom, memory, and structures. Here, as in the Cheyne essay, incarnation is *the* central clue to a Christian understanding of history. There are the trademark sub-divisions and precise teasing out of meanings. History is clearly interpreted in relation to providence and providence is seen in the light of incarnation. Incarnation is redemptive and recreative. It is creative, prospective, and integrative—there is no talk of *The Myth of God Incarnate* here! For McIntyre, there are no easy answers or trendy fixes. Typical is this sentence:

> While it must be said that the Christian doctrine of history "makes sense" of history, this statement requires the gravest qualification. For at the same time it introduces profounder depths of meaninglessness into history than any other of the competing views.[2]

The death of Christ, as a consequence of our sins, underlines the mystery of the cross at the heart of the nature of the loving God. This is a robust theology with no concessions to the fashions of the times.

In his introduction to John McIntyre's last book, *Theology After the Storm*, Gary Badcock perceptively says this of *The Christian Doctrine of History*: "One might, in fact, describe it as the most Barthian of all McIntyre's books."[3]

At the same time, it is no accident that much of *Theology After the Storm* is devoted to the humanity of Christ and the theology of prayer. The accent may have changed, but the substance in no way reflects the trendy modern professor of anything vaguely religious at the University of Barrow in Furness. At the centre of the discussion of the humanity of Christ is a telling section on Humanity as Historicity. Again, history and incarnation are indissolubly linked. He looks with disbelief at the retreat from history:

> The flight from history—one might even call it a stampede—has taken a number of forms. . . . If the kind of meticulous analysis had been given to *kerugma* as was given to its running mate in that celebrated vaudeville act, *Kerugma and Myth,* then I feel that theology generally and New Testament theology in particular would have been considerably better served than it has been by the demythologisers over that period.[4]

2. McIntyre, *The Christian Doctrine of History*, 114.
3. McIntyre, *Theology After the Storm*, 14.
4. Ibid., 108.

Even more emphatically:

> In a sentence the dehistoricisation of the faith which is thought to be implied by existential theologies as critical theories is the docetism of the twentieth century, because by its skepticism it takes humanity out of the only milieu in which it can possibly exist, namely, historical process.[5]

For McIntyre God is active in the world. Not through some shortcut of salvation history, but through the dimension of prayer. God invites us to respond to his call in active discipleship:

> It has to be said right from the start that a belief in the efficacy of prayer in relation to events in the world, in history and within persons and their relations to one another is an inalienable part of the Christian understanding of prayer.[6]

Here is a sign of God's intervention in our world: "To deny that is both to invalidate the doctrine of *creatio continua* and to subscribe to the noninterfering God of Deism."[7] And his own prayers memorably combine trust in God with realism about ourselves:

> O God, the world in which we are called to live is not one of black and white but of different grays;
> not of truth and falsehood but the compounding of both;
> not of light and darkness but the twilight between.
>
> Give us, therefore, wisdom this day in our choices,
> courage in our decisions, and a continual discontent with anything less than the best that Thou hast revealed to us so wondrously in Jesus Christ. Amen.[8]

In the final essay in *Theology After the Storm*, on "The Cliché as a Theological Medium," John hammers away again at the easy accommodations of theologians to historical skepticism. He called for a new analytical philosophy of history. But such is the crooked history of thought that before the end of the century intellectuals were pronouncing the end of history.

If we want to be quite precise about what John was saying about history towards the end of the twentieth century—and precision was

---

5. McIntyre, *Theology After the Storm*, 116.
6. Ibid., 233.
7. Ibid., 235.
8. Ibid., 258.

important to John—we can turn to a highly significant piece which he produced in the Festschrift for James Barr in 1994. The piece is called "Historical Criticism as a History-centred Value System." Here he mounts an incisive critique of the ideas of history as homogeneous and of a uniform historical method "from Kierkegaard to Pannenberg," as he puts it. This is partly inspired by James Barr's own critique, which will be familiar to you, of "the high value currently assigned to 'history.'" And, by the way, as a guest and long time admirer of both of them, may I suggest that you might think of having a Barr Day. As James of blessed memory himself put it: "What I have called story is an absolutely essential and central aspect of the Old Testament; it cannot, however, be too simply identified, indeed it cannot be identified at all, with history."[9]

For John McIntyre in that essay, history is a field-encompassing field, involving geography, anthropology, philology, and much more. So there is no single entity called "historical criticism." John traces this back to his old subject Collingwood's criticism of F. H. Bradley. He acknowledges debts to Stephen Toulmin and Van Harvey, but criticized Harvey for ultimately selling the pass as it were to history: there are no theological magic wands, pleas for exemptions to the rules, or retreats behind the covered wagons. Theology is theology, strong enough to stand on its own feet and argue the issues out openly and freely among the other disciplines.

The Christian Doctrine of History came out in 1957. Coincidentally, in the same year (and this is now half a century ago), Pannenberg and a group of his friends published the collection of essays under the title *Revelation as History*. The theme of the Pannenberg circle was that, as they put it, kerugma without history is a meaningless noise. The preaching of the Word of God is an empty assertion if it is severed from what really happened in history. John would have agreed heartily. Faith cannot live from a kerugma which is detached from its historical basis and content. For, after all, the kerugma is itself nothing but the declaration of what God has actually done in the course of the events of ordinary human history. The standard history of salvation theology has always foundered on a dualism between revelation and history. It fled from the historical flood tide into the harbour of a supra-history. The theology of existence withdrew from objective history to the "historicality" of the individual.

---

9. Barr, *The Scope and Authority of the Bible*, 11.

But revelation comes not merely in or through history but *as* history. 1. The self-revelation of God has occurred indirectly through his historical acts. 2. Revelation happens not at the beginning but at the end of history. 3. Historical revelation is there for anyone who has eyes to see. It is universal in character (external clarity of Scripture, I hear you cry). 4. The universal revelation of the godhead of God was not yet realized in the history of Israel, but first in the destiny of Jesus of Nazareth, insofar as the end of history occurs beforehand in him. 5. The Christ event does not reveal the godhead of the God of Israel as an isolated event, but only in so far as it is part of God's history with Israel. And so on.

The accent on the universal historical scope of revelation is, of course, the big break from Barth and Bultmann. The totality of reality as history is not just the world, but God's world, which he created and through which he reveals himself. Pannenberg would agree that he borrows much from Hegel—but Hegel was wrong in identifying his own philosophy with that end standpoint from which one could view the whole. The final revelation has taken place in the resurrection of Jesus from the dead. But what has happened to him still remains outstanding, unaccomplished, for us, and so history goes on and promises have yet to be fulfilled.

It is not possible to base the gospel on the Christ of faith. The Jesus of history himself must be the actual starting point of Christology. Even and precisely, a theology of the resurrection, must establish itself squarely upon the earthly Jesus.

The resurrection did not happen in a vacuum. Judaism already expected a resurrection from the dead. For those who already hoped, the resurrection would be a sign of the coming of the end of the world, a corroboration by God of Jesus' claim to authority.

The key to history is apocalyptic. Here John would certainly have switched to watching the cricket on another channel: "Why the man Jesus can be the ultimate revelation of God, remains incomprehensible apart from the horizon of apocalyptic expectation."[10]

But how is primitive Christianity as a whole to be related to the present, if not through the Word? Pannenberg's answer is framed in terms of a theology of universal history, which deals with what he calls the horizon of the historical process. The gap between past and present is bridged by the continuing history of God's unfolding plan for the world.

---

10. Pannenberg, *Jesus, God and Man*, 83.

The church and its tradition have a structural significance in a hermeneutic of universal history.

What then of the Protestant tradition of *sola Scriptura*, the Bible alone? The subject matter of Scripture, the person and history of Jesus Christ, can no longer be found in the external clarity of the text. We have to find a new understanding of the relation between past events and present faith by creating a new hermeneutical bridge. We can't just call for obedience to the authority of the word of God. But alas, the "totality of History" to which Pannenberg calls us may prove to be at least as elusive as the Word mythology which he rightly questions.

For Pannenberg, Israel came to understand itself in terms of its own history, and understood its God as a God who is active within that history. This understanding was reinforced by God's revelation in Jesus, in whom the end of history has broken in anticipation.

History and hermeneutics become the magic wands. Unkind critics mutter the Marxist mantra that the theologian must be concerned not only to interpret but to transform the world and human history. Of course if you change it without first understanding it you end up in trouble. Don't just do something, stand there!

Everything turns into history. Pannenberg draws connections between contingency in physics and contingency in history. Skeptics might think there is no obvious link between a statistically indeterminate future and the eschatological future of God, and so Pannenberg's "fusion of horizons," which should create universal historical meaning, never quite happens. Nevertheless, Pannenberg's criticism of the verbalisation of the gospel in much of the tradition, especially the Protestant tradition, may still be important.

Everything is served with history, like with diet coke and fries. Man is by nature an historical creature. The combination of events in a man's life gives him his individuality, and drives him forward to seek a meaningful future. By looking at man in his historical environment we can see who he really is and we may come to see that this existence can only be fully realized in the light of Christ, the key to true humanity. Skeptics may complain that God's prophetic word may cut across the development of human history, which occasionally leads to genocide.

Now you may wonder why I have dwelt on Pannenberg at such inordinate length—and of course one has to respect the power and comprehensiveness of Wolfhart Pannenberg's vision. What I want to bring out by contrast is the immense care and precision which characterizes John's work. He never wraps himself up comfortably in that woolly blanket of dogmatic complexification that the rest of us turn to when we feel the chill of rigorous intellectual scrutiny. You may say that this is a rather austere perspective on Christian faith. But it is always at least honest. This is what we can say. It may not be all we would love to claim but we can justify what we have set out. Is that all there is? It appears to be more than enough to undergird a generous and catholic vision of Christian community as empowered by prayer, by worship, and by discipleship. That is why we remember John today with gratitude and with fond remembrance.

And if you think I've been a little unfair to Pannenberg—whoever said theology was meant to be fair? I should perhaps add that he is the soul of clarity compared with more recent writers on history and events. I quote:

> The moment the real is identified as event, making way for the division of the subject, the figures of distinction in discourse are terminated, because the position of the real instituted by them is revealed, through the retroaction of the event, to be illusory. There is no doubt that universalism, and hence the existence of any truth whatsoever, requires the destitution of established differences and the initiation of a subject divided in itself by the challenge of having nothing but the vanished event to face up to.[11]

> In reality, the Pauline break has a bearing upon the formal conditions and the inevitable consequences of a consciousness-in-truth rooted in a pure event, detached from every objectivist assignation to the particular laws of a world or society yet concretely destined to become inscribed within a world and within a society. What Paul must be given exclusive credit for establishing is that the fidelity to such an event exists only through the termination of communitarian particularisms and the determination of a subject-in-truth who indistinguishes the One and the "for all."

Well exactly.

Whatever we may think about the destitution of established differences, John was dead right to stress that history can always come back to bite us. Take this month's little sensation about finding the lost tomb of Jesus. Here is a comment last week of some worth, of Professor Charlesworth, to be precise: "There is nothing that archaeology can provide that

---

11. Badiou, *St Paul—The Foundation of Universalism*, 57–58, 108.

can be damaging to Christian faith. Archaeology cannot form faith; it can only inform faith."[12]

But I expect if archaeologists found an authentic diary from Jesus recounting a happy retirement in the Bahamas this might somewhat impinge on faith! History is important.

In the preface to *The Christian Doctrine of History*, John refers to the many conversations he had with Reinhold Niebuhr during his tenure of the Fulbright Fellowship in Union Theological Seminary New York in 1953. What does it mean to be a Christian and to imagine Christian community? Niebuhr says this, using I think for the first time that expansive word "Christomorphic" which was to be used later by so many theologians:

> They know themselves to be Christian when they see their companions in need in the form of Christ; there echoes in their memory in such moments the story Christ told which ends in the well-known statement, 'inasmuch as you have done it to one of the least of these my brethren you have done it unto me.' The symbol is not a mere figure of speech. Symbol and reality participate in each other. The needy companion is not wholly other than Christ, though he is not Christ himself. He is a Christo-morphic being, apprehended as in the form of Christ, something like Christ, though another.[13]

I think John would have had a lot of sympathy with these sentiments. Christians in community believe that in God's purpose for humanity, Jesus Christ plays an indispensable and decisive role. This is a pointer to a Christomorphic mystery.

All our theories are only pointers in the direction of the divine love. We participate in the life of God, but as pilgrims on the way to a mystery, a mystery which will reveal itself in all kinds of ways in the future. Christian truth is true, but it remains a suggestion.

The norms of our theology will be determined by the kenotic shape which is the hallmark of Christian faith and the catalyzing contribution to human dialogue about the most serious issues facing humanity. Such norms are sensitive to cultural and political marginality, to the dialogue of world religions, to humanist projects of various sorts. But they are not infinitely inclusive. Faith remains decisively opposed to evil in all

---

12. www.ptsem.edu/NEWS/images/Charlesworth%20comment.pdf
13. Niebuhr, *The Responsible Self*, 154–55.

its forms. This paradigm sets priorities as always related to those at the greatest point of need—especially in a political context in which there is often a huge gulf between appearance and reality. It is through a conception of divine action, through a sense of the divine love in history, social, political, and personal, that theology comes to speak most readily of God. For Christian faith, the Christomorphic paradigm is the icon of God's unconditional generosity—both self-subsisting and self-relating. How this is so remains the divine mystery.

The omnipresence of luck, good and bad, and random evil, raises a question mark about all this. We become aware that faith is sometimes effective despite the appearance of things. Most of the time we see fragments, sometimes hardly a trace, of a Christomorphic element in the complexities of society. Yet it is the Christian vision which "traces the rainbow through the rain" and may provide an antidote to indifference. This is a *trace* which we may recognise in other religions and in humanist action, wherever we recognize the lineaments of the signature of the divine love. These lineaments are more likely to be found in coordinated instances of attention to grinding poverty than in sentimental reflection.

Looking back to 1995—now light years away, and the 150th Anniversary of New College's[14] *Disruption to Diversity* volume—I see that I wrote of one of his books, "[a]s often, a cool sense of humour is just about allowed to emerge, in the entitling of a chapter, 'Universalisers, Relaters and Contemporanisers,' and the work ends with a focus on forgiveness."

I went on to note that McIntyre followed Baillie in combining appreciation of the constructive content of Barth's theology with skepticism about the doctrine of revelation which was integral to his theological programme. He reinforced the influence of the liberal evangelical tradition, and though not especially liberal by contemporary standards was widely held to represent the best of the broad church inheritance in Scotland.

And I ended with the testimony that: "Those who had the privilege of sitting under Torrance and McIntyre had the benefit of a uniquely valuable double perspective in systematic theology."

Looking at the world of systematic theology in 2007, and with the distinguished exception of the current incumbent of John's chair, this is even more apposite now than it was then. It is truly meet, right, and our bounden duty that we should now praise famous men, and not least John McIntyre.

---

14. Wright and Badcock, *Disruption to Diversity*, 129–30.

9

Religion and Democracy

NOSTER symposium, Amsterdam, August 2009

Is RELIGION AND/OR SECULARISM a threat to democracy? Yes and No. It all depends on what sort of religion, secularism, threat, and democracy you have in mind. Historically, we know that religion has sometimes been a threat to democracy and sometimes a support. The same can be said of the secular. And democracy has meant many different things in history, some of which might be thought desirable by some Christian theologians today, others not.

In preparation for this session you will no doubt have read again that fine seventeenth-century text *Den Schotschen Duyvel*, probably by Johan de Wit,[1] which argued violently for toleration, against the supposed Scots Calvinism of the Voetians. The Scots are the source of all our troubles. You may feel that not only is religion a threat to external spheres of society and democracy. But because the religious are always quarrelling bitterly among themselves, their animosities spill over into the secular sphere and create strife where there was previously peace. Of course there is always a possible religious response. The penalties prescribed for Anabaptist heretics in seventeenth-century Holland could be said to be a model example of recognition of the distinctiveness of women: while men were to be burned at the stake, women were to have the privilege of being buried alive. Democracy allied to multicultural, gender-aware sensitivity. What more could we wish for?

---

1. Israel, *The Dutch Republic*, 673.

I'm delighted to be included in this conversation. Already back in the Dark Ages, in 1993, John Witte summed up what needs to be said about democracy:[2] "The cardinal *social* ideas of democracy are equality and freedom, pluralism and toleration.... The cardinal *political* idea of democracy is that government must be limited and self-limiting."

Democracy, however, has no paradigmatic form. Democracy is modest in its minimal requirements and malleable in form. Christianity and democracy complement each other. Christianity provides democracy with a system of beliefs that integrates its concerns for liberty and responsibility, individuality and community. Democracy provides Christianity with a system of government that balances its concerns for human dignity and depravity, social pluralism and progress.

That, I think, still stands. I'm a little less optimistic than John about the Calvinist tradition. Calvin liked aristocracy. The Reformation only came in Scotland when the aristocracy decided it was in their interest. The Lutherans came along a little too early, and lost their heads. John's 1993 collection offers a couple of other important reminders. What about women? "Feminist theology works towards the transformation of democracy into multicultural forms of social and personal flourishing."[3] Calvin might not have liked this.

And just how proud of the Christian contribution can we be? "Christianity and the church must start off with a massive mea culpa when it comes to speaking of their records relating to democracy and human rights."[4] But we are talking of democracy here, not human rights. Well, perhaps there is a connection: "What we need is not democracy but human rights."[5]

I have recently been working on human rights. (I should, of course, have also been working on democracy: health warning—I have no expertise in political science or constitutional law.) This paper reflects much of what I originally argued in my *Christ and Human Rights*. In this field some scholars maintain that religion is almost incompatible with human rights (Louis Henkin), while others hold that religion is the keystone of human rights (Michael Perry). It seems to me that is never wise to restrict strategies for addressing complex issues to single focus perspectives. For

---

2. Witte, *Christianity and Democracy in Global Context*, 2ff.

3. Chopp, "A Feminist Perspective," 126.

4. Tutu, "To Be Human Is to Be Free," 311.

5. Ignacio Ellacuria, 1998, quoted in Sobrino, "A Critique and Unmasking of Present-day Democracies," 69.

example, a Marxist analysis which tends to dismiss all liberal tradition as simply a tool of the market and an epiphenomenon of global capitalism is particularly susceptible to this problem. I do not myself see any credible way of cutting the Gordian knot of complexity and the need for careful differentiations.

This is swiftly confirmed in my view by a glance at the philosophical study of geopolitical problems involving democracy, rights, and religion by Jeffrey Stout. In the discussion of rights, especially in communitarian[6] thinking, considerable doubt has been cast on the notion of democracy as a reliable support for rights. This is a common aspect of the critique of liberal, post-enlightenment values. In his *Democracy and Tradition*, Stout defends democracy as a rich and living tradition, involving the activities and conversation of a wide variety of citizens with differing views, holding each other responsible in the creation of communal ethical agreements.

Democracy is a tradition of huge significance for social development:

> It inculcates certain habits of reasoning, certain attitudes towards deference and authority in political discussion, and love for certain virtues, as well as a disposition to respond to certain types of actions, events or persons with admiration, pity or horror.[7]

Character creates an attitude of what Whitman called piety. Piety can be constructive, but it can also be destructive—he cites Baldwin and West in criticism of aspects of Black National piety. Democracy gives rise to a hope, the hope of making a difference for the better by democratic means.

Stout turns to the role of religion in political discourse. Rawls and Rorty have questioned the legitimacy of religion in public reasoning. But religion need not inhibit conversation, and may be a factor in the construction of positive rather than negative freedom. Secularization as the questioning of infallible religious authorities does not necessarily lead to an equally doctrinaire secularism, *contra* the arguments of Radical Orthodoxy. Likewise the new traditionalism of Macintyre, and the appeal to virtue ethics by Hauerwas, misunderstands the liberal tradition. A positive step would suggest a convergence by the liberals and their critics

---

6. See the fine appreciation of Stout by David Fergusson, "Beyond Theologies of Resentment." I have also learned from discussion of *Democracy and Tradition* with Gretar Gunnarsson.

7. Stout, *Democracy and Tradition*, 3.

on "a form of pragmatic expressivism that takes enduring democratic social practices as a tradition with which we have good reasons to identify."[8] He traces connections between the emergence of rights talk and the emergence of modern democratic culture. This involves reciprocity between rights and responsibilities.

Aligning himself with Annette Baier, he sees rights: "[A]s an alternative to begging on the one hand, and to certain kinds of coercion, such as torture and religiously motivated warfare, on the other."[9]

It involves specific attitudes: charity towards strangers. Whatever we conclude about God, "[o]ur grasp on the objectivity of obligation is firmest in these ordinary contexts where we fully understand the point of requiring one another to live up to the demands of the decent relationships in which we take part."[10] Ethical discourse is a social practice.

Stout concludes that:

> Democracy, then, is misconceived when taken to be a desert landscape hostile to whatever life-giving waters of culture and tradition might still flow through it. Democracy is better construed as the name appropriate to the currents themselves in this particular time and place.[11]

It may be thought that we are straying too far here from the highroad of theology. I do not think that we can avoid these issues.[12]

The Ingredients of Consensus?

What kind of democracy is desirable? This is where I am enthusiastic about bringing in the dimension of human rights.

8. Ibid., 184.
9. Ibid., 206.
10. Ibid., 269.
11. Ibid., 308.
12. Traditional liberal notions of justice and democracy have long been the subject of severe criticism. Derrida has written of "The Mystical Foundation of Authority." He speaks of Justice as the indestructible condition of deconstruction. Justice, for Derrida, is a messianic concept—unattainable (somewhat perhaps like Reinhold Niebuhr's notion of the relevance of an impossible ideal). But, as Richard Amesbury notes, Derrida seems both to deny the relativism of the concept of justice and at the same time to be unable to offer any specification which would make justice recognizable. ("Force of Law," 15. Cf. Critchley, *The Ethics of Deconstruction*. I am indebted to Richard Amesbury for this understanding of Derrida.)

It is widely recognized today that there is not, and is never likely to be, a single agreed perspective on human rights, at least in its theory. But with all due caveats and definitional variations, there is an increasing consciousness, except in totalitarian regimes, *that the cluster of human rights values will include tolerance, acceptance, mutuality and reciprocity, liberty of conscience and equal respect.*

There is, I hope, the future prospect of approaches to a *modus vivendi* in the manner of Rawls's proposals or to an overlapping consensus. It begins to be possible to compile an agreed list of basic and necessary goods as ground for agreement.

We may borrow here the language of wide reflective equilibrium and of agonistic liberalism to help us chart rational grounds for such beliefs. To cut a long discussion as short, as decently possible, it may be possible to contrast an "essentially contestedness" view of differing perspectives with coherence theory, searching for a wide reflective equilibrium.

Despite a potential lack of convergence, it is possible, however, to offer standards of justification—standards of *appropriate* coherence— according to which a conception generated by one wide reflective equilibrium is superior to one generated by another.

The problems of balancing liberalism with equality and democracy were much discussed by Rawls in *A Theory of Justice* and *Justice as Fairness*, in what has been described as a complex egalitarianism.[13] Similar problems arise with rights theory. I have indicated the advantages as I see them of notions of sympathy and solidarity. These may be necessary, but may not be sufficient. They could be backed up by other principles/constructions of rationality—perhaps along lines suggested in his modified theory of rationality by Alan Gewirth. Hilary Putnam[14] draws attention to Dewey's criticism of sympathy and suggests that what is required is transformational sympathy, i.e., education into the ethical life in community. This would also go some way to meeting Wolterstorff's critique of sympathy.[15]

---

13. Daniels, "Democratic Equalities," 150ff. *The Cambridge Companion to John Rawls*, edited by Samuel Freeman, discusses the very real problems of arriving at a stable account of political liberalism which is compatible with equality and democracy, and makes possible a real *modus vivendi* without privileging particular views.

14. Putnam, *Ethics without Ontology*, 102. Cf. Nussbaum, "Radical Evil in Liberal Democracies," 171ff.

15. Wolterstorff, *Justice*.

Cultivating a Thick Culture of Democracy— Tolerance and Its Allies

Can we enhance a democratic culture by encouraging tolerance? Freedom from fear of persecution, after all, is better than nothing.[16] Bernard Williams suggested that

> the practice of toleration has to be sustained not so much by a pure principle resting on a value of autonomy as by a wider and more mixed range of resources. These resources include an active skepticism against fanaticism and the pretensions of its advocates; conviction about the manifest evils of toleration's absence; and, quite certainly, power, to provide Hobbesian reminders to the more extreme groups that they will have to settle for coexistence.[17]

In the light of the checkered history of toleration, Williams' proposals seem to me to have much to commend them, not least the hint that in a democratic society toleration may on occasion have to be effectively enforced as well as abstractly proclaimed. "A wider and more mixed range of resources" will be deeply unsatisfying to our purist longings, but it may be the most practical way forward.

David Richards sees toleration as part of a continuing struggle against prejudice, exemplified in the parallel battles against racism in America and against anti-Semitism in Europe, but applicable also feminist and gay concerns. Against this, Andrew Murphy, after a rigorous historical investigation of myths about religious toleration, defines the scope and limitations of toleration more narrowly, against John Rawls and David Richards. Murphy notes that blacks and others are discriminated against not because of their conscientious beliefs but because they are perceived to be inferior as a group.

Though there is a real difference of perception here, it would seem that there is also a considerable area of overlapping consensus concerning

---

16. ""Freedom from fear" could be said to sum up the whole philosophy of human rights.' Dag Hammarskjold, speech on 180th anniversary of Virginia Declaration of Human Rights. Quote 20th May 1956. (*Simpson's Contemporary Quotations*. 1988. Houghton Mifflin).

On human rights, cf. Witte, "A Short History of Western Rights," and Wolterstorff, *Justice*. I do not agree with Wolterstorff that a secular grounding of human rights is not possible, but I do believe that a Christological grounding makes a vital contribution.

17. Williams, "Toleration, an Impossible Virtue," 26. Cf. D. Richards, "Toleration and the Struggle against Prejudice," and A. Murphy, *Conscience and Community*.

the practical issues to be addressed, since there are inevitably connections between individual and group rights. Both issues of conscience and belief on the one hand, and social respect and equal treatment on the other. Here Williams' notion of multiple resources seems apposite. This does not of course mean, for any of these writers, unlimited pluralism in toleration. In this theological study, the Christomorphic dimension is an indicator of the centre and limits of toleration.

Murphy's historical study of toleration issues in New England and in England in the seventeenth century, brings out the central role of political, as much as theological, judgement in the arbitration of toleration, and the complexity of a situation in which tolerance was often highly selective. He opposes three "myths"—that religious toleration is a self-evident and unqualified good, that toleration came about through the efforts of skeptical Enlightenment rationalists, and that toleration provides a basis for multicultural and identity politics. There were genuine reasons for tension between conscience and community. Toleration easily dropped when the political situation changed, and the tolerant could become intolerant. Liberal views were combined with the belief that a civilised society could only function within an orderly community, and there was often genuine fear of civil unrest. Toleration leads not to the celebration of difference *per se* but to search for a way of living together in peace, a *modus vivendi*. Interestingly for our study he highlights the religious nature of the argument:

> The arguments made by seventeenth century tolerationists were almost exclusively religious in nature: the true Christian displays humility and forbearance towards those with differing views; Jesus commanded preaching and not coercion; belief is beyond the control of the will and can only be brought about by persuasion; true belief requires the possibility of acting on those beliefs without the fear of penal sanctions.[18]

Though non-religious views have made important contributions in later times, religious views do not have to be coercive, and may make a distinctive contribution in particular circumstances.

Toleration of beliefs, liberty of conscience, concern for equality and equal respect for difference, a raft of issues are involved in the evolving emergence of a human rights culture. This is a very uneven development, involving interruptions and tensions. There is always the danger of the

---

18. Murphy, *Conscience and Community*, 14.

modus vivendi breaking down. The existence of monographs, conventions, and treaties is no guarantee of fair and equal treatment *ubique et ab omnibus*. We cannot presume that one instance of an effective human rights regime will set the benchmark for future conduct. Historical study, such as Murphy's analysis, suggests the need for a constant reinforcement of human rights culture from different directions. Where religion is involved in the political equation, as it often still is, it becomes important that the theological contribution also makes an explicit commitment to human rights.

Murphy's account of toleration reinforces the picture of *complexity* in the development of issues connected with rights which we have already noted in earlier periods. Nicholas of Cusa in his *De pace fidei* allows that different nations may legitimately observe different religious practices. "Where no conformity in manner can be found, nations should be permitted their own devotional practices and ceremonies."[19] We need not be scandalized that different writers approach human rights from different angles. A desire for certainty and uniformity seems to be an increasing attribute of the contemporary religious consciousness. Perhaps this should be resisted.

The notion of sympathy may be another marker for the optimum quality of democratic process—I think of the deployment of the notions of sentiment/sympathy, from David Hume and Adam Smith, to Richard Rorty. But sentiment without enforcement may be entirely useless, as the record of abuse in prison regimes throughout history amply demonstrates. The need for sympathy has to be expanded to include a vehicle for enforcement—otherwise sympathy may just be ineffective. In her *Religion and Faction in Hume's Moral Philosophy*, Jennifer Herdt[20] explores the notion of "extensive" sympathy in Hume's philosophy. We have to cultivate a sympathy for the point of view of others, even when we do not share their beliefs, and we can have no dogmatic certainty about our own beliefs. This paradigm of sympathetic understanding provides a way of entering and appreciating the point of view of others, and of avoiding unnecessary conflicts harmful to society.

Sympathy may be helpful. But is it enough? Michael Walzer in his *Spheres of Justice* analyzed the complexity of the notion of equality, in its political and economic dimensions, and in its implication for such

---

19. *De pace fidei*, 62, quoted by Nederman, 94.
20. Herdt, *Religion and Faction in Hume's Moral Philosophy*.

important areas as education, public health, work, leisure, political office, and personal relationships. He concluded that "[m]utual respect and a shared self-respect are the deep strengths of complex equality, and together they are the source of its possible endurance."[21]

In my view it is possible to learn from Rorty on solidarity, and the tradition of sympathy, without subscribing to all the implications which he draws. Richard Amesbury has recently shown this in his excellent *Morality and Social Criticism*. Amesbury sets out from Rorty's proposal to replace objectivity by solidarity. He wants to replace human rights foundationalism by a human rights culture based on sentimental education. Amesbury objects that "his anti-authoritarianism—while ostensibly liberating—ironically renders Rorty incapable of seeing how it could be possible to dissent from the vast majority of one's peers without ceasing to be rational." Rorty dislikes the idea of obligations. But "[i]t is difficult to see how Rorty can hope to continue to talk of 'a human rights culture' while abandoning talk of obligations that obtain irrespective of whether or not one's peers happen to hold one accountable to them."[22] People have felt obliged to rescue strangers in danger, people outside their own communities. Realism without Platonist foundationalism can be reserved as a basis for social action. Amesbury's approach fits well with stress on the postfoundational.

William Talbott also supports the thesis that sympathy is important but not all that there is. He notes the importance of empathy—as a feeling, but more than this:

> The feeling of empathy itself cannot be separated from a judgement about what it is like to be the other person, and that judgement provides the basis for a moral judgement about how the other person ought to be treated.[23]

He discusses Rorty's theory of moral sentiment, concluding that reason *and* sentiment are at the basis of moral judgement: "Sentiments themselves are often a manifestation of reason and can essentially involve judgements of what is true and false."[24]

Human rights, sympathy, justice, these then are some of the basic structural elements which characterise the sort of democracy which

---

21. Walzer, *Spheres of Justice*, 321.
22. Amesbury, *Morality and Social Criticism*, 14, 16.
23. Talbott, *Which Rights Should be Universal?* 66.
24. Ibid., 170.

I imagine most of us would want to support. They can be fostered by religion and by secular perspectives. What matters is not the source by the final balance. Christian faith understands these elements as part of the Christomorphic trace through which God is inviting the whole created order towards eschatological reconciliation. As such, theology supports these developments, as a contributing partner to a wider human conversation.

Faith, Politics, and Economic Crisis

Is that all there is? It is not possible in the real world, especially the world of global recession, to speak of democracy without addressing again the vexed question of the relation of faith to politics. The gospels speak about the values of the kingdom, money, talent, and investment. "You should have given my money to the money-changers, then at my coming I should have received my own with interest." In 2009, international news has been has been dominated by bankers talking to politicians. What has faith to do with politics and economics? Theologians become involved. Is it lawful to give tribute unto Caesar, or not? Asked the members of the Department of Theology and Religious Studies. Jesus said, "Show me the money." And they came unto Jesus and presented him with a blue chip share certificate. And he saith unto them, "Sell, sell, sell. For the IMF has issued dire warnings, your GDP is falling and deflation is at hand."

How can we begin to speak about faith in relation to politics? Seeking examples we encounter the working out of untrammelled faith in the political arena. Here is an Archbishop.

> Ordinarily, it should be our joy that an African American is popularly nominated for the first time in American political history. We should however be concerned that this is a politician considered to be a far left wing liberal for whom all that counts is victory at the polls.... We urge Senator Obama to prayerfully reconsider some of his ultra liberal dispositions, not only for the sake of 'God's Own Country' but in the interest of the world.[25]

The Archbishop might take comfort from the New Testament assurance that "We are of God. He that knoweth God heareth us," as the King James Version puts it. "He that is not of God heareth us not. Hereby know we the spirit of truth, and the spirit of error."

25. Archbishop Peter Akinola, 16th September, 2008.

How are we to understand these mysteries? What is faith? Well faith is trust, confidence, assurance, sometimes a sense of certainty against the appearance of things, a sense of an overarching providence. Sadly, history seems to show that people who have a sense of certainty are often a complete menace. Trust me. Absolutely. Christian faith is part of a complex, we may say, which moves on to hope. But sometimes those who hope are destroyed and those who act with the force of desperation survive. Well faith is sort of the hope of love. Faith would seem to be at best as secure as a kind of philosophical sub-prime mortgage. As for politics, the public does not rate politicians. British ones employ their extended families with salaries funded by the tax-payer. American ones have an insatiable taste for pork, pork barrel politics. Our joint gift to the world is democracy—and the most modern model democracies have a curious tendency to become totalitarian.

Confronted by the faith/politics issue, Jesus looked at a silver coin and he said, "Whose head is this, and whose title?" He invited his hearers to think, and not to be content with the standard answers. He did not say that political issues are a waste of time, and he did not say, "We don't do God." When we give up politics, demons tend to rush in to fill the vacuum. When we exclude the whole dimension of ultimate meaning we may easily diminish ourselves and our capacity to be there for our fellow human beings. There are no quick fixes in the sight of God. Christianity understands faith always in relation to Jesus who IS the instantiation of the presence of God among us.

Patrick Deneen has made an attractive case for the value of religion for democracy.

> In contrast to the "democratic faithful," whose belief in human malleability frequently leads them to reject traditional religious belief as undemocratic, "democratic realism" finds, in the religious stress on human fallibility, an extraordinary chastening and democratic resource.[26]

Religion can stress a shared belief in common neediness and a kind of "democratic *caritas*." He cites Reinhold Niebuhr, who identifies democratic humility with the long tradition of religious humanity. Above all, there is Lincoln, in his Second Inaugural Address:

> With malice towards none; with charity for all; with firmness in the right, as God gives us to see the right, let us strive to finish

26. Deneen, *Democratic Faith*, 11.

the work we are in; to bind up the nation's wounds; to care for him who shall have borne the battle, and for his widow, and his orphan—to do all which may achieve and cherish a just, and lasting peace, among ourselves, and with all nations. (2.687.)

We must just be careful not to tie particular political preferences to appeals to the command of God. Human beings, religious or not, have a perplexing capacity to twist meaning into its opposite. It is not an accident that Christian faith understands the incarnation of God to involve torture and identification with agony. The mystery of God remains in significant ways unfathomable to us. The consequences of that mystery include the implementation of a justice which is always built on compassionate hospitality. Christianity understands politics in the light of the particular compassion and solidarity which Jesus embodies. Christian people are invited to offer this trace of engaged faith in hospitable exchange with people of other faiths and none. Jesus didn't say, "Blessed are those who always close ranks and never rock the boat." Jesus, it has been said, was a man who played to lose. Yet this drama of defeat is also the hope and ground of the persistence of love. Herein is love, not that we loved God, but that he loved us. Not perhaps a strategy for a successful political campaign—but a reminder that there is more to life than politics, and that faith without love—is a fairly transparent example of a credit crunch.

Hospitable Politics

God's hospitality is expressed in personal commitment and in church engagement. But it has implications in almost all areas of human life, perhaps not least in politics, in its theory and its actualities. Though it does not explicitly reflect on hospitality, much weight is placed on dimensions of hospitable politics in Jim Wallis's classic, *God's Politics*, a moderate evangelical critique of the politics of the American Christian Right. Against this he advocates a different kind of religion:

> Prophetic faith is the best counterpart to fundamentalist religion. We bring faith into the public square when our moral convictions demand it. But to influence a democratic society, you must win the public debate about why the principles you advocate are better for the common good. That's the democratic

discipline religion has to be under when it brings its faith to the public square.²⁷

In their *Guidebook for Putting Your faith into Action,* Jim Wallis and Chuck Gutenson make an impressive effort to encourage engagement with basic Christian values at a practical as well as a theoretical level. Amesbury and I make a similar plea at the end of *Faith and Human Rights.* I underline again here the absolutely crucial importance of the difficult task of encouraging and facilitating the transition from theory to practice, to move from a rhetoric to a culture of hospitality. Faith believes that God's creation and reconciliation are shaped for universally instantiated hospitality.

Prophetic Hospitality?

What does prophetic religion look like? It is concerned with justice, with fairness, and therefore, above all, with poverty. Often religious fervor acts as a convenient but toxic diversion from the basic realities of deprivation, sickness, and neglect, the crushing burdens of absolute poverty. Often too, ethical action can become a substitute for faith. Both are involved. The hospitable God is committed to the elimination of a state of affairs in which governments, through international agreements, collaborate to produce a world in which the rich get richer and the poor get poorer. Wallis highlights the Jubilee 2000 campaign as a concrete attempt to address this issue on a realistic scale. Despite a massive effort at the time, all too little has been achieved. But the vision remains central to a continuing challenge. Organizations like Adam Taylor's *Global Justice Organization*²⁸ are needed to maintain effective action.

Thomas Friedman produces detailed and specific examples of these developments. America is a giant consumer of resources. The acceleration of energy and resource demand is exemplified worldwide—e.g., in the very recent growth of new cities—he specifically mentions Doha in Qatar and Dalian in China. There is huge demand for energy to service these highly sophisticated developments. He instances the growth of luxury communities near the pyramids in Egypt where yesterday there were none. Some of these pyramids:

---

27. Wallis, *God's Politics*, 11.
28. Ibid., 289ff.

> [A]re now basically surrounded by gated communities filled with McMansions on quarter acre-lots—gated communities with names like Moon Valley, Hyde Park, Richmond, Riviera Heights and Beverley Hills. There is a ninety-nine hole golf course. There is a French-based Carrefour big-box store and a modern supermarket round the corner.[29]

Petropolitics is influential in changing custom and culture in small ways—notably in Islamic societies though "Saudification."

Climate change has been a much disputed topic, as special interests on various sides of political divides have argued about its existence. It has become clear, even to most skeptics, that there are here the makings of imminent catastrophe, partly due to natural causes and partly due to human action. Some countries may gain more than they lose from climate change, at least in the medium term. But the losers are those who are already among the world's poorest and most vulnerable people:

> Take just one country: Rwanda. In most of its countryside, there is no grid, and generators that run on gasoline and diesel are becoming more expensive by the day to operate. How are the Rwandans going to maintain vaccines, provide clean water, run climate change, without reliable energy—clean, dirty or expensive?[30]

A hospitable God is opposed to violence and coercion—with the sole exception of violence used to protect the most vulnerable from harm. Such a perspective will inevitably remind us of causes for which churches and politicians have often campaigned—opposition to nuclear weapons, the fight against poverty. Yet along with these headline-making issues there are even more deadly sources of violence and coercion in the world, more deadly because they are harder to pin down. Commercial and trade pressures are notoriously elusive. Arms control is one such issue.

Closely linked is the issue of trade connections and investment in brutal and totalitarian regimes. The considerable UK investment in Myanmar is a classic case.

It is always argued that if our country did not participate in such investment others would simply step in—one may point to ever increasing Chinese investment in Africa. Yet if Christian communities are serious about discipleship in following a hospitable God, then there is a need to

---

29. Friedman, *Hot, Flat and Crowded*, 64.
30. Ibid., 159.

be involved effectively in these issues. God is as concerned for situations in which he is apparently absence as when he seems manifestly present. There is no situation with which God is not concerned.

Democracy means embracing justice, not simply benevolence. This brings us inevitably into the public square, and the realm of politics. The Tocqueville Symposium at Harvard in 2006, led by Hugh Heclo,[31] brings out the very different ways in which the relationship between Christianity and democracy in America may be viewed. The picture is of constant fluctuation, of internal migration of Christians from society but also of constant return and influence of democracy in culture and society on the churches. The discussion brought out well the distinctively American strands in American Catholicism and the local, congregational nature of much churchmanship. Progressive Christianity in America does and may derive strength from Catholic and evangelical, as well as liberal resources.

Why should Christians become involved in politics? Franklin Gamwell has argued that they have a duty to do so: "Because their faith means that God as re-presented through Jesus Christ is present to and understood by all humans, Christians may without pause pledge that this faith can be redeemed through reasons authorised by common human experience."[32]

This engagement has specific consequences, God calls us all to the community of love and thus to justice as general emancipation. He instances abortion, affirmative action, and economic distribution as spheres for the deployment of the idea of maximum mutuality.

The actualization of hospitality in specific instances will include the addressing of political dimensions in almost every case—poverty and development, conflict resolution, environmental destruction and population explosion, the proliferation of minor wars, often proxy wars which cause unimaginable suffering. The global problems of peace and security, of weapons and disarmament are even more bound up with politics, the geopolitics of the major powers. Hospitality as justice is eternally bound up with solutions to these perennial tensions.

Let justice roll down like waters and righteousness, like an ever-flowing stream. The multifaceted and omnipresent scope of justice is neatly captured by Walter Burghardt in his *Justice—A Global Adventure*. Burghardt analyses justice as legal, ethical biblical, social, and

---

31. Heclo, *Christianity and American Democracy.*
32. Gamwell, *Politics as a Christian Vocation*, 75, 130.

environmental. Hospitality without justice would remain a hollow simulacrum:

> The hungry person needs bread, the homeless person needs shelter, the one deprived of rights needs justice, the undisciplined one needs order, and the slave needs freedom. It would be blasphemy against God and our neighbour while saying that God is closest to those in deepest need. We break bread with the hungry and share our home with them for the sake of Christ's love, which belongs to the hungry as much as it does to us. If the hungry do not come to faith, the guilt falls on those who denied them bread. To bring bread to the hungry is preparing the way for the coming of grace.[33]

Can We Dare to Get Real?

Thomas Friedman's *Hot, Flat and Crowded* provides a comprehensive and compelling reminder of the deeply challenging geopolitical realities faced by the twenty-first-century world, realities not easily faced with the aid of our traditional religious resources. Friedman lays out impressively the basic geopolitical challenges currently facing the world. The world has become flattened out through the technological revolution, through widespread access to the internet, and the possibilities for working and for information sharing which this has brought. The world has become hot, through the emission of greenhouse gases and the struggle for ever increasing energy supply. The world has become crowded, as population growth has rocketed exponentially throughout the world. Friedman identifies a challenge to innovation, determination, and effectively targeted aid to the weakest. The key players will be the United States, China, and India—each will have its own mountains to climb.

In all these countries democracy will involve inevitable tensions between popular control and issues of legitimacy—benevolent despotism, elective despotism, protection of minorities. Finally, there is another challenge to democracy—the role of the super-rich. In his remarkable *Who Runs Britain?*, Robert Peston underlined the immense influence of the complex financial derivatives, etc. The super rich can move money around the world at will, avoiding taxes and depleting government

---

33. Bonhoeffer, *Ethics*, 163, quoted by Lovin, *Christian Realism and the New Realities*, 204. Cf. A. Lijphart's plea for "a gentler, kinder democracy," in *Patterns of Democracy*.

revenues. Political parties depend on their donations for support. Kevin Phillips has done the same for the USA. Here is an area where the secular can indeed be a challenge. Except that the super-rich in the USA may also be identical with the Christian Right. Nothing is simple.

Christianity is concerned for the most vulnerable. We have to privilege these issues if we are to have any sort of hospitality worthy of the name. To reflect expansively on alterity or reconciliation without taking account of what is required to run the generators can only immunize us against facing the realities. Global hospitality is extricably linked to global economics. Obviously the Christian theologian cannot resolve these challenges, but should try to make an informed contribution to their solution. If we can try to constantly reflect on God's hospitality for the world with our eyes wide open, rather than with our eyes wide shut, that at least will be something.

Is Christianity a threat to democracy? It all depends on what sort of Christianity, and what sort of democracy. In ancient Athens only full citizens could participate in the democratic process. But at least that was an important beginning. As we discern more about equality, freedom, solidarity, and human dignity we may hope to move towards a more just democratic world order. But this will certainly not happen automatically. It has been suggested that as many people have been killed in the Congo in the last twenty years as died in the Holocaust.

Faith believes that the Christian gospel has an indispensable role to play in the human future, for this is part of that movement from creation to reconciliation which is centred on the incarnation of God in Jesus Christ, the concrete instantiation of the hospitality of God.[34]

---

34. Since writing this paper I have been encouraged by the stress laid on justice and tolerance in a partnership democracy by Ronald Dworkin in *Is Democracy Possible Here?*, and on empathy in the face of radical evil by Martha Nussbaum ("Radical Evil in Liberal Democracies: The Neglect of the Political Emotions." The suggestion that abstract ideals are not enough is stressed by Sen in discussing John Rawls—though Rawls would not himself have favoured abstraction. On the theological dimensions of justice, cf. too, Newlands and Smith, *Hospitable God*. I have much appreciated the many perceptive contributions made at the VISOR seminar on Democracy at the VU in Amsterdam in August 2009, for which this paper was written.

10

Incarnation

Doctrine Committee of the Scottish Episcopal Church, 2011

THIS SERIES OF ESSAYS continue to explore central issues in the life, thought, and worship of the church today, and looks towards the future. It is based around the Nicene Creed—a basic part of the Eucharistic liturgy of the Scottish Episcopal Church, as it is for much of the wider catholic church. Here we shall be concerned with incarnation, a concept at the heart of the creed, and the key to the salvation which it promises to humanity. Why incarnation? Would it not be a very good idea to free ourselves from some of these ancient formulations in the twenty-first century? This is a very fair question, and not a new one. To answer it we shall take a look at incarnation in the tradition and the contemporary life of our church.

The Eucharistic liturgy is a central part of the worship of the Scottish Episcopal Church, bearer of that sacramental tradition which complements the liturgy of the Word. Together they promise and they deliver to us that Sacramental Word which invites us to embrace salvation. Salvation is not just a verbal promise. It is embedded, concretized, and instantiated in the material world of which we care ourselves a part. The Word became flesh. The Word became human. All humanity is valuable in the sight of God because God himself has embraced humanity in all its forms. He has embraced life in all its experiences, death in its worst horrors, and out of this experience has brought salvation. This is what incarnation involves. It is central to the tradition of the gospel which the church lives and relives in every generation in its own way from the time of the first Christians. This is why we call the tradition apostolic. It reminds us of the character of faithful discipleship.

But faithful discipleship is not served by mindless repetition. Radical discipleship is unafraid to try new pathways. If the old language has got to the stage of obscuring rather than illuminating the true meaning of incarnation, perhaps even immunizing us against the risk-laden reality of incarnational discipleship, might it not be time to jettison the notion of incarnation in the name of true incarnation. This option was explored exhaustively by some scholars who were mainly devout Anglicans some years ago. The result was a fresh appreciation of many aspects of incarnation. But, in time, there was a realization of just how much that is vital to Christian life and action would be lost.

Nevertheless, this movement was a valuable reminder that even key concepts cannot simply be taken for granted, precisely if they are to have the dynamic effects today that they had for their original creators. These papers are an attempt to encourage and invite readers to do just that for themselves.

Incarnation is a word deeply embedded in Christian tradition. More recently, it has been the subject of vigorous theological controversy. But whatever the advantages and disadvantages of the word incarnation, the substance of the matter has become fruitful as perhaps never before in contemporary Christian thought, action, and engagement. That is why we believe it is worth continuing the long conversation about incarnation in the twenty-first century. This is a conversation with consequences. Here are some suggestions for kicking off some conversation.

God was incarnate in Jesus Christ. The Word became flesh and lived among us. God is here, among the everyday things of life, the bus tickets, the credit cards, the takeaways and the takeovers, the politics and the economics. God is where we are, most importantly God is where the people are at the point of greatest need.

Incarnation as a dimension of faith is central. Yet the concept itself is full of paradox—critics would say contradictions, others would say mysteries. The idea is not a trump card to resolve all problems. It is possible to think and act in profoundly incarnational ways without using the word incarnation, and it is equally possible to think and act with a lofty notion of incarnation in ways which actually mask and neglect the entire basic thrust of incarnation. That is why we are inviting you to share in our conversation. As with everything in Christian tradition, this is always an open conversation, always a beginning rather than an ending, but a conversation which focuses on one central reality, the faith that God was in Christ reconciling the world to himself.

Incarnations, as instances of the divine in human form appear in many though not all of the world religions—perhaps a useful reminder of the overarching unity of humanity in the sight of and in the care of God. The writings of the Hebrew Bible are concerned at different times and in different ways to God who is not only transcendent but immanent—God is Creator of heaven and earth, but God is also in the midst of, and active in, the lives and affairs of the peoples, and especially the people of Israel. When we come to the New Testament we hit what we might see as one of the paradoxes. The Synoptic Gospels, which speak eloquently of the day-to-day life of Jesus in the world of fish and fasting, do not use the concept of incarnation. We have to wait till the Fourth Gospel, apparently the most theological of the Gospels. The Word became flesh, and lived among us, and we saw his glory, full of grace and truth. It might seem that St. John's gospel is furthest from the real world, and the others are down to earth. Yet some scholars might argue the opposite—no gospel is more aware of the darkness in which the light shines. So much the worse for scholarship? All the gospels narrated the tale of the events concerning Jesus, his life, his death and his resurrection, his identification with his fellow human beings and his identification with God.

Here already the man Jesus and the Christ of faith are characterized in different ways. To understand this diversity the early Christian communities needed a Christology. Inevitably, and actually reflecting this diversity, they produced different Christologies. For good and bad reasons there developed a tendency to search for *the* one correct Christology, and this was to produce gains and losses. Some versions were clearly less than adequate to express the central burden of the experience reflected in the early communities and their writings. The most acceptable versions took due account of the affirmation of incarnation. Jesus in the New Testament is portrayed as a man with a unique relationship to God, as Messiah, the Lord, the Word of God, the Servant of God, greatest of the prophets, the Christ. He sacrifices himself "for us." He is the mediator of the salvation expected in the Hebrew Bible. He is in various reflections shepherd, prophet priest and king, witness to God, a teacher, and perhaps even a magician.

As the churches began to consolidate into larger groups, there developed a stream of reflection which we now recognise as a version of a doctrine of incarnation, and which became the major current among numerous other currents. It's worth pausing to set this out in some detail.

In the incarnation, the embedding of the divine love in the created order, the full presence of the divine, and so the unity of the divine and human, in Jesus Christ takes place through a continuous giving on God's part and a continuous human receiving by Jesus. Jesus is the person he is only through a continuous receiving of God's gift: he receives in a truly human way, in faith, prayer, and obedience. God comes into human existence, vulnerability to temptation, openness to suffering. He does this through his divine power. The infinite assuming finitude for the salvation of humanity. This self-giving, of which only God is fully capable, is seen on the cross. Self-giving is brought to self-fulfilment in the resurrection.

For Jesus of Nazareth, the meaning of the incarnation is that God gives him participation in his divine nature, within the limitations of human nature. He participates in God's power to heal the sick, to forgive, and to renew. In devoting himself to his father, he receives the power to act in the way he does for the salvation of humanity. The full divinity of God is united with the man Jesus, but in such a way that the divinity is not changed into humanity, and man is not in any way divinized. Jesus is at once the bearer of the presence of God and the medium of its hiddenness. The mystery of union is complex beyond our understanding. We come to understand who Jesus was by looking at the pivotal events concerning Jesus. Through his life, death, and resurrection there takes place a costly reconciliation, in which the relationship between God and humanity is renewed, to await the perfection of the eschatological peace of God.

All of this was to be disputed fiercely in the centuries which followed. Sadly the desire for doctrinal uniformity was to lead, then as now, to quarrels which negated the affirmation of unconditional love incarnate, and led to the suppression of minorities whose views were perceived, rightly or wrongly, to be inadequate. To kill a man, as was famously said, is not to defend a doctrine but to kill a man.

Let's try to put this history into a nutshell. While the Docetists emphasized the earthly side of Jesus as the Christ, the Ebionites seem to have done the opposite—of course the eventual majority wrote the history. Justin Martyr saw Jesus as the eternal logos or Word of God—the governing principle of the ancient universe. But the Logos was then secondary to the Godhead.

The problem was how to express the affirmations which arose in the realm of worship in conceptual terms. All kinds of variations on the Logos Christology arose. Paul of Samosata thought that the man Jesus united with the divine logos by willing the same things—one in will with God. His opponents argued that the very essence, and not just the will, of the Logos is incarnate. But where in a human being do you locate essence? How could you combine the essence of the nature of God, who did not change, with the nature of a man, who was crucified, died, and buried?

The Arians pursued this line: the logos or Word suffered in Jesus' suffering, but God remained unchanged. How then could we be saved, if Jesus was not identified with us and with God in his humanity? Christ was the incarnate Logos. Christ was subject to change. Therefore, the Logos was subject to change. But granting that God the Creator could not suffer, that he did not change, the Logos could not be identified with God.

Schools of theology in Antioch and Alexandrian followed rival lines of argument. The Council of Nicaea (325 CE) insisted that the Logos or Son was of one essence or substance with the Father. The Cappadocians, Basil, Gregory and Gegory of Nazianzus refined the arguments, especially around the definitions over which the battle was mainly fought—substances, persons, and natures.

In Gregory of Nazianzus' famous phrase, what is not assumed is not redeemed. If God himself did not come right into human life, then we remain imprisoned in our sins: in Pauline terms, the incarnation did not work. Aware of the difficulty, Apollinarius of Laodicea proposed that in the incarnate Christ, the place of the human mind was occupied by the divine Logos. But within the current understanding of the human as body, soul, and spirit, this looked like a diluted Christology.

Battle was often the appropriate word, for there were awesome geopolitical dimensions, as rival politicians and emperors hijacked the theological slogans. The Chalcedonian definition of 451 CE sealed the definitive understanding for much of Christendom—though again, huge tracts of the known world were to disagree and often to pay dearly for their convictions. Two natures, divine and human, were affirmed so stressing the full humanity of Jesus. At the same time, Christ is only one person—though person was not quite the modern personality. Chalcedon was probably the best solution to the insoluble available, and was to last, in different formulations, more or less up to the eighteenth-century Enlightenment. The meaning of Chalcedon remains hotly debated. Sarah

Coakley (at last, a female name) has described the definition as a kind of horizon with which the mystery may best be imagined.

Thinking about incarnation went on. The Christologies of the West, following Augustine, tended to be interested not so much in the nature and person of Christ as in the salvation brought by Christ to humanity. Luther asked, "How can I find a gracious God?" and the Reformers concentrated on the nature of the gift of divine presence, especially in the Eucharist. Luther followed the Fathers in stressing the exchange of divine and human attributes in Christ, while Calvin stressed the divine transcendence. The Lutheran tradition developed a new Christology of the two states of Christ's humiliation and exaltation in the cross and resurrection, leading to further reflection on kenosis or self-emptying, in Jesus and in God.

The European Enlightenment brought a new stress on history and the historical Jesus as key to the understanding of the mystery, rather than traditional metaphysics—though of course all discussion of "ultimates" have metaphysical dimensions. Jesus is typically seen, in the tradition of Schleiermacher, as a man of pure compassion and kindness, who sets a moral example in all that he does, and is God for us. In nineteenth-century Britain, incarnation, rather than atonement, was often the preferred way into the understanding of reconciliation, salvation, and the implications for discipleship in social outreach. The twentieth century brought the dialectical theology of Barth, who returned to reaffirmation of Chalcedon, and Bultmann, whose existential interpretation of the Word stressed the mythological, rather than historical, nature of much of the New Testament. Recent interpretations have seen Jesus as the key to faith, to hope, to history, to cosmic process, and to science and to art. Rahner saw Jesus as the ideal form of humanity and Schillebeeckx as the key to Christian experience.

Every age thinks that its own preferred interpretation most faithfully reflects, at least in an indirect way, the original interpretation—and that is, of course, a legitimate aspiration. In the twenty-first century the emancipator theologies, liberation, post-colonial, feminist, gay and lesbian, black and Asian, human rights—orientated Christologies have come to complement and challenge the prevailing perspectives.

Reflection on incarnation is a rich and always changing development in the stream of Christian faith. But that does not mean that we cannot try to find some ways of expressing it. Let's imagine an account along these lines. The parables of Jesus, his life and his teaching, are *the* examples for Christians of self-giving love. Self-giving (kenosis) is incarnation and service is the way of the cross. Through the suffering humanity of Jesus Christ in humiliation, comes resurrection. God is compassionate and creates compassion in us. Jesus Christ is God for us, answering God's self-emptying in his own life of sacrificial love, a love eschatologically effective through resurrection. Such an account says more than a little about Jesus, about God and humanity, and the way of discipleship in the world today, and most Christians might agree with it. The task of constantly improving our understanding is left to us all to work out in creative tension and conversation. This diversity may be no bad thing. In any case, however we come to think of incarnation, the decisive issue is how we seek to implement this understanding through engagement in the complex globalized world in which we live. This might be a Christomorphic, incarnational response to the challenge of the form of Christ in the world. Now it is time to attempt to open out further the rich variety of some Christian reflections on incarnation.

11

Adolf von Harnack

Introduction

ADOLF VON HARNACK, 1851–1930, was one of the greatest historians of Christian life and thought. Today, he is remembered chiefly for his monumental *History of Christian Dogma*, and also for his firm support for German aspirations in the First World War. Harnack represents, it is often thought, the clearest indication of the bankruptcy of modern liberal theology. Yet events like the delivery of the annual Mildred Fish-Harnack Lecture on Human Rights in the University of Madison-Wisconsin should perhaps alert us to a much more nuanced view of the Harnack intellectual legacy. Mildred was the only American citizen to be executed by the Nazis for civilian resistance of Hitler, along with her husband Arvid Harnack and his cousin Ernst, son of Adolf von Harnack. Harnack's daughter Agnes, an early champion of feminist causes, was also associated with liberal opposition to Hitler, as part of the circle around Martin Niemoeller in Berlin-Dahlem.

Harnack was born in Dorpat (now Tartu), Lithuania, in 1851, and was educated originally at the University of Dorpat (1869–72), where his father was a distinguished Lutheran professor of theology. Christianity was at the centre of his life from the start:

> The longer I live (and how brief a time we as yet have behind us), the more daily I learn by experience how all problems and conflicts run back finally in to the realm of religion and find their issue there, and how therefore a Christian viewpoint can never be gotten rid of.... But here among my school comrades I am often forced to bear witness to my opinion, and in that have

had the experience that I am always best understood when I speak out most frankly what is in my heart.[1]

The family moved to Erlangen, where Harnack was much influenced by the learning and piety of his teacher, Moritz von Engelhardt, then back to Dorpat, and on to study and teach in Leipzig.

Appointed a professor extraordinarius in Leipzig at twenty-five, he moved through an effortless academic career, from Giessen to Marburg and then to the Chair of Church History in Berlin in 1888. At Leipzig he joined a group of friends who were to be stimulating and influential colleagues in the development of a contemporary theology and church history. At this point the great figure in German theology was Albrecht Ritschl, professor for many years in Goettingen. Ritschl was then what Barth was to be a century later—apparently the arbiter of theological truth and sanity. Harnack became a disciple, but not an uncritical follower. Producing a huge number of brilliant articles on patristic theology, notably textual studies, he came to espouse an increasingly liberal stance on issues of theology and church, which created tensions with his solidly confessional Lutheran father and with the Lutheran church. These tensions were not lightened by Harnack's incorporation, again not uncritically, of much of the historico-critical work on the bible of the Tübingen School, the work of F. C. Baur and his pupils.

The appointment to Berlin was fiercely contested by the church. Harnack was thought to be unsound, and indeed he never received any recognition or acknowledgement from the church, though he always understood his work as in the service of the church, and indeed taught generations of its leaders over many decades. Things came to a head in a fierce battle over the legitimacy and utility of the so-called Apostles' Creed. Harnack survived numerous accusations of heresy, and attacks from liberal and conservative quarters alike, to become one of the world's most influential scholars. Students flocked from the United States, Britain and elsewhere to attend his lectures and compete for a precious place in his seminar.

Harnack was excluded completely from church affairs, but soon gained wide recognition—Rector of Berlin University, twice offered a chair in Harvard, member of numerous international academies, invited to be German ambassador to the USA. His lectures on *What is*

---

1. Letter to Wilhelm Stintzen from Dorpat to Erlangen, by A. Harnack aged seventeen, cited in Glick, *Adolf von Harnack*, 33.

Christianity?, published in 1900, were an instant worldwide success, and his seminar lists were to include the names of Barth and Bonhoeffer. Like his predecessor Schleiermacher, he was much involved in the development of education in the humanities, joining the Berlin Academy of Sciences in 1890. In 1902 he founded the Evangelical-social congress, and in 1905 became director of the royal library. He became the founding director of the prestigious new Kaiser-Wilhelm Gesellschaft in Berlin, Germany's premier academic institution, in 1911. The first decade of the new century was also a decade of heated church controversy, into which he was often drawn. Perhaps his main achievement in the Academy was his direction of a magnificent edition of the pre-Nicene Greek fathers (*Griechische Christliche Schriftsteller*), which ran to thirty-six volumes. Through his connections with government and with the Emperor, he was ennobled in 1914, becoming Adolf von Harnack, and helped to draft the Kaiser's justification of the Great War.

Harnack's role in the production in 1914 of the manifesto of ninety-three leading German intellectuals in support of the war famously led Karl Barth to reject finally as worthless the entire liberal theological tradition of which Harnack was the epitome. It is true that Barth was already moving in that direction. But the manifesto was the tipping point, and has continued to be the ultimate damning evidence of the hollowness of liberal theology. It is true that theologians and churchmen, liberal and conservative, on both sides supported the war with an enthusiasm which it is hard today to imagine. Harnack and his colleagues should have known better. The concluding passage from Harnack's reply, defending German policy and dated 27 August 1914, to a letter from eleven British theologians, including P. T. Forsyth, read as follows: "I would not unnecessarily break any bond that joins me to the true Christians of your country and its scholarship. But at this moment this connection has absolutely no value for me."[2] The results of this policy were to be catastrophic. Yet, as I suggested at the beginning of this article, it remains a question how far the episode can be extrapolated into a universal principle.

Harnack continued, in 1916 and beyond, to support the war policy—as a bulwark against Bolshevism on the one hand, and British imperialism and "Americanism" on the other, in defence of what he saw as the unique spiritual and intellectual tradition of Germany. After the war he remained engaged in public theology in support of the Weimar

2. Harnack, *Aus der Friedens-und Kriegsarbeit*, 299; an essay collection which makes for extremely dismal reading.

republic, sitting on the 1919 government commission for church and educational reforms, concentrating on ceaseless academic research and on higher education, both in the humanities and the sciences. His multivolume *History of Dogma* was now an influential standard work. He was interested in social reform, and opposed the rise of anti-Semitism. When he died in 1930 the storm that was to engulf members of his family in the resistance to Hitler was not yet fully unleashed. He would not have enjoyed the fact that participants in the Wannsee conference of February 1942, which planned the murder of millions of Jews, gypsies, homosexuals, socialists and others, included PhDs in the humanities from leading German universities.

Academic Writings

Harnack was a leading member of the school of theology which dedicated itself to the construction of a school of critical contemporary theology, developing the insights of the European Enlightenment, and especially the philosophy of Immanuel Kant. This was a process to be applied equally to all the theological disciplines, church history, systematic theology, biblical and practical theology, and to employ the new theology in the service and reformation of the structures and practices of the church. The father of this school of modern theology was Friedrich Schleiermacher, and the leading proponent of the systematic theology in the next generation was to be Albrecht Ritschl, with whom Harnack was to conduct a voluminous correspondence over thirty years. Stress was laid on a repudiation of traditional metaphysical claims and structures, and a stress instead on contemporary Christian experience of God. The school of Ritschl divided into two main sections, a more rightward leaning group which took a generally more positive view of traditional notions of revelation and history, centred around the work of Wilhelm Herrmann in Marburg, and a more left-leaning dimension, intensively engaged with the relationship of theology to the newly emerging social sciences, and associated particularly with Ernst Troeltsch and his colleague Max Weber, in Heidelberg and in Berlin. Harnack was to stand somewhere in the middle of this group, showing confidence in the possibility of an historical reconstruction of the life of the Jesus of the Gospels as the centre of Christianity, but completely committed to rigorous historical critique of the tradition. He was committed to the position that while history might not have the last word in theological study, it should always have the first.

Harnack followed the classical route for the modern German theologian by beginning with study of the early church, based on the great classical education at which the German gymnasium in the nineteenth century, building on the vision of William von Humboldt, excelled. From schools like Maulbronn, students made their way to the theological faculties at Tübingen and elsewhere—a tradition in part at least still alive today. This was the time of such giants in the humanities as Mommsen and Wilamowitz, whose masterly critical editions of the classical authors spurred readers of Christian texts, not least the Scriptures of the Old and New Testaments, to new levels of precision.

Harnack's doctoral thesis dealt with the fragments of the work of the second-century thinker Marcion, a wealthy ship owner who founded a community at Edessa on the Black Sea, and is associated with Gnosticism, a movement which sprang up in various places around the ancient Mediterranean. For Christianity, Gnosticism involves emphasis on the spiritual side of faith, to the detriment of flesh, of substantive incarnation, suffering, crucifixion. Harnack was to return again and again to Marcion, culminating in his magisterial *Marcion* of 1921, and to be embroiled in controversy about his own supposed Gnosticism, and Hellenization of Christianity.

Despite a very full engagement in public life, Harnack maintained throughout his life a truly formidable volume of immaculate scholarly output—1,611 items are listed in his bibliography. He knew not only where important texts might be found but he knew exactly what they said. He had forgotten more than many later scholars ever knew, part of a fast diminishing band of consummate patristic scholars. (The author had the privilege of being advised as a graduate student in Heidelberg by Hans Freiherr von Campenhausen, another Baltic scholar. Campenhausen combined immense personal generosity with ferocious *Wissenschaftlichkeit*.) In 1876 Harnack began publication of a new critical edition of the Apostolic Fathers. In 1881 there appeared a comprehensive study of Monasticism, and he became joint editor of *Theologische Literaturzeitung*. The following year, he began, what is still the authoritative German review of theological literature with Leopold von Gebhardt, a series of studies on the early church, soon to become famous, as *Texte und Untersuchungen zur Geschichte der altchristlichen literature*—forty-nine of the monographs were his own work.

1885 brought the first version of what was to become his most influential work, the multi-volume *History of Doctrine*. For Harnack, Christian life and thought, doctrine and cultural context were inextricably bound together. It was always controversial. Though it is today largely outdated and in need of correction in the light of more than a century of further study, to read it through as an organic whole remains a hugely rewarding and challenging task. More immediately accessible to his contemporaries was the careful and radically crucial reappraisal of the tradition around *The Apostles' Creed* of 1892. Though often portrayed as an archetypal figure of the German establishment, Harnack was never afraid to follow the conclusions of his research wherever they might lead him. It did not increase his standing in church circles.

Harnack's liberal Protestant view of Christian theology was to provoke interesting critical responses in Catholic as well as Protestant circles. Apart from the predictable dismissals of conservative Catholicism, he became involved in a fascinating discussion with the French Catholic Modernist writer, Alfred Loisy. Loisy's 1902 study, *L'Evangile et L'Eglise*, was a response to Harnack's *What is Christianity?* Loisy maintained that the essence of Christianity was to be found not simply in the teaching of the Jesus of the Gospels, but in the developing faith of the church under the guidance of the Holy Spirit. The fact that Christ may not have founded a church, or indeed instituted sacraments, did not take away from their central role in the life of the church. Loisy followed this work with further studies, intended as a defence of the Catholic Church. But his modernist critical studies drew devastating criticism from his own church, forcing him to resign his priesthood and continue his work from a secular chair in the College de France. It is ironic that these two inquiring minds were to be equally disdained by their churches. In recent years Loisy, like Harnack, has come to be more seriously appreciated.

Throughout this period, Harnack continued to produce learned short monographs, interspersed with major works—two volume works on the history of early Christian literature in 1893, and on the mission and expansion of Christianity in 1902. The New Testament itself did not escape his critical scrutiny—*Luke the Physician* in 1907 and *The Sayings of Jesus* in 1908. But the general public around the Western world was perhaps most awakened to and challenged by Harnack's vision with *The Essence of Christianity* at the turn of a new century—1900. *The Essence of Christianity* spelled out as "trust in the message, which Jesus delivered, of eternal life in the midst of time." Jesus taught "the kingdom of God and its coming," which meant "the rule of the holy God in the hearts of individuals."[3] Beyond this he emphasized the fatherhood of God and the infinite value of the human soul. Jesus' message is essentially about God the father and not about himself. The external forms of religion are less important than obedience to the moral teaching of Jesus. Here is the Enlightenment turn to morality as the clue to transcendence. Here is stress on inward religious experience rather than the external instantiation of God embodied in incarnation and reconciliation. As people are liberated to enjoy the freedom of the children of God, so religion must be liberated from the accumulated detritus of external forms and rigid ecclesiastical institutions. This instinct has advantages, but a faith without some firm structures, however admirable, is always open to manipulation and misappropriation.

Unlike Troeltsch, Harnack stressed the unique salvific role of Jesus in human life. Christianity is *the* true religion. "It is THE religion, because Jesus Christ is not one among other masters but THE master and because his gospel corresponds to the innate capacity of man as history discloses it"[4] However, Harnack and Troeltsch became good friends and were to remain so—a friendship eloquently documented in Troeltsch's contribution to the Festschrift for Harnack's seventieth birthday in 1921 and in Harnack's funeral address for Troeltsch in 1923.

The contemporary social consequences of Harnack's vision were spelled out further in the collection of essays by Harnack and Wilhelm Herrmann in 1907—in which Harnack supported the education in universities of women—on condition that they attended different courses from the men. But Harnack continued throughout his life to be deeply involved in social issues. His work has been documented in a thesis by Binsar Nainggolan, who claims that his thinking is highly relevant to the work of the worldwide churches today. The social mission of the church, like the social gospel in America, was much criticized by conservative churchmen. But the Evangelical-Social congress was heavily involved in social outreach from its inception, and Harnack, addressing the congress, spoke of the need for the equality of all persons and freedom from oppression.[5] In 1905 he had expressed sympathy with striking miners in

---

3. Harnack, *What is Christianity?*, 51ff.

4. Harnack, "Die Aufgabe der theologischen Fakultaeten und die allgemeine Religionsgeschichte," 172ff, quoted by Pauck, *Harnack and Troeltsch*, 31, 97.

5. Harnack, *Aus der Friedens-und Kriegsarbeit*, 109.

the Ruhr valley—which he saw as a struggle to discover themselves as human beings.

Harnack's programme was developed alongside a growing controversy about the "Hellenization" of Christianity. Harnack sought to disentangled the simple, primitive message of Jesus' gospel from the trammels of Greek metaphysical speculation, which, for him, culminated in the doctrine of the two natures of Christ, divine and human, promulgated as authoritative at the Council of Chalcedon in 451 CE. He believed that such a basic teaching could be unearthed from the gospels, especially the Synoptic Gospels of Matthew, Mark, and Luke. More radical critics, notably Ernst Troeltsch, disputed that such a historical core could be reconstructed. Karl Barth was also to dispute Harnack's historical reading, not in the name of historical skepticism (though there were interesting similarities to the views of Troeltsch which he profoundly detested), but in the name of an appeal to pure revelation.

Harnack was always concerned to stress the importance of history for theology, in an age when secular history was being reassessed in new ways and the Christian tradition was, in many respects, leading the way in the science of hermeneutics, of textual interpretation. Yet he was not concerned with history alone, far less a mere historicism. He could actually have agreed with his friend Rudolf Bultmann, and indeed with Barth, that history was not sufficient. But he thought it was vitally necessary, in ways that Barth could not follow. He always understood himself as a theologian. His theological views interacted with his historical interpretation, and this brought advantages and disadvantages. Beyond history he was deeply immersed in other dimensions of Enlightenment thought—philosophy, politics, and a hugely comprehensive knowledge of German literature. Goethe was much quoted, and may well have influenced his idea of an essence of Christianity.

The Barth-Harnack correspondence is one of the classic exchanges of modern theology. Harnack was always concerned to stress the importance of reason in theology. The irrational was always seen as dangerous, and Barth's appeal to the pure Word, beyond the reach of human reason, alarmed him. He saw Barth's archetypal Christian as walking along a "glacial bridge" on a tightrope between disasters. Barth was, of course, to develop beyond the sharp paradoxes of the commentary on Romans and explain the complex rationale of his thought in his later work. Harnack and his pupils perceived a methodology which insulated the logic of theology, however meticulously pursued, from the critical procedures of other academic disciplines.

Harnack saw clearly that Barth's early theology constituted a deeply serious challenge to the liberal tradition of close engagement with the whole range of academic disciplines. And he had hopes that an appropriate academic dialogue might lead Barth to mitigate his stance. Hence he took the trouble to engage in a prolonged correspondence. The last of his initial Fifteen Questions to Barth illustrates his anxiety about the strategy of a theology independent of other disciplines:

> Granted that there are inertness, short-sightedness and numerous ills, yet is there any other theology than that which has strong ties, and is in blood–relationship, with science in general? Should there be one, what persuasiveness and value belong to it?[6]

Barth's response was characteristically considered and courteous, rather different from the open disdain which later Barth followers have sometimes poured on the Harnack tradition:

> I do not intend to entrench myself in these positions in which you, honoured Sir, and our voluntary-involuntary audience in this conversation have seen me, simply because I know how frighteningly relative everything is that one can say about the great subject which occupies you and me.[7]

Harnack was not persuaded.

> Revelation is not a scientific concept. There is no future in the attempt to grasp a "Word" of this kind as something so purely "objective" that human speaking, hearing, grasping and understanding can be eliminated from its operation. I have the impression that Professor Barth tries something like that and calls in a dialectic in this attempt which leads to an invisible ridge between absolute religious skepticism and naive Biblicism—the most tormenting interpretation of Christian experience and Christian faith! . . . But can it create a community and are the blows justified with which it beats down everything that presents itself as Christian experience? Will there be any room left on that glacial bridge for the children and friends of him who, interpreting Christian faith in this and never in any

---

6. Rumscheidt, ed., *Barth-Harnack Correspondence*, 31.
7. Ibid., 52.

other way, has been able to find a foothold on it? Would it not be better for him to admit that he is playing his instrument only and that God has still other instruments, instead of erecting a rigid either-or?[8]

The need for an interdisciplinary approach to theology has been the major theme of Harnack's famous rectorial address in the University of Berlin in 1900, and was of course a hallmark of post-Enlightenment European theology. Yet unlike Troeltsch and many of his contemporaries, he held to the belief that Christianity is *the* true religion, and all other religions have only glimpses of ultimate truth. Christ is the centre. History is crucial. The historical Jesus can be recovered by meticulous historical research, and is key to the understanding of faith. He is the founder of Christianity, the supreme teacher but much more than a teacher, for he instantiates uniquely in his person and activity what he teaches. This means that the history of the church must be judged by the standard of the gospel, rather than, as historians of religion were increasingly stressing, by the changing cultural standards and circumstances of changing times. In this respect at least, Harnack was closer to Herrmann and Barth, an heir of the right wing of the Ritschlian school, than to Troeltsch and the left wing Ritschlians, for whom the discipline of comparative religion, and the work of Max Weber, would become increasingly important.

The Barth/Harnack dialectic is well reflected in the life and work of Dietrich Bonhoeffer. The Bonhoeffer family were friends and neighbors of the Harnacks, related by marriage and constantly in and out of each other's houses. Bonhoeffer attended Harnack's seminar, but was also, in the 1920s, increasingly and deeply influenced by Karl Barth (who had of course also attended the famous seminar). The family connections and the political and theological influences were well documented by Carl-Jurgen Kaltenborn. Caltenborn notes the stress on the humanity of Jesus in Bonhoeffer's Christology, the accent on the oneness of reality, the unity of creation and redemption. Jesus Christ is *the* reality within the reality of the world. Ethics is important, and the ancient world is a valuable source of reflection. The world of penultimate things is to be taken seriously. This relates to the proper worldliness, orientation towards the world, of Christianity, and a hint of anti-clericalism. The importance of honesty in matters of confessions, of non-religious interpretation and even of "secret discipline," can all find echoes in Harnack.

8. Ibid., 53.

Throughout the 1920s Harnack continued his educational and scholarly work. He continued to support the Evangelical-Social Congress, to pursue his research, and to expand the library extensively. He did not actively engage in politics. His enthusiasm for monarchy waned, and he condemned the increasing violence of right-wing parties, not least their anti-Semitism—"to adorn the flags of Evangelical Christianity with anti-Semitism is a sad scandal." In 1926 he was to speak of the folly of the Great War—a complete change from his views of a decade earlier. In 1927 he wrote a memorandum for the Lausanne Faith and Order Conference in which he expressed the hope, not to be fulfilled, that the churches would reach an agreement about Christology that did not involve the traditional two natures model. In 1929 he saw the opening of the *Gesellschaft*'s Harnack House before dying the following year.

Adolf von Harnack was without question one of the greatest scholars of his age. But great scholars, perhaps somewhat removed from the preoccupations of ordinary people, do not always make wise administrators or politicians. Why was Harnack so bewitched by the deeply unpromising figure of Kaiser Wilhelm II? Perhaps his modest academic background back in Lithuania may be a clue—flattered and overawed by the royal connection, his judgment became clouded. Scholars may perhaps be allowed to be as fallible as the rest of humanity. On the other hand, it is significant that so many members of the Harnack family and friends were actively involved in the resistance to Hitler. As the Volksgericht verdict of 1 February 1945 authorizing the execution of Ernst von Harnack put it bluntly, "Der Angeklagte hat durch seine Handlungsweise schwer gegen Führer, Volk und Reich vergangen" ("Through his actions the accused has caused serious damage to Führer, people, and state"[9]). Though the collapse of the German church into Nazism is often attributed to the continuing failure of liberal theology, it could also be imagined that if the church had not excluded Adolf Harnack so rigorously from all its official bodies, the spirit of resistance might have been more widely influential.

There has been much misunderstanding about Harnack's theology. It is often thought that he was concerned only with God the Father, and that Jesus was a mere example of the appropriate human response to God. But Harnack explicitly offered a much more robust view of Jesus as the centre of the gospel. For him, the gospel of Jesus Christ is a dynamic reality, not simply a beautiful idea. Jesus the Christ is not simply a component

9. G-A v. Harnack, ed, *Ernst von Harnack, Jahre des Widerstands, 1932–45*, 224.

part of the gospel. As Bultmann emphasized in an introduction to *What is Christianity?*, for Harnack, "He was its personal realisation and its strength, and this he is felt to be still." This is incarnation back in the time of primitive Christianity, before the effects of Hellenization began to transform Christendom. Harnack laid stress on the notion that the earliest forms of the gospel came gradually to be encrusted and transformed by concepts derived from Greek philosophy, a process which reached a climax in the doctrine of the two natures of Christ, a process culminating in the decrees of the Council of Chalcedon of 451 AD. The centre of Jesus' message is the proclamation of the kingdom of God, and the assurance of the presence of the fatherly care of God which the kingdom brings, and which awaits a wider fulfilment. Here there was a privileging of the poor, and an injunction to seek actively for social justice, which was to lead him to take an active interest in social democratic politics during the Weimar republic. *What is Christianity?* achieved a huge circulation in Germany and beyond, especially in the United States, and helped to consolidate Harnack's reputation as the leading European Protestant theologian of the age.

Conclusion

In this article I have emphasized Harnack's contribution to theology. But we should not forget his seminal contribution of textual studies and to patristics in general. His legacy includes such outstanding figures in the field as Hans von Schubert, Hans von Soden, and Hans Lietzmann, then in the second half of the twentieth century, Hans von Campenhausen. This tradition has continued to flourish in the present (Gerhard May, Katharina Greschat, and others). If one word may summarize this dimension it is *Marcion*, the title of his brilliant 1922 monograph. For here the textual and the theological come creatively together in Harnack's work, in studies stretching from the very beginning to near the end of his professional life. Marcion, wealthy founder of a Christian second-century sect in the Black Sea area, was greatly influential in the development of the New Testament canon, and on the writing of commentaries on the Scriptures. Harnack thought he abandoned the Old Testament and was essentially an instance of the much wider movement known as Gnosticism, which spiritualized the gospel and denied many of the essential tenets of later orthodoxy. Later research has cast doubt on a number of his conclusions. But here, as elsewhere, the volume of high quality research generated is a tribute to the central role which he played in stimulating the development of contemporary academic theology. As the late Gerhard May most recently put it, "Harnack understood with masterful, historical power of portrayal how to conjure up from tradition the vibrant image of the Christian and theologian Marcion"[10] That characterization of his work may perhaps serve as an epitaph for the huge achievement of Adolf von Harnack.

---

10. May, *Markion, Gesammelte Aufsaetze*, 13.

12

Faith, Slavery, and Human Rights— Appearance and Reality

Rochester Cathedral, 2007; Athenaeum London 2009; Sydney and Otago, 2011.

I: Belief and Action

THE 200TH ANNIVERSARY OF the Abolition of Slavery, or rather of the carrying of slaves for trade on British ships is being widely celebrated this year, in the media, and not least in the churches. I am not going to add to the many repetitions of the story of slavery, with which you will be, or soon will be familiar. Instead I want to look at slavery within the particular context of human rights. There is still slavery today—perhaps there are more slaves today than at any time in history, and that is important. But there is also a wider issue which is important to faith, in human rights. Some would say—and others inevitably would disagree—that there is a fundamental human rights issue at the heart of the global conflict in the Anglican Communion today.

Human rights are not an obvious feature of the early traditions of the church. The New Testament struggles to make sense of the events concerning Jesus, his life, his teaching, the horrific and humiliating circumstances of his death. Different and sometimes conflicting interpretations swiftly arose. The early Christian communities began to understand Jesus as the resurrected one, or as a unique messianic prophet. Christians began to worship Jesus as God. In a community based on minor cultural groups and facing hostility, there was no obvious motivation to consider social deprivation and human rights issues in the existing majority communities. More important was the need to plead for tolerance and protection for the small and vulnerable congregations. The main emphasis of the influential Pauline communities was to refrain from asserting rights, but rather to act in humility and kenosis. The development of theology brought the need for agreed doctrinal criteria, and often led to harsh treatment of those who produced minority reports. Christians were persecuted. Christians persecuted. Biblical tradition seemed to point in opposite directions. Christians constantly heard sermons on texts exhorting compassion—on Matthew 5:43, love your enemies, on John 15:12, love one another, as I have loved you, on Galatians 2:20, and many other passages. Lactantius defends all freedom of religion: "Liberty has chosen to dwell in religion. For nothing is so much a matter of free will as religion, and no one can be required to worship what he does not will to worship."[1]

Beyond this there is evidence of a raft of concerns for what we would today regard as human rights issues—explicit concern for widows, the poor, and the sick, the development of alms-giving, arising out of biblical exposition. Gregory of Nyssa, almost alone among the theologians, clearly condemned slavery.

The Middle Ages

Throughout church history there is the well known paradox of amazing variety in faith and practice in many local areas, of cultural pluralism and intercultural thinking shining through the work of a theologian like Augustine, the great definer of orthodoxy. The other side is an enduring tendency to confuse unity with uniformity, and to seek to force Christianity into a doctrinal and ethical strait-jacket.

Heresy and persecution could be linked easily by St. Thomas Aquinas, unfaithfulness is an act of the intellect, but moved by the will. Against this rather bleak narrative we may place the impressive charitable work done by monasteries, as an example of a positive Christological influence on society. The monasteries looked after the poor and the disabled. But biblical texts against the handicapped remained a powerful counter-force.

There were, however, other pointers towards rights. The idea that all persons possess natural rights appears to have arisen around the twelfth century. *Ius naturale* is discussed extensively by Ockham. Stress on the

---

1. Lactantius, *Divinarum Institutionum*, V.19, *Fathers of the Church* 49, 364.

dignity of man and on humanity, as made in the image of God, created possible conditions for the development of a human rights culture. Development of the doctrine of the just war, building on Roman law, illustrated the highly developed state of Christian moral theology in the period.

St. Thomas uses the *Imago Dei* metaphor extensively to show that human beings, quite distinct from other animals, are made in the image of God and capable of knowledge of God. But slaves remain inferior, for slavery is a punishment for sin. The treatment of slavery remains under the influence of Aristotle's notion that slaves are naturally in servitude.

Las Casas in America was generous towards the Indians but harsh towards heretics—then, as now, respect for difference is usually selective. On the other hand, he could invoke the legal maxim, *Quod omnes tangit debet ab omnibus approbari* (What touches all should be approved by all) to call for government by consent, which could have had potentially enormous consequences for church as well as society.

Reformation and Rights?

What then of Reformation? Despite Luther's strongly Christological emphasis on Christian freedom, and Calvin's proclamation of the absolute freedom of the sovereign God, freedom did not extend to freedom of life and opinion over against the covenant community. "It is the saints who burn the saints." This striking phrase about the saints, from Roland Bainton, who pinpoints a problem at the heart of Christian reflection on human rights.

Enlightenment

There were increasingly theological pleas for tolerance and for religious liberty. William Penn said, "I ever understood an impartial liberty of conscience to be the natural right of all men" (*England's Present Interest Discovered*, 1679[2]), though even Penn found it necessary in particular circumstances to advocate coercion.[3]

From our survey so far it may seem that the churches' record in human right issues is at best ambiguous. Christians could support slavery in the nineteenth century. Yet many Christian groups were strong

---

2. Quoted by Witte, *Christianity and Democracy in Global Context*, 42.
3. Murphy, *Conscience and Community*, 232.

anti-slavery advocates. In the USA, besides Las Casas, protests against slavery went back to the protest on February 18th, 1688 in Germantown, PA, by a group of Quakers including Francis Daniel Pastorius.

In the second half of the twentieth century Christian input to human rights concerns developed, with varying degrees of effectiveness. This is most obviously seen in numerous commissions for social justice and for justice and peace in most churches. The WCC continued to be engaged with human rights at various levels, from UN and government levels, to supporting the work of NGOs. Through the Churches Council for International Affairs, it contributes to UNHRC on a standing basis. Because of its human rights concerns, the WCC was to come under deep suspicion from the 1970s in conservative political and Christian circles. Matters of nuclear war, of environmental issues, and global economic development all had human rights implications. The churches became explicitly concerned with human rights talk in the seventies and eighties.

II: The Bible and Its Interpretation

Where is the Bible in all this reflection?

Support for Human Rights Issues

In the New Testament discussion of most theological issues is naturally brought to focus in relation to Jesus Christ. But the New Testament is built upon the Old, and there is in the Old Testament considerable material relevant to rights issues in Judaism, which had a considerable input into the development of modern rights theories and institutions.

Obstacles to Human Rights Issues

It must also be acknowledged that here is also a considerable body of "texts of terror" that militate sharply against HR in the biblical material. Biblical texts have been used effectively to oppose most advances in modern HR. The abolition of racism, slavery, the emancipation of women and gays, the extension of suffrage, anti-Semitism and xenophobia—all have been vigorously supported on biblical grounds.

Here is a piece from a powerful sermon in favor of slavery.

Excerpts from *The Rights and Duties of Slaveholders: Two Discourses Delivered on Sunday, November 27, 1836, in Christ Church, Raleigh, North-Carolina*, by George W. Freeman:[4]

Discourse I. Colossians IV.I: *Masters give unto your servants that which is just and equal, knowing that ye also have a master in heaven.*

The strict meaning of the word here rendered *servants*, is bondsmen or *slaves*. In this sense, particularly when applied, as here, to a distinct class of men, it is believed to be uniformly employed in the New Testament, especially in the Epistles. Slavery, it appears, is of great antiquity. It has existed in the world, in some form or other, even from the times immediately following, if not before the flood. It may be regarded as one of the penal consequences of sin. Though this sentence was passed upon mankind generally, it was not to be expected, that its effects would continue for any length of time to be felt by all alike. There would, of necessity, very soon arise an inequality among men.

Such were the nature and extent of slavery in the world, when our Saviour appeared, to proclaim, "peace on earth, and good will to men"—to preach the glad tidings of salvation to a ruined world—to redeem us from sin and everlasting death, and to, *"open the kingdom of Heaven to all believers."* And how did *He* regard it? What had *He* to say of this institution, as He found it existing among the people He came to save? Did He condemn it as anti-scriptural and unjust? Did He enjoin on his disciples an immediate emancipation of their slaves? Did He so much as caution His followers against purchasing them in the future? Not a word, disapproving the practice, ever fell from His lips. As a settled civil institution of the Empire, He meddled not with it, of *course*—for His *"kingdom"*, as He declared, "was not of this world." He came not to remodel the governments—He came not to reform the civil institutions of the world—He came *"to seek and to save that which was lost."* But in the course of His ministry, He must have come in contact with many *individuals* who were *holders of slaves*; and surely, had He regarded them as living in the habitual commission of a *"moral wrong,"* He would scarcely have forborne, on some occasion, to express His indignation. And did He never rebuke them for holding their fellow-men in bondage? Did He never give them to understand that, if

---

4. Charleston: A. E. Miller, Printer to The Protestant Episcopal Society for the Advancement of Christianity in South-Carolina, 1837.

they would be His disciples, they must set their slaves at liberty? No, Brethren, nothing of the kind occurs in His whole history.

Neither do we find anything in the writings of the Apostles condemnatory of slavery. The relation of *Master* and *Slave* is frequently spoken of, but never with one word of disapprobation. The *relative duties* of each are inculcated with freedom and earnestness, in the same manner as are those of other relations subsisting among men, such as parents and children, husbands and wives, magistrates and citizens; while no intimation whatever is given that *that particular one* is more inconsistent with the principles and spirit of the gospel than the rest. Indeed we are furnished with one remarkable instance, in which an Apostle appears to have been instrumental, *not in setting at liberty*, (as some over-benevolent persons in our day are forward to do) but in *reclaiming and sending back to his master*, A FUGITIVE SLAVE! I allude to the case of Onesimus.

III: Christology for Human Rights

In my book *Christ and Human Rights,* which some of you have generously been looking at, I suggested thinking about a Christology *for* human rights. Christology can never be as self-contained as we often find convenient. We are always thinking of the concrete instantiation of the love of the God who is, Christians believe, *the* Creator and Sustainer of all that is.

We cannot impose a God concept on a rights dialogue which is genuine dialogue. But we can say that Christian communities and individuals, who have worked out ways of living together on the basis of gradually agreed values, have drawn strength from the faith that at the root of all existence there is a power which is entirely non-coercive, and that this power is the power of unconditional love. At least in an informal sense, Christians will say that before God is being, God is love. They will regard it as significant that human beings, to date the most complex entities in the cosmos, are the field in which God has become incarnate in the shape of self-dispossessing love. It is as the shape of the mystery of ultimate reality that faith in God through Jesus Christ transforms hearts and minds and societies.

God Instantiated

Two thousand years of Christianity has shown that the spirit of Christ-likeness is not confined to Christian community. The divine love has been experienced by Christians as active in other religions and in secular spheres, in individual lives, in social and political developments, sometimes from within the church, and sometimes challenging the churches from outside.

Where human agency produces outcomes in love and compassion, Christians may give thanks for Christomorphic traces of divine action, the Spirit of Christlikeness, in the created order. This is the salvific outcome of the dynamic sequence of the life, death, and resurrection of Jesus Christ.

A Christological perspective has both positive and negative value in contributing to human rights issues. Positively, reflection upon Christ has encouraged Christians to work by themselves and with others in effectively addressing many areas of human rights—individual liberty, torture, political rights such as the right to justice, and economic rights like the right to be free from hunger. It has been largely ineffective where scriptural tradition has had a strong influence in inhibiting rights—most notably in the areas of gender and sexuality. Here, perhaps, we have to look elsewhere for guidance. But Christianity has shown the capacity for change and development, e.g., in relation to such issues as slavery and race.

Postfoundational Transformation— Reconciliation and Forgiveness

Healing wounds requires reconciliation. Few countries have shown such an amazing example of the capacity for reconciliation and forgiveness as South Africa.

Archbishop Tutu has said this: "I can testify that our own struggle for justice, peace and equity would have floundered badly had we not been inspired by our Christian faith and assured of the ultimate victory of goodness, compassion and truth against their ghastly counterparts."[5]

Tutu, in *No Future without Forgiveness*, gave an excellent description of the apartheid system itself.[6] He concluded that: "Forgiving and being reconciled are not about pretending that things are other than they are."

---

5. Witte, *Religious Human Rights in Global Perspectives*, xvi.
6. Tutu, *No Future Without Forgiveness*, 217ff, 270.

We have to try to see beyond the failures of the churches, past and present, to the continuing vulnerable love of God. It is true that Christians have supported human rights abuses with great tenacity. There is no quick fix. But as a community response Christian action has had considerable success in mitigating the effects of slavery, racism, and many other abuses over a longer time-scale. We have seen that human rights engagement takes place at different levels. It is important to focus on carefully targeted projects, which correspond to available enthusiasms and resources.

Beyond this, however, lies the eschatological vision. This calls for a theological version of "rooted cosmopolitanism" which encourages a continuing effort of Christian solidarity in tackling human rights enforcement. This means solidarity among the churches and solidarity with all kinds of religious and secular organizations in achieving agreed human rights outcomes. This will not occur until churches and theology learn to distinguish clearly between unity and uniformity.

It may be appropriate to end with one of the sharpest challenges to the theme of Christ and human rights yet seen, the churches' response to AIDS. Donald Messer, in his *Breaking the Conspiracy of AIDS* makes a passionate plea for the Christian church to take a much more pro-active and compassionate approach to AIDS sufferers and AIDS prevention.

The Christian tradition has potential, in reflecting on the dynamic of relationality and respect for others expressed in the events concerning Jesus Christ, to have universal application even in areas where it has largely failed. If it is able to face up critically to its failures it may have a future role in encouraging other traditions, religious and secular, to confront their weaknesses and make appropriate changes of attitude and action. It may also learn from such dialogue to widen its own base of human rights commitments in the long-term future. In the present, it may be important to concentrate action within the Christian tradition on human rights issues where there is a large measure of agreement, while continuing to work on areas of disagreement. It will remain open to respond to the Christological vision by working with organizations outside church structures in areas where these are more likely to be effective. In this way, human rights action may be seen as part of the consequences of the form of Christ in the world.

I come back to the specific issue of historical slavery, and its consequences which extend even into the present.

Brian Blount's *Then the Whisper put on Flesh—New Testament Ethics in an African-American Context*, argues for the model of liberation as a lens for reconfiguring ethics. This enables him to read the Synoptic Gospels as an ethics of the kingdom, John as the Christology of a community of active resistance, Paul as theology enabling liberating ethics, at least on occasion, and Revelation as the witness of active resistance. More precisely, the synoptic gospels set up new paradigms of behavior, "[f]or Mark, discipleship as a narrative theme follows from the realisation of God's own boundary breaking behavior around and in Jesus."[7] In Matthew we see the liberating ethics of a "visible institution," the kingdom of heaven. In Luke there is a bias towards the poor and the oppressed in Jesus' teaching and action, in a reversal of common attitudes. In John love for God and humanity becomes a strategy of active resistance. In Paul there is also a basic liberative ethic of boundary breaking, though Paul's choices might be different in some areas today, notably slavery and sexuality. In Revelation there is a pattern of active resistance in the face of massive evil.

Blount struggles with the question of what exactly the New Testament has to do with ethics, and here he follows Leander Keck: "New Testament ethics may not look like what we have come to expect from a 'critical reflection on morality' because it is its own brand of ethics. It is not ethics formed round a philosophical construct. It is, instead, 'event ethics.' It is ethics orientated and structured around the event of Jesus' life, death and resurrection."[8] This, it seems to me, is precisely why any Christian reflection on human rights needs to deal centrally with Christology.

Why should people who have suffered at the hands of Christians even consider listening to Christian sources for human rights reflection? This basic question is illuminatingly tackled in Blount's discussion of slavery as an interpretive lens. Those who first learned of Christian faith, often in very distorted form, at the hands of their oppressors have nevertheless been able, in the past, to own Christian faith as a humanizing force, through a reconfigured ethics of liberation. "Jesus can understand the pain, the tragedy, the hopelessness, the sorrow, and, most important, the hope."[9] In the lens of liberation the Bible is read contextually, reading,

---

7. Blount, *Then the Whisper Put On Flesh*, 57, 149.
8. Ibid., 17.
9. Ibid., 33.

respecting, sometimes rejecting. African American slaves reconfigured the biblical message in order to retrieve it for their own situation.

Blount's narrative respects equally the value of the narratives of individual and/or community suffering. Are human rights concerned with individuals or communities? The answer, from the slave communities, would seem to be emphatically both.

Brian Blount, in conclusion, faces up to the need for dialogue between black and white American communities who remain separate and distrustful of each other:

> In this dialogue the primary focus would not be on the establishment of universally normative ways of dealing with particular issues. It would instead encourage a cross-fertilisation of different cultural perspectives which would spark in turn new encounters with the text's meaning potential. Then and only then would the real goal be within reach. Then we would approach an interpretive reality where ethics enables the crossing of those boundaries that separate humans from God and disable productive and transformative human contact with one another.[10]

I have quoted this study at length because the issues with which it deals seem to be me to be applicable to other contemporary human rights issues. The love of God in Jesus Christ as a boundary breaking narrative, and a signal of the hope of a different future, is of the essence of a Christian contribution to human rights.

I am going to try to take this a little further and suggest a deeper theological approach to the root of the issue.

IV: Hospitality

God is hospitable. People of faith are called to be hospitable. That is a classical Christian affirmation. Historically, it has often gone along with an assertion of divine omnipotence, domination—in a word, a great deal of bullying. What has gone wrong? Hospitality is, after all, a word easily abused—not every Hospitality Inn is hospitable.

Religion when it's good can be very, very good. But when it's bad, of course, it's unspeakable. What sort of God could we possibly encourage? Not a God of tribal partiality, hate, discrimination,

---

10. Ibid., 191.

punishment etc. But this sort of imagery has been operative in all the major religious traditions.

This is obviously not an issue for Christianity alone. The necessity of more effective interfaith engagement and dialogue has become more sharply obvious since 9/11. The dangers of hospitality talk are obvious. Unclarity and sentimentality loom. Yet all our language about God is human language and fashioned out of human experience. Hospitality is a practice with a long tradition. Today, it is a buzz-word with very modern connotations. The hospitality industry is an important feature of our globalized existence.

Christian Leitmotif

For Christianity, the reality of hospitality to the *stranger* is expressed in the meals taken by Jesus with those who were at the margin of society; here is revelation, sacrament, Word of God. . . . The practice of hospitality was viewed as the concrete expression of love . . .

Hospitality does not, of course, begin with Christian faith. Homer in *The Odyssey* says: "Rudeness to a stranger is not decency, poor although he may be, poorer than you. All wanderers and beggars came from Zeus. What we can give is slight but the recompense great."[11]

The city which forgets how to care for the stranger has forgotten how to care for itself. (No dawn raids on asylum seekers then.) In the New Testament, Jesus was a stranger, "I was a stranger and you welcomed me." "Hospitality to the stranger demands sacrifice: to surrender our biases: to make the interests, joys and sorrows of the stranger our own. As such, hospitality to the stranger is subversive by nature, threatening to the existing powers."[12]

In ancient Israel, the people were united by a bond of covenant, but the outsider might be excluded—a tension throughout its history. Bread should be shared with the foreigner and one should love him as oneself (Lev 19:34). On the other hand, the foreigner should keep the religious laws of Israel (Lev 17:10). In the Qur'an (18.76) to entertain and to give food are synonymous.

Hospitality is vital to the flourishing of a humane society. But it is not without limits. It indicates a texture of compassion and care—not

---

11. Richard, *Living the Hospitality of God*, 5.
12. Ibid., 51.

compatible with violence, coercion and manipulation, the neglect of the marginalized, and triumphalist ideologies. A theology of hospitality is a theology of risk, a theology at risk.

Hospitable and Inhospitable

God in the major world faiths is a hospitable God. But we need to be cautious here. There is a clear danger in the "all manner of things shall be well" approach to religion. Often things aren't.

Inevitably we face problems. The inhospitable and the bleak. Evil and suffering came in the twentieth century in one hundred million people murdered. The hospitable is mocked by the inhospitable.

Postmodern Hospitality

The French philosopher Jacques Derrida reflected famously on the theme of impossible hospitality. To be hospitable, it is necessary that one must have the *power* to host. One must have some control, otherwise one can't be host. There is a need to abandon all claims to ownership—but then one cannot be a host. One must be prepared to accept the truly uncomfortable. So, this remains always an impossible possibility. Christian theology might reflect that hospitality is shown in the out-working of God's love in creation and redemption.

Unwrapping the Gift of Hospitality

Hospitable God is the goal of an emancipatory theology. Above all, with the hospitable God, it is the tone which determines the music.

Desmond Tutu, in his *God has a Dream*, spoke of:

> Ubuntu. A person with ubuntu is welcoming, hospitable, warm and generous, willing to share. Such people are open and available to others, willing to be vulnerable, affirming of others, do not feel threatened that others are able and good, for they have a proper self-assurance that comes from knowing that they belong in a greater whole.[13]

---

13. Tutu, *God Has a Dream*, 26.

Christomorphic Humanism/Cascading Hospitality

For all who believe in God, hospitality is a trace of the presence of God, differently construed in different faiths. It sets up a human rights imperative in an often inhospitable landscape. Perhaps we can imagine a kind of comprehensive cascade of effort in hospitality:

- encompassing all that can be said of friendship.
- embracing radical spirituality.
- taking a fresh look at traditional sources, and unconventional sources, for talk of God.
- facing up squarely to religious pluralism.
- imagining a Christomorphic understanding of historical transformation.
- compassionate commitment breaks through violence in history.

When Christians speak of the vulnerability of God, they envisage a power beyond emptiness and weakening which is innocent of all hubris, a source of energy and engagement, in an invitation to hospitality both universal and local.

Hospitable Praxis

God acts through people. We might think of human progress from the paleolithic to present as a move from more fear to less. But there is clearly no straight line of progress—as many people live in fear today as ever did. Somehow we must try to move towards unforced consensus.

Scots companies profited hugely from the slave trade, through shipping and with connections to American plantations. And historical reference should not blind us to the unpleasant fact that there are as many people in slavery today as there ever were. Hospitality may involve going against the stream.

Hospitality Today

Mark Noll, in an article in *The Christian Century*, brilliantly characterizes the two sides of the biblical debate over slavery in America in the 1860s. He shows how the literal interpretation of texts on the pro-slavery side seemed to correspond to the approach which had made America a free, God-fearing people. Passages such as Leviticus 25:45 and 1 Corinthians 7:20–21 seemed clear enough. On the other hand, the more nuanced hermeneutical interpretation of the anti-slavery argument, moving away from the literal to the sense of the gospel as a whole, seemed contrived, complex, and less attractive:

> In short, this was an argument of elites requiring that the populace should defer to its intellectual betters. As such it contradicted democratic and republican intellectual instincts. In the culture of the U.S., as that culture had been constructed by three generations of evangelical Bible believers, the nuanced biblical argument was doomed.[14]

Noll concludes strikingly that:

> The country had a problem because its most trusted religious authority, the Bible, was sounding an uncertain note. . . . The supreme crisis over the Bible was that there existed no apparent Biblical resolution to the crisis. It was left to those consummate theologians, the reverend doctors Ulysses S. Grant and William Tecumseh Sherman, to decide what in fact the Bible actually meant.[15]

It will not have been lost on readers of *The Christian Century* that this article appeared just before the crucial PCUSA debate on same-sex relationships in June 2006.

The churches today are as split as they have ever been and over the unexpected issue of homosexuality. This issue provides a litmus test for the churches in relation to hospitality and human rights. It has to be recorded that the track record of most religious people here continues to be very ambiguous. In 2005, students were hanged in Iran and imprisoned and tortured in Egypt for being gay. Though there are many sympathetic Christian organizations, particularly in the United States, there are at least as many homophobic bodies, often well funded and influential. The Anglican Communion, pioneers in tolerance, now appears to be moving in a more judgemental direction, valuing denominational unity above solidarity with disadvantaged minorities, while the Catholic and Orthodox Churches, at least in their official pronouncements, continue to be intransigent. Hospitality remains in short supply.

14. Noll, "Battle for the Bible", 49–50.
15 Ibid., 50.

Much of this hostility is legitimated under the rubric of "Biblical Christianity." But Jesus is found ministering to "outsiders" of every sort—the Gerasene demoniac and the woman suffering from chronic bleeding, the child of the Syro-Phoenician woman, the centurion's servant, the ten lepers, the blind beggar. Jesus turns to the untouchables, those beyond the pale, flouting many of the sacrosanct moral, religious, and social taboos of the time. The leper in Jesus' day was the archetypical outsider, forced to live outside the community, living the life of the damned, rejected by God as well as man. Jesus touches the untouchable in all embracing love and grace, challenging the excluding mindset. Touching the leper, the living damned, is precisely the touchstone of God's own hospitality.

Jesus Christ is not a conquering hero. Unlike us, Jesus was not concerned about image, reputation, ego, or power. As has been wisely said, Jesus on earth was a man who played to lose. To lose, for us and for our salvation. He was the voice of the voiceless, until that voice was choked out of him. God has brought reconciliation out of conflict. This is the promise of God, the rainbow that may for ever be traced through the rain, the quiet faith that God will quite certainly gather up all the broken and hurting fragments from all sides into his all encompassing love, however long it takes.

This brings me back to two fundamental points about slavery.

First, it has become increasingly clear how hugely Britain profited from slavery. Africans were, of course, themselves slave owners. But here the Royal Company of Adventurers was formed in 1663 and succeeded by the Royal Africa Company in 1672. By 1720 the South Sea Company included 462 MPs. One hundred members of the House of Lords and most of the Royal Family. From 1761 to 1807, it has been calculated that British ships made 5,693 voyages across the Atlantic, carrying 1.5 million slaves worth an average of £42 each, bringing £60 million to the economy. And that was in 1807 money.

Secondly, today in 2007, there are more slaves in the world than ever before. Slaves are cheaper than ever, and they are disposable. Millions of vulnerable people are potential slaves. They are so cheap that they are not worth preserving. When they get sick, or redundant, they are simply dumped or killed.

What can we do? We can try to identify areas where there is slavery, often hidden—not least in Britain. Look at websites like Free the Slaves. We can help research into solutions. We can advocate the monitoring of areas where labor practices are questionable. We can ask about the sources of the goods we all buy. We can support the rehabilitation and training of former slaves. In 1670, we didn't just talk about carrying off 1.5 million people across the Atlantic. We got on with it, enthusiastically and happily. In 2007, perhaps we should not just talk about the problem of contemporary slavery. I guess we owe it to these 1.5 million who helped to create our economy, to do something about it.

There is a very long way to go, both intellectually and practically. When we look at the churches today, often torn by conflict over what many of us regard as dead issues, we soon realize that the churches themselves are not likely to be in a position to bring the hospitality of God effectively to bear on society by themselves. The most powerful churches are all too often deeply influenced by fundamentalism. Yet signs of a dynamic progressive Christianity still appear, and may, in the future, encourage the hospitable future which is the vision of the gospel, by engaging in concerted action with other groups.

The obstacles are formidable, but the love of God is always transformative. Your own hospitality in listening to a theologian talking about hospitality tonight is a welcome sign of a more hopeful future.

13

Affirmation Scotland, Gay Christians, and Equality

Conversations on Sexuality[1]

What We Believe

AFFIRMATION SCOTLAND'S VISION IS to affirm and celebrate Christ's call to inclusion, generosity and hospitality, and to see all Christians welcomed and affirmed within the Church, regardless of sexual orientation. Membership of *Affirmation Scotland* is open to all who support this vision—clergy or laity, gay or straight, members of the Church of Scotland or those from other traditions. *Affirmation Scotland* seeks to offer a ministry of care, hope and advocacy to lesbian, gay, bisexual and transgender (LGBT) Christians, their families, and supporters. We will also contribute to the debate within the Kirk on human sexuality from a progressive perspective.

1. We affirm that Christian theological reflection is above all about God. The written word found in Scripture points beyond itself to the Word incarnate: God among us. All that the church does is about God, or it is nothing. The church is the Church of Jesus Christ, or it is nothing. The Gospel is the good news that the triune God took flesh and came among us for our salvation.

---

1. I was involved in founding the organization, *Affirmation Scotland*, in 2006, and drafted a statement of beliefs.

affirmation scotland, gay christians, and equality 179

2. We affirm that God is the one who loves in freedom, not as the world loves. We further affirm that God's love extends equally to all people.

3. We affirm that in God's self-giving to humanity in the incarnation in Jesus Christ we find the ultimate expression of divine hospitality. God's greatest gift to us, the source of all our giving, is the Gospel. Central to the Gospel are generosity and hospitality. Christian hospitality is hospitality to the stranger. "I was a stranger and you welcomed me." Jesus was with the lepers. Jesus made himself an outcast and died for the outcast—this was courageous hospitality. We affirm that this is the essence of the Gospel and we pledge ourselves to support those who are at risk, wherever and however we are able. We are called to tell the world that there are no outsiders.

4. We believe that God has brought reconciliation out of conflict. We maintain a quiet faith that God will quite certainly gather up all the broken and hurting fragments from all sides into his all-encompassing love, however long it takes.

5. We affirm our commitment to an ever more open, generous, inclusive, hospitable, and truly evangelical Church of Scotland.

6. We affirm that the Church has been and is richly blessed by the transparent Christian witness of lesbian and gay ministers and laypeople over a long period. The Church should rightly be humbled by their integrity, encouraged by their faith, and awed by their Christ-like generosity, often in the face of daunting adversity.

7. We affirm the need to speak boldly in support of those who feel unable to speak for themselves, in the church and in the world.

8. We affirm with gratitude to God the profound contribution to the mission and discipleship of the Church made by lesbian and gay people today, and we look forward with confident hope to that time when all discrimination will be past, and the peace, love, and justice of the Kingdom will be established among us.

9. We welcome assurances that none of us in the Church wishes to be homophobic. That is a step forward. But however sincere the protestations of compassionate and unconditional love, a theological position that states that homosexuality is sinful gives a green light

to those who believe that God will punish lesbian and gay people because of who they are. Pronouncements have consequences.

10. We remember with sorrow that the literal imitation of Biblical injunctions has caused mayhem in history and may do so again. We do not forget that some of the most oppressed gay Christians are evangelical Christians, who may have to hide their identities with huge attendant anxiety.

11. We affirm the need to maintain the unity of the Church. We affirm the need to be in unity with the outcast and the marginalised. We believe that neither orthodox nor evangelical are the property of a particular section of the Church. We plan to affirm the place of LGBT Christians in the Church of Scotland by doing the following:

- Creating safe places and times for gay people and their friends to meet for worship, fellowship, and support.
- Organising events that promote an inclusive church.
- Providing resources to the Kirk and the LGBT community promoting the belief that God welcomes into God's family all people regardless of gender, gender identity, or sexual orientation.
- Speaking out for the dignity and place of LGBT Christians whenever this is under attack.
- Responding appropriately to approaches by the media for comment on issues related to the Kirk.
- Being a presence—reminding the Kirk in a consistent way that the LGBT community has always been and is present within the Kirk.

Civil Partnership and Services of Blessing.

From *Ministers' Forum*, 2006.

Having said recently that I would accept an invitation to bless the civil partnership of an ordained former student to another ordained minister, (neither is a minister of the Church of Scotland), I was interested to read the recent illuminating discussion of partnerships and blessings. It seems to me that the views expressed by your correspondent probably represent the position of a significant number of Church of Scotland ministers and elders, and indicate the status quo, even though it could be said that the Assembly debates of the last decade introduce an element of provisionality into that stance. I believe that this position is just plain wrong, that it has caused untold damage and hurt to countless people in Scotland and in countries influenced by Scottish Presbyterianism over many years, and that it will continue to underwrite homophobic abuse and violence until it is explicitly disavowed. Should we call for repentance? "Words without thoughts never to heaven go."

This is not the place to rehearse the hoary debates about Scripture and homosexuality. Compared with ferocious pronouncements from American pastors and Nigerian Bishops, his comments are sweetness and light. If the Church of England on this issue has been a church at war, the Church of Scotland has been a church in denial. We just know that all gay people are English, and if the image of God is exclusively the male/female relationship, it's a gratifying bonus to discover that there are no English people in the Bible.

Of course some of the best theological arguments over the centuries have been made in favor of slavery, capital punishment, the subordination of women, condemnation of same sex relationships. In my *Christ and Human Rights* I try to indicate the academic debate. But this is not only an academic issue. It has consequences. If you are gay and vulnerable—living here in an area of multiple deprivation or abroad in many parts of the world—you are quite likely to be attacked and even murdered. If you are gay and vulnerable—a parish minister in Scotland—you are at serious risk of deprivation of your ministry. If you are rich and/or socially secure, you can do pretty much what you like.

Nowadays we all love the sinner and we are not homophobic. But people still die, and we create the conditions of the possibility of murder. The other day my wife and I went to see Ang Lee's brilliant *Brokeback Mountain*. The breathtaking scenery recalled powerfully the wonderful Wyoming country we had travelled through last summer. It also brought to mind Matthew Shepard, the devoutly Christian gay student crucified on a barbed wire fence in Wyoming one winter's night in 1998. This issue is a matter of discipleship. That is why, in my personal view, the stance of our Church on this issue is, quite simply, a disgrace.

This does *not* mean that those who differ from me on this issue are inevitably un-Christian or uncaring. But it does mean that we have to learn to dialogue and to act without exposing the most vulnerable in our midst to further violence and abuse. How to achieve this is by no means easy to discern. There is a need too for positive action. How many churches would dare to oppose the homophobia rampant in football?

Why do I feel deeply privileged to be invited to bless a civil partnership? Because the awkward truth is that I and numerous others have been richly blessed by the transparent Christian witness of a number of lesbian and gay divinity students, ministers and laypeople over a long period, humbled by their integrity, encouraged by their faith in the face of daunting adversity, and awed by their Christ-like generosity. Jesus Christ is straight and Jesus Christ is gay. Desmond Tutu once said that we are made to tell the world that there are no outsiders. "The solid reality is Christ" (Col 2:17).

The Church of Scotland and the Question of Same-sex Marriage—for the Doctrine Committee of the Scottish Episcopal Church, 2011

In the modern period the various Scottish churches have regularly produced reports on the "doctrine" of marriage. Sometimes, as in a fairly recent report of the Church of Scotland-Roman Catholic Joint Commission, these have had an ecumenical dimension, noting agreement and disagreement. In 1994, the General Assembly of the Church of Scotland, after lively discussion, accepted a report on marriage prepared by the Doctrine Committee.

The issue of same-sex marriage has produced further challenges. In the 1960s, the Church of Scotland condemned the recommendations of the Wolfenden Committee on the decriminalization of homosexuality in Scotland. But the 1994 Marriage Report included comments, soon very controversial, on same sex relationships. The Report contemplated recognition of the legitimacy of faithful relationships of a homosexual nature. The issue was debated in the Assemblies of 2000, 2004, 2008, and 2009. In 2009, the assembly ratified the transfer of an openly gay minister to a new charge in Aberdeen. A Theological Commission representing different shades of opinion reported in 2011, and a further committee was set up, promising a further report by 2013. Opinion was sharply divided, here as elsewhere. Movement in sentiment within the wider society influenced debate. Civil Partnerships were introduced into Scots Law, and a consultation on same-sex marriages was announced in 2011. This left open the further question of whether a religious ceremony for same-sex marriage might be offered. The Roman Catholic Church was united with the Free Church in being sharply critical of these developments. Views varied between "the Church does not allow homosexuality," and "this is like saying, 'the Church does not allow rain.'"

A further comment on the Church of Scotland background is appropriate. Marriage and homosexuality were discussed increasingly by the Church of Scotland from the 1970s on. In 1974 the Church reaffirmed that all homosexual acts were inherently sinful, and this tradition has continued to be strongly supported, notably by the "Forward Together" group. A Moderator who expressed liberal views on the subject was barred from preaching in a Highland presbytery in the late 1990s. There were other views. The so-called Scottish Minorities Group was given meeting space in 1967 by the Chaplain of Glasgow University and the Catholic Chaplain at Edinburgh University, and churchmen spoke for liberalization at conferences from the late 1970s. Marriage, sexuality, and the potential legitimacy of different interpretations of Scripture were reported on by the Panel on Doctrine and discussed by the General Assembly throughout the 1990s and beyond. Different committees produced different perspectives on physical relationships and the Assembly made no binding decisions. The issue of sexual relationships between women, never illegal, did not appear till a distinguished woman minister blessed a lesbian couple in the 1990s. Support for an inclusive Church was given by organizations such as One Kirk, while pastoral safe space was created by the ecumenical Clerical Consultation in the 1980s, and by the Presbyterian Affirmation Scotland from 2006.

The Scottish Episcopal Church has been generally regarded as more progressive than other denominations on this issue. The documentation from General Synod meeting June 2011, demonstrates a perceptive awareness of the complexities of the issues, and of the importance of cherishing and maintaining the distinctive character of the Christianity in Scotland. Opinion in the United Reformed Church was rather divided, and the other smaller denominations generally held to traditional views—though the presence of evangelical support groups for gay and lesbian Christians suggests that here too there is a range of perspectives.

14

In Church

Commemoration of Benefactors

John 3:16

Trinity Hall, Cambridge, 4 February 2007

BENEFACTION IS A GOOD thing. It is better to give than to receive. Academic institutions in the UK are waking up to the painful fact that we do not have a culture of giving on the same level as that in the United States, and so our research suffers in proportion to our funding deficiencies. Heads of academic institutions are increasingly charged with the primary task of fund raising. If we are to move further up the league table of the world's top universities—without which there will be no entrance to the kingdom of heaven—not to mention Goldman Sachs, we need more financial muscle. We begin to feel uncomfortable. Talking of the kingdom, we discover that the Church of England is now so impoverished that our leaders have to avoid giving offence to wealthy pressure groups, in order to stay afloat. Think of Jesus secluded in the wilderness, writing out grant proposals to the Herod Family Research Foundation.

Without benefactors we should not have the unquestionable delights of Trinity Hall today, architectural, cultural, intellectual, and social. Without the crusading Bishop Bateman, perhaps a kind of fourteenth-century cross between Donald Rumsfeld and Pat Robertson, without the rather improbable Sir Nathaniel Lloyd, without the decent and generous

Dr Eden, we should not be contemplating this chapel of sanctified memory and the prospect of memorable dinners. As a college we have reason to be grateful for the provision of that five letter word which churches are reluctant to mention—money. Without resources visions remain unrealized, ivory tower pipedreams: in the real world the hungry remain unfed. As individuals we are only too aware of how much we depend on funds. No money, no mortgage payments, etc.

Yet the benefactions that we receive personally are very often of a different kind. There are often the imperceptible acts of concern and thoughtfulness which cumulatively enrich our lives in many ways. There are the friendships and the collegiality which create the most positive aspects of our working lives. There are the gestures of love which create the most basic foundations of our personal and family lives.

In Trinity Hall, I would guess that most if not all of us have had tangible and enduring experiences of this kind of basic benefaction. I certainly have, as my life has been touched at various points—by the great and the good, archbishops and masters, by the less great but still good, college staff and undergraduates, by the moderately great and tolerably good, other members of the fellowship. Indeed, I was lucky in this place to have experienced the undeserved friendship of a number of amazingly generous people—whom I shall not embarrass, in life or in death, by naming here and now. So yes, it is most right and our bounden duty to commemorate our benefactors, and to mean it.

But what, you may well ask, has any of this to do with God? What benefactions has God given to this college, and indeed to the world? Why should we be grateful to God? The traditional answer is still the best one. God loved the world so much that he gave his only son for our salvation. Over the years we have largely phased out the meaning of this breathtaking claim: we have rendered it culturally innocuous. Not least, we have wrapped it in pious jargon which has effectively removed it from serious discourse. Let me try to spell out this claim to truth again.

It is not so long since Christmas. God, the hospitable God, came down at Christmas. The world turned upside down. In the sign of transformation of the wondrous birth in Bethlehem, God, as Luther put it, was made small for us. The Creator of the universe comes to be in the being of another, in the being of a fragile, vulnerable child. *Ave verum corpus natum ex Maria virgine.* Women are the witnesses of incarnation, crucifixion, and resurrection. The Christ child grows in wisdom and in stature, not by magic but by experience. Tears and smiles like us he knew.

He loved us from the first of time. He loves us to the last. It is always hard for us to get our minds round complex and counter-intuitive imagery. But that is partly what we are at university for.

The gods of the ancient Mediterranean world were in many ways terrible gods, imposing all kinds of dire penalties on their followers to drive them to submission and obedience—and Christianity was soon to follow suit. But to substitute one tyranny for another was to miss the breathtaking radicalism of St. John's Gospel.

Love came down at Christmas. Love came out at Christmas, we may say, reflecting on the current traumas of the Church of England. The real daring is not the daring of ecclesiastical pressure groups, but the daring of God in Incarnation. Calvin (patron saint of miserable Scottish religion) said, reflecting on the gospel, "[w]e ought to embrace the whole human race without exception in a single feeling of love; here there is no distinction between barbarian and Greek, worthy and unworthy, friend and enemy, since all should be contemplated in God, and not in themselves" (*Inst.* II.8.55). You, all of us, are made in the image of God, the image redefined in Jesus the Christ. This is an image of relationships, not limiting but transformational. Jesus Christ is the icon of unimaginably unconditional love, of self-giving undetectable, of everything other than coercion, manipulation, and domination. Here now is God, for us and for our salvation, fully divine, and fully human. For our salvation, black and white, gay and straight, male and female, Jew and Arab. This is a gospel for those at the bottom of the league tables, and a call to those of us near the top of the statistics to be generous and hospitable in turn.

God is a generous God. Not a God of tribal partiality, hate, and discrimination. Who would believe this today? Negative imagery has been operative in all the major religious traditions. Against this, there is a persistent tradition in Christianity, and in other major religions, that there is a God of love, compassion, justice and fairness, forgiveness and reconciliation. There is an urgent need to re-imagine this God. I want to suggest tonight that the imagery of hospitality may be one useful avenue towards realizing this goal. Think hospitality as the deep substructure of all worthwhile religion. Hospitality comes in many shapes and forms, and this concept too, potentially has positive and negative elements. Hospitality has to be conceived: it also has to be actualized, if it is to be a gift which can be unwrapped and enjoyed.

God in the major world faiths is a hospitable God. There are of course contrary readings. God has been, and still is, often envisaged as a savage God, even a brutal, tyrannical God whose chief delight is to punish those who disobey him by causing havoc, suffering, and death on a grand scale. Followers of such a God replicate these characteristics in their conduct towards other human beings. But to major on this tradition would be a kind of ironic tribute to an evil God. I want to focus on the broad stream of reflection and action based on the recognition of a gracious and loving God, who is *par excellence* hospitable. I concentrate on Christianity, with which I am most familiar.

A long tradition of Christian hospitality stems from an attempt to respond to the perception of the call to service of a loving God. Beyond explicit mention of hospitality, there is a rich stream of reflection on the nature of God as unconditional love, unconditional generosity and compassion, and unconditional hospitality. We are accustomed to think of the doctrine of God in Christian doctrine as a reflection on divine being and action. I want to suggest a concentration on the hospitality of which Augustine speaks. For Thomas Aquinas, the hospitality of God is not as strange as is often thought. Luther and Calvin can speak of hospitality—Calvin sees it as a duty to migrants. Schleiermacher's Christmas Eve dialogue is a celebration of hospitality. Hospitality may not be what we think of initially in these contexts—the great theologians were by no means uniformly hospitable. But the leitmotif is always there.

We can find the same confidence in divine hospitality in poetry, e.g., in Auden and Hopkins, in music, in the Christian Mozart and Bach, and the Jewish Copland and Bernstein, in Alf Houkom's "The Rune of Hospitality." We find hospitality in art, in Leonardo and Michelangelo, in the famous Rublev icon of Trinitarian hospitality, in Chagall's Mainz stained glass.

God is understood differently in different world religions. To minimize the differences is not to facilitate but to stifle constructive engagement between them. But they do have aims and aspirations in common, arising from their different visions of God but targeted towards the same human race. Different Gods, same human race. There are some bridge concepts which link the religions in their quest for the realization of God's will for humanity: one of these is the divine hospitality. It is often said that in a religious context only God has rights and humanity has only duties and responsibilities towards God. Yet there is a kind of reciprocity between the divine and the human. This is not assimilation but an affinity of opposites. In Islam and Judaism, the asymmetry is privileged. In

Christianity, the asymmetry is qualified by the paradox of incarnation. In Hinduism and Buddhism, there are other visions of interaction.

A Christian version of this relationship will bring to dialogue the recognition that God has given his rights as the unconditional source of love over into the human realm through Jesus Christ, as a catalyst and energizing source for human compassion. Other religions will construe this contribution through their own channels. There remain for all the world religions equivalents in different ways of the visions of the compassion of Allah, the righteous love of Yahweh and the self-dispossessing love of God in Jesus Christ. I want to suggest that each of these visions can make substantive contributions to the realization of the divine rights of God as the ground of human rights, and the notion of hospitality as central to God.

The divine rights of God are shared rights. God is a God who cares. Here is a link, if you like, with a humanist as well as a religious vision. A theological humanism has links with a secular humanism, in sharing the framework of ultimate care. Its distinctive contribution is the suggestion that human caring is also a matter of grace and spontaneity, not simply of enlightened self-interest. Human grace is an aspiration to which all human beings, religious and non-religious, may aspire, and may draw upon an a vehicle for the delivery of human rights at the point of greatest need. For those of us who believe in God through Jesus Christ, this human grace is the fruit of the self-dispossession to us of the divine rights of God. For all who believe in God, it is a trace of God, differently construed in different faiths, of the will of God for the created order. But however construed, the crucial point is the human rights imperative as the consequence of the reality of the hospitable God in an often inhospitable landscape.

Thinking this through further, for Christian faith, God acts through Word and Sacrament, through participation and embodiment, in the created order. God's Word is a hospitable Word, both in shape and in content. The Word of God is likened in the Bible to a two-edged sword. Can we think of a sword of hospitality? I rather doubt it. We must in all probability abandon the sword metaphor. We may retain the underlying truth that hospitality is not always welcome. It may divide and create tensions, it may be refused, because of self-interest or misunderstanding, because it is costly and inconvenient. We should not expect hospitality to be always achievable without careful preparation.

The content of God's word is a word of counsel, a basis for understanding ourselves and relating to others. Word is further communicated as sacrament, as signalling the embodiment of the divine hospitality in the created order and especially in human life. The concrete instantiation and source of word and sacrament is Jesus Christ in the events of his life, death, and resurrection

Since the hospitable character of God is understood to be recognizable in the life of Jesus, his words and actions, in his death in solidarity with the marginal, and in his resurrection through and beyond death, we may understand the Holy Spirit as the Spirit of hospitality. The divine complex, which we call Trinity, as a matrix of hospitality in which we are enabled to participate and empowered to offer hospitality to others. If this is true, resistance to the hospitable in the created order is not an intractable problem for all time, but a situation in the midst of which God's vision of love, peace and justice is promised.

How does the hospitable God act? God acts through people. There is a rich strand of reflection on the hospitable frame of mind in the tradition of Christian spirituality. We do not always have a hospitable frame of mind—usually due to our insecurities. If we are to move and encourage others to move from the selfish to the selfless, we need to encourage personal as well as corporate structures of hospitality. Psychology has a significant role here—perfect love casts out fear etc. We might think of human progress from the paleolithic to present as a move from more fear to less. But there is clearly no straight line of progress—as many people live in fear today as ever did. Somehow we must try to move towards unforced consensus.

God's hospitality is expressed in personal commitment and in church engagement. But it has implications in almost all areas of human life, perhaps not least in politics, in its theory and its actualities. Though it does not explicitly reflect on hospitality, much weight is placed on dimensions of hospitable politics in Jim Wallis's classic, *God's Politics*, a moderate evangelical critique of the politics of the American Christian Right. Against this, he advocates a different kind of religion:

> Prophetic faith is the best counterpart to fundamentalist religion. We bring faith into the public square when our moral convictions demand it. But to influence a democratic society, you must win the public debate about why the principles you advocate are better for the common good. That's the democratic

discipline religion has to be under when it brings its faith to the public square.[1]

God is a hospitable God. Anything else associated with God is simply wrong. Of course, human religion has added numerous laws, rituals, purity codes, taboos, etc., to its understanding of God. As far as these are consonant with the love of God, they are unlikely to be harmful and remain a matter of culture and custom. Where they contradict the unconditional nature of the divine love, they are undesirable and may have to be opposed. This will apply to many of the practices in the sacred texts of the major world religions. The text is important, but not in itself a sufficient guide to the nature of the God who has revealed himself as unconditional love in human experience.

God is pure hospitality, unconditional love. This theme is instructively underlined in a *Times* article by Martin Amis on the film *United 93*, a film about the passenger revolt on board a 9/11 flight. In this bleak, but immensely moving account, love is the vital thread. Ziad Jarrah, the pilot and leader of the hijackers, phones his fiancé just before boarding the plane and says just six words into his cellphone—"I love you, I love you." Mark Bingham, one of the group who attempt to rush the hijackers, (and incidentally gay, like the Fire Brigade Chaplain who died under the towers—bad news for the Herod Research Foundation), phones his mother and simply says, "I just want you to know that I love you." Amis comments:

> Love is an abstract noun, something nebulous. And yet love turns out to be the only part of us that is solid, as the world turns upside down and the screen goes black. We can't tell if it will survive us. But we can be sure it's the last thing to go.

We are to be mindful of human rights. Of course. We are to contribute to Amnesty and its sister organizations. But this is only first aid. God, the generosity of complete self-dispossession, calls us to look at the deep structures of our world with different eyes. Hospitality is not just for special occasions, like tonight. God's hospitality in incarnation invites us to look again at global economics, at market structures, at the depth structures of our political and social arrangements.

At Christmas we hear the Nine Lessons and Carols from Kings across the way, and the bidding prayer touches us with its very familiarity—"And

---

1. Wallis, *God's Politics*, 67.

because this of all things would rejoice his heart, let us at this time remember in his name the poor and the helpless, the cold, the hungry and the oppressed, the sick and them that mourn, the lonely and unloved." Perhaps we ought to think that this is a call as relevant to February, to June and September, as it is to Christmas. It is a call not to charity, but to solidarity and effective structural change.

Yes, we should remember our benefactors. And because we have been given much, we need to be benefactors too. Not to make us more sensitive, or more caring—if that happens fine, but it's hardly the point, but to respond to the call of God to let hospitality and benefaction permeate the created order. Of course we shall not succeed in doing this as we should. Perhaps we can make a small difference here and there. For this it is worth remembering our benefactors, not least the God who gave us life and love, by giving us his life and his love. In the end, love is all we have left, thoughtfully targeted, and persistently directed love.

Commemoration of Benefactors

Trinity Hall, 5 February 2012

How does one commemorate the benefactors, especially since we have quite possibly been doing this for 650 years? I have been preaching on this Sunday myself for some time, though actually not yet for quite 650 years. I can imagine that when the preacher for 1352 uttered his words of wisdom lots of undergraduates said to themselves, "Hell this is *so* 1340s." And so it goes. Well, at least the Scripture readings for the appropriate Sunday change. And this year's perhaps speak especially to our condition. We may soar on wings like eagles—Virgin Atlantic. Lead me Lord in thy righteousness. Bring ruin on my enemies—especially on those who didn't like my last essay or book review, and everybody who hissed my mystery lectures. Jesus says, "where are we tonight?" and promptly heals the demon-possessed. Masters contemplating the Governing Body meeting, students going into uncomfortable supervisions, cooks trying to please everybody at once—all must have resonated to the thought that there be demons in Trinity Hall, at least occasionally.

No doubt we ought to be truly thankful today for the great and the good, the world class scholars who maintain our reputation at the cutting edge of knowledge and the immensely rich who maintain us in the manner to which we wish to continue to be accustomed. Without the continuing momentum in education and research, we don't deserve to prosper. Without continuing generous financial support we just cease to function—full stop. There's much to be grateful for here. We just have to look for a moment outside our comfortable college to see that.

Christian faith is all about looking outside the magic circle. St. Paul encourages us to be all things to all men—and women. We are here to enjoy ourselves, but to help other people to enjoy their lives too. We are here too to appreciate the well-balanced, sane, intelligent, and always generous community which is Trinity Hall—well hopefully most of the time!—but all men includes the people who, from time to time, seem to us, and often to themselves, to be possessed by demons—whatever demons may be. We might even reflect that none of us is immune from a little fit of demon possession ourselves from time to time—well I am something of a Scots Calvinist after all!

So where are my Strictly Come Benefaction winners for 2012? I want to mention four people who come to mind from the time when I was Dean. None of them won a Nobel Prize and none was unspeakably rich. I was not particularly close to all of them. But all of them seem to me, looking back, to have been benefactors to our college community, in ways which were remarkably consonant with the Christian gospel. They would no doubt deny this furiously!

My first victim was the Master's wife when I arrived—Marian Sugden. Master's wives have a particularly hard time of it. They come into what looks suspiciously like an academic version of Downton Abbey—big, old house, loads of staff, splendid grounds, formal meals, and all the quotidian minor tensions of a strong minded family, multiplied by X. Whatever they do, not to mention whatever they don't do, is going to be scrutinized and analyzed continually, and probably compared with the last incumbent, and the one before that. Lady Sugden managed to have a quite amazing rapport with just about everybody in the place. She entertained them, actually did things with their kids, whether they were the Vice Master's student offspring or the assistant chef's toddlers, and picked up the undergraduates who were feeling lost or the fellows who were divorcing their sixth wives. She had strong opinions, she was not afraid to speak her mind, and she was unquestionably a benefactor to us all.

The next contestant for benefactor 2012 was a student here, even a member of the Chapel community—I trust you appreciate this tactful move on my part. Charlie Beale was organ scholar and choirmaster in my time. He studied music, later did a PhD on jazz piano, and became a professor at the Royal College of Music. Charlie was a fantastic organist and a hugely persuasive leader of the choir and the music society, not to mention a centre of their decidedly colorful social life. But he also had principles—a rare thing in an organist, you might think—and so he felt unable to receive communion in Chapel, as long as the Church of England practiced discrimination on grounds of sexuality. Charlie is today the conductor of the famous New York Gay Men's Chorus, still working for inclusion. Benefaction and generosity do not mean losing sight of what you believe in and what you stand for.

My third contestant was a fellow, and is happily still with us, as a retired fellow, John Collier. He will hate this. But John was by any standards a considerable benefactor. Collier is not a name to rank with Blackstone, or Dicey, or the stacks of Appeal Court judges whom we produce as a matter of course. The fellows did not always agree with him on every issue. But he had a quite unique gift of the capacity for friendship with undergraduates, endless students whose lives and study were supported, and greatly enhanced, through his consistently supportive presence. So what, you may say. In the academic life in 2012 we are increasingly encouraged, mandated even, to be ferociously competitive with every sinew, neuron, synapse, whatever. Sad losers don't count. John was not like that. Shocking—but if his contribution is not benefaction, I don't know what is.

Finally, there was, and I guess still is, a good field to choose from, when I think of benefaction, I think especially of Mrs Jeffs, then the Senior Tutor's secretary. Thelma Jeffs was an angel, in not too heavy disguise. Trinity Hall is a well-organized, efficiently run, generally benevolent institution. It ticks all the boxes for equality awareness, health and safety, equal opportunity requirements, and all fellows are certified to work with emotionally challenged youth (though the youth may not be certified to work with emotionally challenged fellows!). But there are moments when someone, through no fault, or perhaps half fault of their own, feels that they have come up against a brick wall and they don't quite know where to turn next. That's where Mrs Jeffs was a godsend. People knew that they could turn to her and she would somehow find a way through the brick wall. She knew what she knew and was totally discreet. And that was benefaction, even blessing.

In my version of Strictly Come Benefaction there are no winners. None of my contestants were remotely interested in winning. And so they all win.

In thinking of these four very different people I have tried to show how they made a difference where they found themselves, and this was extremely good news for our college community. But these folk also had interests outside. They were not obsessed by their local involvement, and that was good news too. This brings me back to the "Hall" men and women that I rather rubbished earlier, the scholars and scientists, and the wealth creators. Benefaction brings obligations to contribute to a wider society, to take advantage of the benefits we enjoy here, and to add something to the lives of folk who don't have the experiences we have. The 1 percent but also the 99 percent—I guess there is an absolutely fundamental and ever present challenge here. And somewhere in the middle of all this, there are a surprisingly large number of benefactors, members of the college past and present, who are not in the Zuckerberg bracket, but who still contribute most generously to our 650 year old project, and for that we are deeply grateful.

All things to all men. What about the demons, our demons and others' demons? Jesus was there where it was needed. End of story. Perhaps not quite. In our 2012 world of post-theism, post-modernity and post-post, it is not entirely unthinkable to imagine that through these still vaguely familiar stories there are pointers to a God who is there, who is benefaction instantiated in, the not always so comfortable, life of Jesus of Nazareth. In that deeply challenging drama of death and resurrection, suffering and celebration, murderous violence and the hope of compassion, there comes a call to attentive benefaction. It echoes in every situation in which we find ourselves, comfortable and uncomfortable—even in Trinity Hall.

Being prepared to be open and accepting to all the huge variety of people we encounter here and outside the college, trying to be alert to the situations of the more difficult people we meet, and to face the contradictions in ourselves, is that the sum of our Christian faith? Actually it's not. Though the liberal vision of reasonableness, tolerance, affirmation, and inclusion, serves to help keep the church honest at times of huge pressure to retreat into a tunnel of blind fideism, of dogmatic intolerance.

2012. What will benefaction look like in 2112? The one sure thing one can say about prophets is that they are almost always wrong. However. We all know that most of the churches in Europe are in a bad way. We can tell ourselves that they are believing if not belonging, that the disastrous decline of ecumenical action has been succeeded by a higher form of togetherness, etc. We can say that our lot are declining more slowly than theirs, because we have a better theology or liturgy or whatever. But there it is.

We know that the more classically liberal Protestants have declined the fastest, and the others feel safer with their richer liturgical traditions. But even very progressive Episcopal churches are withering on the vine, and Catholicism is in retreat all over Europe. In America, the most forward looking and enlightened Christian communities, from the UCC to the Quakers, are losing numbers fast. The future seems to lie with the millions of devout Protestants and Catholics who will sing hymns at the inaugural of President Gingrich. The next fastest growing church is the alternative community of Governor Romney.

In Asia, Africa, and South America, easily the fastest growing churches are charismatic and pentecostal, often deeply conservative in social and political areas. Paradoxically, as we try in Europe, entirely sensibly, to introduce more contemporary music for a younger generation, in Asia large congregations may well be singing the music and the words, literally translated, of Moody and Sankey, with huge enthusiasm. As Christianity declines in Europe, it grows elsewhere. The work of world ecumenical bodies is likely to be shaped decisively in much more traditional directions, not least if there is, as there may well be, an exponential expansion of Christian presence in and from China.

So, what's not to like about all this? As far as global Christianity goes, it may well soon be our Christian duty to work in committed conversation and engagement with all sorts of new and sometimes uncomfortable people. But benefaction does not mean that anything goes. I would guess that there are understandings of some core elements of the gospel, relating to theology and pastoral care, ethics and belief, that we would be concerned to maintain in all circumstances. We can all talk the talk, but we have to try at least to walk the walk.

So where do we go from here? I have painted such a dark picture that you may think it can only get better. It gets better. People who say this sometimes have a disconcerting tendency to cease to be with us shortly afterwards. The seed has to fall into the ground and die before there is new birth. But there's a lot of evidence of falling and precious little of new growth.

My own take on this is that indeed, we have to be resolute for the very long term. I guess the Dean will have talked to you about Bonhoeffer's secret discipline. In terms of practical action, no one-size-fits-all approach will do. Sometimes more traditional, sometimes more radical approaches, often a judicious mixture of both, will be required. Things may well remain difficult. Churches may continue to decline despite our best efforts. But as they decline, it becomes even more important to maintain a witness. I don't mean, to prop up institutions which have had their day and can only benefit from reconstruction. But rather to point, in word and action, to the heart of the Christian gospel—unconditional love in action, as the motive force of God's creation. Despite the superstructures of ecclesiastical triumphalism, Christian faith always has a built-in sense of "nevertheless," and often "against the odds." If the light shines on in the darkness, and I believe it does, then there is every possible reason to maintain a sane and consistent witness to it in the world. And in any case, the darkness will never extinguish it.

We need progressive values. But to make them stick, we may sometimes need to pray for a resolute faith against the odds. The gospel tells us, the evangelical gospel of the catholic faith, that even while we are searching for answers, for values, for effective actions and solutions in the face of all the challenges (translated into English as horrendous obstacles), that face a quest for the triumph of love and well-being in the world of 2012, God is already there before us. This is the great benefaction, the benefaction that has already taken place, improbably and against the appearance of things, through the catalyst of one single human life in the history of the universe, the incarnation of the cosmic Christ. What it means is that in 1412, in 1512, in 1612, in 2012, in 3012, in life, in death, in our future with God, we are not alone. Of course there need not have been a benefactor. Faith promises us that there is one.

Spirituality and Human Rights

Glasgow University Chapel 12 October 2003

> O Lord Jesus Christ, who hast said that thou art the way, the truth and the life: suffer us not at any time to stray from thee, who art the way; nor to distrust thy promises, which art the truth, nor to rest in any other thing than thee, who art the life; beyond which there is nothing to be desired, neither in heaven nor in earth, for thy Name's sake. (Erasmus/Glasgow University.)

Micah 6:1–8: Justice and Mercy; Luke 10:25–37: Good Samaritan

What is spirituality? Discuss, in 1500 words, and remember to put your matriculation number on your paper. Spirituality can mean many different things to many people. I suppose spirituality has an inside and an outside, and these are connected in different ways. You can see the effects, as it were, of spirituality in the presence of a worshipping congregation in a huge cathedral, in a little country chapel, or in a great spiritual gathering on the banks of the Ganges. You can think of spirituality in the work of an artist, and in the humanitarian work of caring agencies throughout the world. You can think of true spirituality and you can think of false spirituality. There certainly appears to be something there, something which we can and do assess.

Spirituality seems to have something to do with an attitude, a way of acting and thinking which puts our thoughts and actions in the perspective of relation to God, or to transcendence, whatever that may mean, to a more ultimate ground of meaningfulness. People sometimes do this consciously or unconsciously.

In the Christian tradition, which is where I am coming from, spirituality is often understood as listening for the voice of God in our world and in our lives. There have of course been great spiritual giants in the Christian past. But for us, it means perhaps just stopping to think occasionally and trying to imagine the reality of God in relation to our world and the way we live our lives. Creating this space for reflection affects us all differently, and affects each of us differently at different times. We may respond by paying more attention to private prayer and meditation. We may respond by getting more involved in public worship and in the work of the churches. We may simply come to see our daily lives as being themselves an expression of spirituality, of lives lived and relationships developed, with an integrity which seeks to reflect the decency and justice which the prophet Amos long ago identified as God's will for his creation.

And that is good. Of course we struggle sometimes, when we look at the decidedly ambiguous state of the world, and the churches, to ask ourselves what sort of prayer and meditation is best, what sort of worship, what sort of church work, what sort of daily lives? And here Christian faith offers us a kind of icon, a pattern and a shape for a spirituality in the events concerning Jesus.

Christian response to this pattern has been very mixed through the ages, sometimes very extreme. Jesus Christ is the way, the truth and the life. Here is the most precious thing, the divine love incarnate. People who do not see this, are the enemies of God and of life. Let's kill them all, from the Jews of Europe to the Muslims of Srebroniza. A spiritual vision, you might begin to think, is like a loaded gun, and it is irresponsible for people like us even to touch it. It has often been as bad as that. But fortunately, it has not always been as bad as that.

Despite what sometimes seem to have been our best collective efforts, something has shone through the icon of the Christ event which has also inspired countless, often unremembered, acts of compassion and generosity. These have transformed human lives in great ways and small. If you read the kind of reports about the churches which hit the newspapers, you may have the impression of bodies which are eternally consuming their own smoke and being pathetically self-absorbed.

If you take away just one thing from this sermon, I'd like to suggest to you the thought that the Christ of the New Testament is just not like that, and that is why he is worth our lifelong attention. Like all of us, Jesus of Nazareth depended heavily on his family and friends. But his words and his actions were surprisingly and strikingly outward looking rather than inward looking. The parable of the good Samaritan is typical, and it breaks most of these rules of tribal behavior by which we all still tend to live. It is all about inclusion, not about exclusion.

Religion is so often about exclusion. In Scotland, those of us with Presbyterian links are familiar with a Calvinism one of whose main planks is the doctrine of election. When we wake up in the morning and say to ourselves, "We are God's elect," it's almost better for our endorphins than going to the gym, and a lot less hassle. Problem is, when some are elect, the others become unelect. The Anglican Archbishops, rather curiously self-designated primates, are meeting currently to talk about sex. What do we know about the sexual behavior of primates, I hear you ask? Are these gentlemen—there are no women—in the business of inclusion or of exclusion? That is where the trouble usually starts.

This is where I begin to think of human rights. Spirituality can be an important vehicle for concentrating our attention—for good or for bad. Jesus comes through the New Testament as always there for those for whom no one else will speak up within the tribe, as the voice of the voiceless in all circumstances.

Human rights are important, not just as a language, but as a culture. They are not unproblematic either. The language of human rights is constantly hi-jacked by people who abuse rights. Human rights language can obscure issues as well as clarify them. It can elevate individuals at the expense of groups. It can become a plaything of diplomatic spin. But it is still one of the most potent symbols of our time.

I want to suggest that Christian spirituality which is centred on Jesus has a lot to do with support for human rights. Jesus comes across as someone whose whole existence is moulded and illuminated by his compassionate relation to others, not only in giving but in receiving, in teaching and in learning, in amazing mutuality and reciprocity. Jesus is totally devoted to God. But God relates to him through this self-giving which is, at the same time, the self-dispossession of God. Jesus reluctantly but deliberately puts himself at risk. Unsurprisingly, he is tortured and killed. Utterly surprisingly, that does not appear to be the end of the matter. The women, minor characters to this day in the Christian narrative, come to understand that the world has been turned upside down.

Do we need to know this? Give us Barabbas. As they say, be careful what you wish for . . . the last two thousand years have produced plenty of victims. But the spirituality of Jesus suggests that victimhood is not the last word. There is always hope of transformation, because the world has once been turned upside down, and nothing is ever again quite as static as it looks. The love of God is not quite dead, and may do awesome things in unexpected places. It is not owned by any tribe, the Glasgow tribe, the Protestant tribe, the British tribe, the Christian tribe, the white tribe, the male tribe.

It is for you, whoever you are, because through you, God is still in Christ reconciling the world to himself.

Christmas

Cambridge University Staff and Graduate Students. Great St. Mary's, 18 December 2007

In St. Matthew's Gospel, chapter eleven, Jesus talks about the expected advent of the kingdom. The blind see, the lame walk, the lepers are made clean, the deaf hear, the dead are raised to life, the poor are hearing the good news.

When those of you who are students leave this university, quite a lot of your time will probably be taken up in preparing presentations, reports, lessons, or even sermons—and most of us do lots of this sort of thing—too much of it—already. Let me try to set you an example—the most useful examples are often the *bad* examples—so here we are. We begin by looking for a text, which rather often turns out to be only a pretext. The lectionary around this week offers quite a lot from the birth of Jesus narratives. But we hear these so often . . .

Try again. Psalm 137 is offered. By the waters of Babylon we sat down and wept. Well that can wait till nearer the tripos exams of the PhD vivas. Next on the list is Matthew 11:2-11. Actually, let me begin by telling you about our summer holidays. Last resort of the anxious minister as he wonders what to say this week. In September, Elizabeth and I spent a couple of weeks in Crete to celebrate our 40th wedding anniversary.

Among other things we took a short cruise to the island of Spinalonga. Apart from the beach and the sunshine, Spinalonga's main claim to fame was its use as the last European leper colony. Now that was providential. Because the text offered from Matthew is about lepers. And it's very suitable—not that I usually think of this university as a leper colony, you understand. Lepers are not good news, as far as much of the history of our religious tradition is concerned. In the book of Leviticus, lepers are pronounced cursed, unclean, and to be totally isolated to avoid sacred pollution. The good news is that Jesus changed all of that. Jesus was not afraid of lepers. He ignored the tradition of thousands of years. He related to them as human beings like himself. He broke the chains of isolation and illness. Behold, I make all things new.

The bad news is that the influence of Leviticus continues right up to the present. Lepers were thought to be punished by God for their hidden sins. Nowadays we are more regularly punished by the *News of the World* for our hidden sins. But the religious tradition of illness, or just difference, equals sinfulness, has been extraordinarily effective. There are still issues: disease is curable—but the money to buy drugs is not there. And the notion of a curse is still potent. So what has gone wrong? I come back to Jesus and the lepers. What was this all about? Your faith has healed you, says Jesus. I want to suggest that this is crucially a question of faith. The faith of the gospel is not to be confused with maintaining all the traditional certainties of the religious cultures. That way lies radical fundamentalism, with all its destructive power. The light of the world is come to bring illumination, not to scorch and burn.

What has any of this to do with Christmas? In any case, Christmas is not always popular. Sir Kingsley Amis, former fellow of Peterhouse, to Philip Larkin, 27 December 1947:

"My dear Philip . . . Myself I am not too happy at this season: Christmas comes but once a year, and it makes you feel *sodding fed-up* because you remember all the Christmases when you were a child and enjoyed yourself . . . and now you don't enjoy yourself. God rest you *dismal*, gentlemen; may all things you dismay; O come let us *debauch* them."[2]

Cheerful stuff!

God of God, Light of Light, Very God of Very God, Who for us and for our salvation came down from heaven. But do we actually believe it? Love came down at Christmas. The world turned upside down. In the sign of transformation of the wondrous birth in Bethlehem, God, as Luther put it, was made small for us. The Creator of the universe comes to be in the being of another, in the being of a fragile, vulnerable child. *Ave verum corpus natum ex Maria virgine.* Women are the witnesses of incarnation, crucifixion, and resurrection. The Christ child grows in wisdom and in stature, not by magic but by experience. Tears and smile like us he knew.

Love came down at Christmas. But the real disclosure is the Incarnation. All of us are made in the image of God. This is an image of relationships, not limiting but transformational. Christ is the icon of unimaginably unconditional love, of self-giving undetectable, of everything other than coercion, manipulation, domination. Here now is God, for us and for our salvation. And because this of all things would rejoice his heart, let us at this time remember in his name the poor and the helpless, the cold, the hungry and the oppressed, the sick and them that mourn, the lonely and unloved.

What does this have to do with Christmas? I think this is something at the heart of faith. Let's go back to the Psalm suggestion in the lectionary—not the waters of Babylon, but Psalm 111. "Praise ye the Lord," it says in the King James Version. "I will praise the Lord with my whole heart, in the assembly of the upright, and in the congregation." Well, at least in Great St. Mary's we are firmly in the assembly of the upright—or at least, in the right postcode. But that's not the whole story. Cambridge has a long tradition of caring for people with the wrong sort of postcode—and people with no postcode at all. That is the breakthrough of the Gospel. What had been implicit in the tradition is now made stunningly explicit. The good news is there for the upright and the not so upright

---

2. Amis, *Letters*, 128.

alike. It is those at the point of greatest need who are the constant focus of Jesus' concern. He died a death devised for slaves, and out of death came new life.

What are we called to do here? Ministry—and there is a basic sense in which we are all ministers to one another—has been famously defined as constructive loafing. And constructive loafing importantly means offering hospitality—physical, emotional, and intellectual hospitality. Hospitality helps to make life fun. I want to suggest that God is hospitable, and invites us all to be hospitable in turn. Trouble is, religion is often anything but hospitable, as we see in the news every day. This is obviously not an issue for Christianity alone. The need for more effective dialogue has become more sharply obvious since 9/11.

In the New Testament Jesus was a stranger, "I was a stranger and you welcomed me." Hospitality does not of course begin with Christian faith. Homer, in *The Odyssey*, says that: "The city which forgets how to care for the stranger has forgotten how to care for itself." No dawn raids on asylum seekers then.

In ancient Israel, bread should be shared with the foreigner and one should love him (or her, one might think) as oneself. In the Qur'an, to entertain and to give food are synonymous. So what *is* the problem? But what your average punter knows about the churches, and the mosques, in Britain today, is that they are still often none too hospitable. They divide in bitter conflict on issues which are really non-issues.

As Jesus said, have nothing to do with any sort of dodgy people—mix only with the assembly of the upright.

Well that's quite long enough for a mini sermon. Faith believes, often against the odds, that the impossible can happen because God is radically hospitable, and we may begin to believe it. That brings me back to tales from our summer holidays. If we try to remember Jesus and the people suffering from leprosy, perhaps we won't go terribly far wrong. But then I know from many years spent in this University long ago, that hospitality is not something which you need to hear a sermon about. Merry Christmas when it comes, and God bless you all. Amen.

Christian Unity

St Edward's, Cambridge. 21 January 2011.

The people who walked in darkness have seen a great light.

The gospel is not all sweetness and light, Mills and Boon. There is always a fair bit of darkness around, and it doesn't go away—think Elie Wiesel's "Night." And if we can truly say that "the darkness comprehended it not," it sometimes comes pretty close. Yet there is perhaps one striking thing. You only need a tiny bit of light to point the way in the middle of a huge expanse of darkness. And of course there are different sorts of darkness. Without darkness we should never be able to sleep!

Which brings me neatly to the small matter of Christian unity. A sermon on this topic in 2011 will perhaps inevitably have more darkness than light in it, but we shouldn't forget that the light is, in the end, what really matters. Christian unity, it often seems today, is a lost cause. Dead as the Dodo—though actually there's a much better chance of resurrecting the Dodo's DNA. After a century of meticulous schemes for organic unity between the Christian churches, the results are not impressive. *Ut omnes unum sint.* That they all may be one. The Johannine Jesus' great prayer for the community of his followers is as fashionable today as hula hoops and television sets with twelve inch square screens. Perhaps if they brought back Latin . . . ?

There have been some remarkably generous schemes involving considerable sacrifice for some of the denominations. Forty years ago some of the best brains in Cambridge were deeply into ecumenical dialogue—I think of Gordon Rupp and Anglican-Methodist unity.

Nothing much came of it. Buried in bureaucratic wrangles about who would present the chasuble to whom on the great day, and unspoken anxieties about money, property, and power, it has all largely faded away. True, magnificent words are uttered every year. New "ecumenical instruments" are born. In Scotland there is a grand sounding body called ACTS—Action for Churches Together in Scotland. But the constitution is expressly designed to ensure that action is the last thing that ACTS can take—all can be gracious and none shall be embarrassed. And the churches are strangely reluctant to provide the modest financial resources which might make any concrete action possible. Scottish Churches House is to close in the summer.

But, I hear you cry, isn't this rather overdoing the doom and gloom? Surely there have been successful schemes for organic union: united and uniting churches exist in many parts of the world. This is true, and anyone who has had the good fortune to get to know the life of uniting churches, in India, Canada, Australia, New Zealand, the USA and wherever, can testify to the lively spiritual lives of congregations no longer comprehensively bound by arrangements made for an age long since gone (though, of course, all of us in St. Edwards would die in the last ditch for 1662!) On the other hand, it is notable that some of the Uniting churches are becoming smaller, while bodies more focussed on traditional certainties flourish—fundamentalism trumps ecumenism every time. The ecumenical train seems to have rusted quietly away.

Shall we then sit down by the waters of Babylon and weep? No way (footnote: here St. Paul might have used a double negative). I'm inclined to think (on the rare occasion when I'm still inclined to think) that the game may have changed in a way that makes the usual paradigm shifts as up to date as twelve inch television tubes. There was a time when ecumenical effort was inspired by the great theologians—Reinhold Niebuhr, Bonhoeffer, William Temple, Bishop Bell, the Baillies, etc. Then the churches dropped the pilots and the torch was carried by senior churchmen. Then the process fell, as everything eventually does, into the hands of church bureaucrats, all with different designations but all essentially alike. Then in the name of democracy—a good thing in itself—the task was to be inherited by the most intellectually challenged delegates who could be mustered after meticulous search. You think I exaggerate somewhat. Well, you're right. But essentially, give or take a few philosophical discussions about the postmodern meaning of unity, the goals remained the same.

Prophecy is never a sure thing, and most prophets have been wrong. But, with that insurance clause in small print, I am inclined to think that the game is beginning to change in ways which could not have been anticipated. I imagine that the traditional wings of churches will continue to devise elaborate canons for rebaptizing Methodists and burning Baptists to taste. But they will be increasingly overshadowed by much larger conservative Protestant and indeed, Catholic, bodies for whom all such delicacies are irrelevant. These will be the Christians who will have a considerable attraction for the worldwide post-twitter generation. And how about the liberals, if, by then, the last of them has not already turned out the light?

Some of them will still quite probably find homes in the remains of the traditional churches. Others may seek unity with likeminded Christians across the denominations, and this may lead to the formation of new uniting churches. One might imagine porous structures in which different sorts of Christians work together to create an unforced consensus, a kind of rainbow alliance of different but mutually respectful perspectives. How this may work out we don't yet know—cultural identities change and become more inhabitable as we begin to embrace them. And then there are the Pentecostals, of different sorts, a hugely energetic and transformative force across the world.

A sad tale of woe? Well perhaps not. I guess it is true that the failure of the ecumenical effort of the last half century has its shameful aspects. Too much obsession with power—was Jesus obsessed with power? Too much nationalism, racism, and plain old-fashioned snobbery posing as piety. Obviously, a uniting church constitution is an obvious way of breaking up the logjams in faith and action created by ossified institutional structures over the centuries. I think of Scottish presbyteries, you can find your own examples. And papering over the cracks with much hand wringing about the pain of our divisions did not help. Yet it is also true that the notion of institutional organic unity had its own problems. Holisitic schemes for organic unity were sometimes not without a hint of imperialism, and one size will not necessarily fit all. I say nothing here of Anglican Covenants, etc.

There is perhaps another angle to ponder here. For the last couple of hundred years at least, we have become used to the idea of solid national churches ploughing like dreadnoughts over the ecclesiastical ocean. But actually, there have always been breaks and shifts in Christian community since the early church. And it is not perhaps entirely clear that God has ordained the Church of England, or the Church of Scotland, by law, to remain forever in their current forms—not to mention Roman Catholic or Orthodox polities. Even within traditional frameworks, founding fathers like, for example, Richard Hooker, envisaged a freedom to develop in distinctive and diverse currents within a particular church. A kind of institutional "Animal Farm" was definitely not on his agenda.

By now, if you're lucky, you will have fallen asleep, before going back to your friends, who may include Buddhists, Muslims, Jewish people, etc. How strange is that? And while I have been displaying these ecclesial delicacies before you, children have died of malnutrition in Africa, Asian women have been exploited by their husbands, gay teens in the United States have been made homeless by their parents, asylum seekers in the UK, and Europe generally, have been locked up in even more boring confinement than your current situation. It is true of course that progress in any direction will not be achieved by a statutary nod in the direction of the suffering millions. Given a choice, most of the world's poor would probably embrace a deeply conservative version of faith, Christian or otherwise. There are no quick fixes for complex issues.

When we look for light in our darkness, we are encouraged to turn back to the gospel. The people who walked in darkness have seen a great light. The Lord is my light and my salvation; whom shall I fear? (To say this from Latimer's pulpit reminds us too that lighting candles carries a quantifiable degree of risk.) Be united in the same mind and purpose. The cross is foolishness to them that are perishing. Repent, for the kingdom of heaven has come near.

In the last few years I have thinking a bit about themes like generosity, human rights, and hospitality, especially in our churches. A long time ago, the American theologian, Reinhold Niebuhr, wrote a book called *Moral Man and Immoral Society*. His central thesis was this. As individuals in society we are often hugely kind, generous, and hospitable. But when we gather together into interest groups, quite often behavior patterns change and we become increasingly rigid and aggressive. We may seek to impose our perspectives and our goals on all the other people we encounter. In ecumenical dialogue, it is sometimes said, it is always more blessed to give than to receive.

This is a particular challenge for those of us who have faith in God. Because God in love has emptied himself in incarnation and self-dispossession, because Jesus was, as has been well said, a man who played to lose, we are invited to give ourselves, in love, to God and our fellow human beings. We are invited to generous and hospitable practice. This pattern of life, of lifestyle if you like, is by no means exclusive to Christians. But people of generosity and of hospitable practice have often been deeply immersed in a tradition of prayer and spirituality. Perhaps the outstanding contemporary example is Archbishop Desmond Tutu.

Hospitable practice does not mean simply niceness. It needs to get into the structures, the DNA of our churches, and it has to be proactive.

> We are meant to do the hard work of the Gospel. We are meant, not only to pull the drowning people from the raging river, but we are required to go back upstream and find out who's throwing them in.

That's from the Bishop of some obscure American diocese—New Hampshire I think it is—Gene Robinson.

What is the truth of this for us in our generation? Asked Peter Walker, who presided over one of my ordinations. Jesus went throughout

Galilee, teaching in their synagogues and proclaiming the good news of the kingdom, and curing disease and every sickness among the people. If the medieval kings of Europe had two bodies, perhaps the Christian church has two unities—at least. One is the unity of the institution, which is truly important. The other is unity with the poor and helpless, the cold, the hungry and the oppressed, the sick and those who mourn, the lonely and the unloved, the aged and the little children. We are called to work our way through these incommensurables, with patience and with faith. It would be nice to end on a good satisfying note of dramatic conclusion, of apocalyptic resolution of all the issues. But the way of the whirlwind, earthquake, and torrent is not always as effective as the way of the still, small but constantly persistent voice. Perhaps this too has something to do with the foolishness of the cross.

The church we may think is called to a unity in diversity, and not every unity in diversity will do. Oneness, perhaps, is unity in the vulnerable hospitality of Christ, in the fragility of goodness in a fragmented world.

Remembrance Sunday

Glasgow University Chapel, 14 November 2004

Remembrance Sunday lends itself to simple sermons. Batman and Robin, the goodies versus the baddies, the axis of evil. The Scriptures of the major world religions supply us with plenty of ammunition. There are groups around the world who are positively longing for Armageddon, the battle to end all battles, and would quite like to speed up its arrival. Of course we all know that this is nonsense. History seems to show that countries can easily be hypnotized by the rhetoric of "us" and "them." As Joan Baez used to sing in the 60s, we could all march off "with God on our side."

Ever since we members of Homo Sapiens began to knock the Neanderthals on their heads back in our caves, very successfully it has to be said, people have struggled to cope with violence, its limits and its justification. We have learned to be skeptical of the doctrine of the just war. But it was a major step forward. On the other hand we may think that, as that wise archbishop Robert Runcie, MC and some time tank commander, used to say, no wars are just, but some wars can be justified.

The passage from Matthew 24 has Jesus speaking in the apocalyptic language which was common currency at the time, and which has returned today with the X-Box, Halo 2 and all that. None of us can jump out of our cultural skin, and God, in coming among us as a human being, clearly did not want to either. The language of total chaos, famine, and earthquake began to seem a little exaggerated to sophisticated Christians a hundred years ago. But it has come back to us with a vengeance: "shock and awe" is on the menu, and it has a nasty habit of turning back to bite us.

None of us can jump out of our cultural skin and you will perhaps forgive me if my sermons begin to sound like extracts from our departmental minutes, or whatever. But though we speak in the culture of our time and place, most of us have come to think that our judgements and decisions are not entirely culturally relative. Just because we may all be *persuaded to think* this morning that we can jump from the top of the University tower and not have an uncomfortable landing, won't actually make it terribly comfortable. We have to take account of external events and the experience of other people in similar situations at different times and places. People have reached a sort of informal consensus that jumping off the tower without some backup is not necessarily conducive to your health.

The Jesus of the Gospel story begins from where people are. Then he points out a crucial fact in the situation. Men's love for each other will grow cold. It happens. (There were no women in theology till about 1980!) Jesus suggests an alternative sequel. The man who holds out to the end will be saved. And the gospel of this kingdom will be proclaimed throughout the earth as a testimony to all nations; and then the end will come.

The alternative is the alternative of love. Now if you go home and type "alt.love" into Google and persevere to the end (but please not with the university's computers!) you may get some fascinating suggestions. Things may be bad but they're not yet desperate.

No wars are just, but some wars may be justified. It may not be very Christian to maintain armed forces just to promote the national interest—conducting diplomacy by another means. But suppose other people, not ourselves, are being murdered.

The gospel, we often hear today, is for the marginalized and the oppressed.

The Glasgow poet Eddie Morgan, in a poem called *The Trondheim Holocaust*, captures in a few lines the Nazi murder of the:

Jews, (The Yellow Triangle)
We entered by the gate of fear
We exited without hope, as smoke
The chimneys pointed at the sky
In silence, unaccusing, unaccused.

The Gypsies: (The Brown Triangle)
Who shall chronicle our suffering?
We have no lobby and no voice
Where is our home, where is our country?
Is that why our destroyers destroy?

The gays: (The Pink Triangle)
We were the lowest of the low.
Further down you could not go
Nature itself, they said, abhorred us.
How should the Third Reich reward us?

Blessed are the poor in spirit: should we ever just sit on our hands and watch the vulnerable being destroyed? And how should we feel about those soldiers who die bravely for their country and for their families? Think Black Watch.

Well, of course, the horrors of war in the past were perpetrated by other countries. It wisna me! Yet war makes us all desperate because in conflict we are usually terrified. John Baillie in his war diary for 10th October 1915 writes, "[o]ne Gordon who was in the recent advance said to me, 'We took no prisoners. That is the Gordon motto. We believe in finishing them, wounded and all.' One hears many things that do not make good telling.[3]

What we are left with is not only a few famous victories but the loss of thousands of uniquely valuable lives—lives soberly documented in the names of a quarter of all the University of Glasgow students of the time. And that is almost certainly not the whole story. There were students from Germany in Glasgow then as now, and some of their names can be found in the books of remembrance dotted around the universities and colleges.

What can be said as we contemplate the long lists on these black tablets, and the tablets everywhere from here to that other black tablet, the Vietnam Wall and beyond? In 1918 people looked to a bright future created out of all that sacrifice, and were often cruelly disappointed. But they

---

3. Newlands, *John and Donald Baillie*, 54.

had a point. If there is to be any scrap of meaning out of holocaust, then men's love should not grow even colder. Can we say that in our society in Britain in 2004 our solidarity with the marginalized and the oppressed is more clearly demonstrated in action than it was in Central Europe half a century ago? Well, we may not have too much anti-Semitism, but is our current Western Islamophobia any better? What about the Gypsies? The local papers still show that there is a fair bit of resentment against travelling people in all sorts of places, and what do we actually think of the homeless people we meet most days in Ashton Lane in Glasgow? As for the gays, well, we who are in the churches are not exactly in the forefront of respect and affirmation.

And where is God in all this? The silenced, are remembered only by chance, and even God seems to forget them. Professor Edwin Morgan makes the point with some elegance. On *Janet Home*, the last woman burned as a witch in Scotland in 1727, he comments:

> Dear God, were you sleeping
> You were certainly not weeping
> She was not in your keeping.

None were more enthusiastic for the murder of poor harmless women in this country than the guardians of the God tradition, Presbyterian clergymen like myself.

So what's left? Well, certainly not space for a mawkish wallowing in post colonial, post modem, post everything feelings of guilt. One of the criteria for an old fashioned Thomist doctrine of the just war was the reasonable and responsible expectation that the result would be effective, positive, and good. It would contribute more in the end to love, peace and justice than *not* going to war. Well, we've heard that one before. The war to end all wars just doesn't happen. There have been hundreds of small but deadly wars in the last fifty years. A just war includes preparation for the organization of the sequel, a just and peaceful society.

War is a pretty blunt instrument at the best of times. And yet, tyrants may have to be resisted, if not for our own sakes, then to preserve the most vulnerable. Otherwise all is lost. Biology student Sophie Scholl lay anxiously in her condemned cell in Munich in 1943 and had a dream, a day or two before she was beheaded for resistance to the Nazis, a dream about a child:

> *Ich trug an einem sonnigen Tag ein Kind in einem langen weissen Kleid zur Taufe.* One sunny day I was bringing a child in a long white dress for baptism. The path to the church led over a steep hill. But I held the child firmly and safely in my arms. Then suddenly there was before me a crevasse. I had just enough time to lay the child down safely on the other side—and then I fell into the depths. The child is our ideal, it will prevail despite every obstacle. We may be pathfinders, but we must die before our goal is reached.[4]

The Gospel texts point us firmly to the goal of all this talk. Man's love should not grow cold. The Bible speaks of the fruits of the Spirit—love, peace, justice, patience, kindness, active compassion. Human beings will probably never agree in the nature of the case on principles and methods for the organization of society—freedom or democracy, majoritarian or judicial decisions, individual or communal values, the bases of human rights talk. But there may just be the possibility of an unforced consensus about the goals we want to achieve—even an inter-civilizational consensus on what makes for human flourishing, the freedom to exercise all our human capacities in the best interest of ourselves and our communities.

The gospel is not a trump card which settles all arguments and closes down conversation. But it is a word of encouragement. It suggests that the nature of all reality has a bias towards constructive rather than destructive activity. That we are encouraged to see a little way beyond ourselves. The promise of the gospel is that there is a loving God, often almost despite all appearances, that there is compassion even beyond the shock and awe, the beheadings, and the genocides of our time. There is aspiration beyond expectation, hope after hope. It is not all pointless, actually.

Das Kind ist unsere Idee, sie wird trotz all er Hindernisse durchsetzen. The child is God made small for us, perhaps just perhaps, even, the Christ child. Where is God ever to be found in the fog of war and the obscenity of suffering? Here is part of a poem by Godfrey Rust, *11 September 2001*:

> Where was God on September the Eleventh?
> He was begging in old clothes in the subway
> beneath the World Trade Center
> he was homeless in Gaza,
> imprisoned in Afghanistan,

---

4 Aicher-Scholl, *Die Weisse Rose*, (my translation). Cf. Scholl, *The White Rose*.

> running the gauntlet to her school in the Ardoyne,
> starving in Somalia,
> dying of AIDS in an Angolan slum,
> suffering everywhere in this fast-shrinking world; and boarding a plane unwittingly in Boston, heading for an appointment on the 110th floor.
> When the time came he stretched out his arms once more to take
> the dreadful impact that would pierce his side.
> His last message on his fading cellphone
> once more to ask forgiveness for them all before
> his body fell under the weight of so much evil.

I can't say much about the discipline of War Studies. I can say a little about faith. An open, porous vision of Christian faith will respect the mystery of God. It will perhaps encompass a touch of mysticism, in so far as it will have reservations about doctrinal absolutes and infallible authorities, whether of sacred texts or sacred communities. It will continue to respect those who differ on these issues, while seeking to advocate alternative perspectives. As a Christian vision, it will continue to be centred on Jesus Christ as the way, the truth and the life, but in an inclusive way. It will be open to dialogue both with other Christian cultures and with non-Christian and non-religious visions. It will be democratic without being either majoritarian or exclusively defined in terms of Western culture, Protestant, Catholic, or secular. As a Christian vision, it will understand rights and privileges, and national interests, as servants of the gospel concern for all humanity rather than an alternative gospel. It will hope to work with all who seek to promote human welfare through justice and reconciliation. And it will continue, despite all, to trust in the unconditional love of God. Amen.

15

Christian Futures

For Professor Mark Chapman. Ripon College, Cuddesdon, March 2012. Revised for One Kirk, Perth, March 2012.

I

PROPHECY IS A STRIKING feature of ancient Mediterranean religion. It takes many different shapes and forms. But it is united by one striking feature. Most prophets in the Hebrew Bible and elsewhere turn out to be wrong. Today, I risk no prophecy. I shall try to say something from my own very limited perspective. But I strongly suspect that in the future, anything is possible. Some years ago I wrote a chapter under the heading "Faith at Vatican X," a council presided over by a Baptist Pope called Flora. Perhaps Professor Chapman will be made by acclamation the next elected President of the Southern Baptist Conference—or perhaps not.

Churchgoing, as Professor Percy told us in a famous lecture, has not always been a popular sport in Britain. Throughout Europe there has been, and there is perhaps, quite a lot of believing without belonging. Obsessing about statistics will not help. We should concentrate on attracting the young, and indeed the old, and building an in-depth spirituality which will strengthen a legacy for the future—a sound judgement and a sensible strategy.

But do we have, are we likely to have, the resources to achieve this? In my view—gloomy Scotsman—the prospects are not great. (This is known as defeatism—a self-fulfilling disaster!) The mainline churches are withering on the vine—not helped by oversized central bureaucracies which woo the ambitious with promises of preferment, and instinctively stick to nurse for fear of worse—ossified, calcified, petrified. Many of their cherished features are already well beyond the point of no return—but mercifully, the ossified have lost all consciousness of loss. The flourishing communities are often dogmatic and aggressive, and the progressive communities are anemic and constantly apologizing for their own existence. That's how it is.

Faith comes in many forms, and its diversity is sometimes its strength. Change is not new. In the past, Christianity was *always about* to experience different futures in different churches, and even within the same church. Different groups imagined that they had some kind of privileged position for the future, and they were not always rewarded by what they wished for. I want to suggest an understanding of faith, not as a strategy for universal acceptance, but as an affirmation of a tradition which I regard as important for constructive Christian engagement with the global future.

I want to try to re-imagine faith as liberal, catholic, evangelical, and open. Going global by going local, has been a useful mantra, but like all mantras it is not a universal fix. We shall not flourish by drowning in a miasma of globalized slogans and pluralism unlimited. But if Christian faith is concerned for the welfare of some, it is concerned with the welfare of all. We shall not flourish either by pulling up the drawbridge and immersing ourselves in a virtual Little Gidding down some leafy country lane. But without a sacramental core, intelligent preaching and meaningful Christian fellowship there will be no constancy in faith for the future. Liberal churches with liberal theology? Nothing new here.

Key here are concepts of inclusion and incarnation—easier to say than to achieve. Inclusive faith is open to learn from anywhere. The attempt to produce a "pure" liberal presence in Christianity always creates a very thin expression of Christian faith. A broader liberal presence permeates much of Christian life, and is still influential even in unlikely places. I'd like briefly to suggest new ways of harnessing this continuing energy in the future. I do this in the face of evidence to the contrary. Even the Episcopal Church in the United States, which some of us might think of as doing most of the right things, is losing numbers pretty fast. The challenge is not small.

Incarnation roots the Christian project in the claim that in Jesus Christ, God was uniquely instantiated in human life and death, and that in these events concerning Jesus, a decisive moment in the realization of unconditional love in the universe was enacted. If this is true, then the challenge can and will be met, sometime, somewhere.

II

The fashionable critique of liberal values in theology is paralleled in the churches. In the Catholic Church the progress of Vatican II has been systematically dismantled. In Orthodox churches there has been a solid reaction, e.g., in the WCC, against Western liberalism. In the Anglican Communion the Covenant process, supported strongly by senior clergy, breathes a very different spirit from that of the bishops of the previous era—Runcie, Montefiore, Jenkins, et al. In America, conservative evangelicals have powerful influence, intellectual and economic, at home and abroad—not least in Africa.

Given the strong position of anti-Enlightenment theologies in prestigious university departments in the UK, it might seem that here liberal faith is dead. But there is still creative liberal theology today—not least in America. I don't want to forget, too, an earlier generation of phenomenally gifted scholars. In Germany, I think of my old teacher von Campenhausen, in Scotland the Baillies, my late colleague, Geoffrey Lampe, and the Cambridge liberals. When I compare their thinking with currently fashionable despisers of Enlightenment, it is hard to conclude that liberal Christianity has been refuted.

III

I have been writing on human rights, and on hospitality. Sadly, churches are often still highly suspicious of the work of human rights commissions. This usually reflects sensitivities about their own structures of power and control, not least on issues of gender and sexuality. Liberal faith values tradition as a tradition of disruption as well as continuity. It is built on a broad band of appropriation of revelation, reason, and experience stretching back to the early church. It is ecumenical and emancipatory. It is grounded in trust that God is equally near to every generation. Faith's commitments are both serious in their engagement, and yet provisional in their formulation. Some sorts of certainties must await the eschaton.

IV

Liberal church need not be unexciting. Far from being dryly rational, it may be conceived as a church of the Spirit. It will be a church of risk, which engages with serious issues in solidarity and identification.

Liberal faith is committed to the church. But it does not confuse the church with the kingdom of God. It has no brief for ecclesial triumphalism, and for prejudice confused with obedience to God. It can assimilate neither with atheism nor with religious fundamentalism. It can't revert to premodern perspectives. But it can learn from other perspectives, notably non-Western perspectives, and indeed from forms of humanism—the fruit of a humane spirit which contributes to the service of a wider humanity. The liberal spirit may be seen as one current of the Spirit of Christlikeness.

Liberal church manifestly has not always worked. Within liberal circles, illiberal views have prevailed and the truly "Left Behind" have sunk into voiceless anonymity. We should not forget the innumerable human beings whose lives have been wrecked while institutions have gone down blind alleys or waited for a process of "discernment" to take place.

There are pluses. Though ecumenical effort has almost vanished in recent decades, the vision of mutual recognition is still there. Despite intolerance, notions of constructive rather than destructive conflict have been established and will not go away. The development of new themes, taking up older notions such as the form of Christ in the world, signal a continuing theology of resistance and respect. Compassion and flexibility, rather than control and the competitive exercise of power, are persistent challenges. As Professor Chapman has written, "[t]he Church needs ambassadors of Christ who are not afraid of acting in His name, whatever that might do to their cherished tradition."[1]

The turn to art and film, literature, music, and internet media can help us to grow fidelity to traditions. YouTube, Facebook, and Twitter need not be a monopoly for the far right wing. The religious and the secular are not always in complete antithesis. Postcolonial reflection has re-imagined the practice of hospitality without being patronising, while learning that the reverse of the colonial is not always sufficient for substantial development. Good reflection is continuing conversation. A thick culture of hospitality can begin to replace confrontation.

---

1. Chapman, *Ambassadors of Christ*, 22.

I make no apology for this list. Deeply conservative religion is highly vocal, not only in the United States, where it is difficult to imagine the huge influence of such books as the *Left Behind* series, but in Africa and in Asia. The progressive is not inevitably the antithesis of the evangelical. The impressive development of evangelical programmes on social justice issues is a reminder of the significant role of this movement.

For Christianity, there is still a huge opportunity for progressive Christian influence through professions other than theology—notably in law, medicine, and in education. Christian education remains critically weak in the UK. This underlines the need to foster well-grounded preaching, worship, and spirituality. Faith does not flourish by gathering around the aspidistra to utter vacuous platitudes.

The notes of compassion which faith inspires are not always to be expressed in a Western context. There are important lessons to be learned elsewhere, not least around the Pacific Ocean. We have to find fresh ways of continuing to remain aware, and draw strength from the sense that the God of unconditional love is the source and goal of our lives.

Christians look for the guidance of the Holy Spirit. Here are paradoxes. On the one hand, appeal to the Spirit is a call to universal love and open relationality. Yet claims to be possessed, guided, or commanded by the Spirit, have been an excuse for the violation of human dignity, on a small or a massive scale, throughout history. In advocating and acting on a particular understanding of the Spirit, and the work of the Spirit, an awareness of the unavoidable tension between fully committed engagement and the limitations of our own discernment will have to be observed. In Christianity alone the nature of the fruits of the Spirit of the risen Christ remains debated. Both decisiveness and a sense of fallibility are important.

Where does this take us for the churches in Britain? Ecumenical effort is destroyed by denominational bureaucracies scrambling for the last crumbs of power in a deteriorating playground. Churches which mediate a lively sense of the gospel are often exclusive, particularly closed to humanist and secular conversation partners—though these are often still sympathetic potential partners in Europe. Things will get worse before they get better. It may be that existing patterns will gradually change. In Britain it is not certain that the Church of England by law established, the Church of Scotland as is, even the Roman Catholic Church, have been ordained by God to exist in anything like their present forms. In the future there will be surprises which none of us can imagine. Similar shifts may well take place in other parts of the world. It may be that something like a chastened, nuanced and contemporary rendition of Bonhoeffer's secret disciple of humane spirituality is a fruitful way forward. This could be rendered nourished in widely differing contexts, from cell group to cathedral. What matters is not the outward form but the spiritual credibility.

V

Unexpected shifts. Thinking of the great traditional institutional churches, like the Anglican Communion, I suspect that they are undergoing the same pains of transition as the great empires. Established certainties unravel. To be in the midst of change is usually uncomfortable. Futures markets, as we learn in the current economic recession, are highly charged and unpredictable. What of the ecclesial futures? I offer one example of an area which seems to me to have potential to influence change, in different possible directions—the influence of China.

VI

Why on earth should I bring China into a sensibly focussed discussion of the future of the churches in Britain and in Europe? No man, as Chairman Mao might well have said, is an island. Firstly, as long as Western churches understand themselves as linked into global denominational structures, the influence of non-European churches will be significant, especially as gaps widen between them and some Western churches. If 90 percent of churches worldwide were to resolve that the moon is made of green cheese, this would undoubtedly have consequences. Federated church structures would probably leave the nature of the moon to local discernment, more organically integrated denominations would perhaps prefer just not to talk about cheese at the dinner table. Either way, there could be economic and political implications.

Secondly, Western churches might feel that there were new things to be learned about the moon from alternative observation points. And thirdly, the cheese majority would take over and this would eventually impact decisively on all Christians. Next time you begin to think of church futures in Britain, in Europe, in Africa, America, and Asia, please just say cheese. As they say, some people are cheese lovers, just get over it.

In recent years Christian people have begun to engage in dialogue with other religions. The main concern has been Islam, driven largely by the events of 11th September 2001. I think we need to widen the scope of this engagement. In the long term, our relationships with Asian societies may be at least as important as engagement with the Middle East for the development and well-being of our own society. As you know, there has been a remarkable growth of Christianity in East Asia in recent decades.

The tale of foreign interference in East Asia is a sobering one. The legacy of colonial Christianity in Africa is not always encouraging. In South Korea, a strong Christian community witnesses to faith but also on occasion to real intolerance—of members of other religions, of many liberal values. (One of our Cambridge neighbors is Korean, gay, and a Buddhist—I have to say that he is not a big fan of the Presbyterians back home.) Foreign support, notably from the United States and often from the Deep South, may simply magnify the problems. (And we Brits simply forced on China the gift of opium!) What of China? One might think that the best thing for us to do is simply to forget about everything beyond our own borders—after all, in Scotland we already tend to think of Anglicans as aliens—in order to do the least harm. But is that enough?

A search for transcendence. It is often noted that large numbers of modern Chinese people appear to have no sense of transcendence, of anything beneath or beyond the immediate and measurable everyday realities of life, and there is great uncertainty about the status and role of ethical values. At the same time, there has arisen among many Chinese citizens an awareness of a need for transcendent values, and a desire to link this contemporary quest with the long tradition of reflection on spirituality and transcendence in the history of Chinese culture.

In the last twenty years, there has been a quest in China for a "socialist spiritual civilization," to replace the idealism of traditional Marxism. This has proved hard to promote, given the increasing awareness of diversity among the Chinese peoples. What can be offered in fellowship to this complex civilization? Eastern religion, and particularly Buddhism, respects kenosis, humility, and self-emptying—though, of course, it has often been just as authoritarian as Western theologies. Against the taint of cultural imperialism, Western and indeed Eastern, we need non-competitive structures and, we need to listen.

VII

What contribution, if any, may Western theology and church still offer in conversation and partnership with China?

The potential gains in the development of Christian faith in China are great. But there are real problems. We mentioned South Korea. Here there has been huge growth in Christianity, often linked to a perception of Western values as creating material prosperity. This has led to inter-church conflict (there are over 100 Presbyterian denominations alone!) and, on occasion, to an intolerance of other religions. The result is now a decline in Christian profession. In China there is a huge appetite for Western ideas among the young. If Christianity is mainly assimilated on the same basis as Levis, then problems could arise. The growth of a strongly conservative Christianity may also lead to intolerance of other faiths, thus becoming a challenge to the government's declared aim of achieving social harmony and eventually leading to its decline as it has in Europe. There will inevitably be occasions when Christian defence of human dignity will clash with governmental policy. But a Chinese Christianity resembling American fundamentalism would not be a step forward for world Christianity. What has Athens to do with Jerusalem? What has China to do with Cuddesdon? It should, I think, be concerning that one of the most significant Christian exchanges in recent years with other world Christians has been Anglican Global South Primates' visits to China in 2007 and 2011, sponsored by the Chinese government. The Minister for Religion in China also visited African churches in 2011.

VIII

The construction of interreligious hospitality is a vital but clearly delicate challenge. It may be that Christianity in China will settle into being just one of a minority of religions, strong in some places and weak in others. It may become a more significant force. Whatever the future holds, the Holy Spirit may work as a voice against the appearance of things, active only but sufficiently through the unconditional love of God.

Here is a quote from a Cuddesdon source, Robert Runcie:

> If the Church acts as if it possessed answers to life's problems wrapped up in neat packages, it may be heard for a time. It may rally some waverers, but its influence will be lost. It will confirm others in their suspicions and hostility. To them it will mean that

the Church, like every other human institution, is making a bid for power.²

Or, as Mark Chapman himself has written:

> The very incompleteness of the Christian vision, its constant pointing towards an eschatological vision, thus forces us to criticise the provisional representations of truth we have established up to the present.³

IX

A few familiar reflections to end with. *Lux Mundi*, the religion of the incarnation, was a high point of Anglican spirituality in the modern world. A light in darkness. But what kind of light? I believe there needs to be a continuing serious tradition of worship, of devotion, of spirituality. At the same time, there has to continue a completely open, proactive, radical welcome of hospitable affirmation and sharing. The shape of this hospitality will change from place to place. Sometimes perhaps God himself chooses to dwell in darkness, and creates light from within it. *Gott will im Dunkel wohnen und hat es doch erhellt*. Next time we meet someone whom we need to welcome, perhaps an older person with advanced Altzheimer's and we think, "Where is God in all this?" Here is perhaps the beginning of a Christian response. Here O my Lord, I see thee face to face.

The church of the future need never be a church of doom and gloom. Faith trusts that the quality of the light is discovered in Jesus the Christ, as the Sacrament of God for the world. For *I was hungry, and you fed me. I was thirsty, and you gave me a drink*. Circumstances change, technologies of advocacy and delivery change, but the service of the gospel remains the same. That, I guess, is how we are enabled to continue to sing to the Lord with cheerful voice.

---

2 Quoted by Beeson, *Windows on Westminster*, 113.
3. Chapman, *The Future of Liberal Theology*, 16.

16

A Journey into Theology

(Not Quite Autobiography)

I

> I was born in the territory of this monastery. When I was seven years of age I was, by the care of my kinsmen, put into the charge of the reverend abbot.... From then on I have spent all my life in this monastery, applying myself to the study of the Scriptures, and, amid the observance of discipline of the Rule and the daily task of singing in the church, it has always been my delight to learn or to teach or to write.

ACTUALLY, NOT. AS WITH the Venerable Bede, whose *Ecclesiastical History* was a text book in my first year as an Edinburgh student, my professional pilgrimage was a product of a particular time and place. In my case, it was much more unplanned and serendipitous in its outcomes. This is not an autobiography. It is concerned with professional development rather than life—and yet, I suppose this too may be thought to be part of living, or at least almost living.... It is increasingly common to ask a theologian where he or she is coming from into the subject matter—*Theologie als Selbstbiographie*. It is said too that theology is often itself a kind of autobiography, and of course autobiography is always a matter of subjectivity and selectivity.

Born in 1941 in Perth, Scotland, it was said that my grandmother, who stayed nearby, encouraged me to talk, endlessly. Of the war, I had no notion, apart from memories of crossing the local park with my mother at night, with a torch covered in cloth, and the local Victory parade. At the age of five I went to the Southern District primary school, where the head was an old fashioned headmaster with a strong sense of order and a love of English literature. We were well drilled in the basic disciplines, and this was to stand me in good stead, when I moved on to Perth Academy, a state school where the Rector insisted that we all studied Mathematics, Physics, and Chemistry to advanced level. I also took Latin and Greek, and this meant that there was no place for French—the only Scottish schoolboy who never learned French at school? What was I to do on leaving school? My father worked on the railway and my mother helped the family income by working as a cook in various restaurants. She learned the Greek alphabet in order to help me with elementary Greek. We were lucky. In my year there was a bright group of friends with whom contact was to be maintained. One was to become an Oxford professor and a Fellow of the Royal Society, another taught mathematics in Oxford for forty years, and a third friend became head of Scotland's flagship Catholic school.

The 1950s, at least in Perth, were a time of conservative culture. The local member of parliament was Conservative, the local newspapers were socially and politically conservative. We had had the Festival of Britain in 1951, the Queen's coronation in 1953, the Empire had not yet begun obviously to fall apart, at least as seen from Perth. For a number of years we lived on council estates. Ours was not a house of books, but there was a fourteen volume history of the Great War (my father had enlisted at the age of fifteen, though he never spoke of the war). I read this history several times—not a very cheerful tale—and I'm sure it made an impression on me. I spent much time in the local public library, reading whatever came to hand. I edited the school magazine, chaired the debating society and became the head boy—the last gave me some of the confidence which I sorely lacked. But I was to remain much more a product of the cautious fifties than the swinging sixties. I was not into pop culture—probably in reaction to aspects of the culture of the council estate.

University education was an unknown quantity. Only a tiny percentage of the population went to university in the late 50s. A history teacher who was an Oxford graduate suggested tutoring for an Oxford Entrance Scholarship. Alas, the local education authority decreed that they would not pay the extra fees which Oxford would involve—£30 a year—and my father was not inclined to waste money on Oxford. I went to Edinburgh.

What should I study? The sort of people I knew were my teachers, and the local minister—I had been sent to Sunday School. (I must have been a bookish child—at the age of seven I was given a copy of Scott's *Redgauntlet* as a prize—I found it distinctly unreadable!) My father was not in favor of church, though my mother sometimes attended. I was better at the humanities than the sciences, though I did briefly think of medicine. I thought of law—my father had always fervently instilled into us that lawyers are liars, and a close friend's solicitor father had recently committed suicide—perhaps not a good omen. My younger brother Alan was to go into IT.

In October 1959, I went off to Edinburgh University, to Cowan House, then a residence in George Square, with the intention of pursuing an honours degree in English, and took first year courses in English, British History, and Latin. I attended services at the Chaplaincy Centre and was confirmed in the Church of Scotland by the chaplain. I did well in History and Latin, less well in English. I was more impressed by the History teachers and the Latin lecturers (especially Walsh and Wellesley) than by my English tutors. Cowan House was a very good experience, mixing with students of all backgrounds and interests. I was House Secretary. I joined the Student Christian Movement and the Diagnostic Society, an old debating society. For £12.50, I bought a very old car. After much hesitation I decided to try to get into honours Classics, and the Professor of Greek generously allowed me entrance to second year Greek, though I had not taken the first year course. Catching up was something of a struggle, but I did well enough to secure a First and a postgraduate scholarship at the end of the course. What next?

There were a number of options. One of my Greek tutors suggested a PhD in Cambridge, on Pindar's grammar. Another possibility would be a Part II in Classics at Cambridge (there was an Edinburgh/Cambridge axis) and then perhaps the civil service. But there was another possibility. At school, like many of my classmates, I had sung in the Choir at St. John's Church, Perth, where the choirmaster was head of music at school, and at university I had been attracted to the Student Christian Movement, and I began to contemplate the ministry. It seemed to me in 1963 that the church offered a persuasive option for contributing to the flourishing of individual life and of society at a difficult time—for example, October 1962 had brought us the Cuban missile crisis, and I appreciated inclusion in the worship and community of the University Chaplaincy. 1963 brought John Robinson's *Honest to God,* much discussed in SCM circles—religion was becoming more exciting. In earlier years, I had seen at close hand the need for a continuing "bias to the poor" in British society.

Beattie arranged an interview with the Professor of Divinity in New College. John McIntyre suggested that an extra two years Classics at Cambridge, followed by a three year BD and another three years for a PhD, would be a very long student term, and that it would be better, if I decided for Divinity. (He probably reflected judiciously that two years in Cambridge might have set me off in different directions than the ministry of the Church of Scotland.) I applied to the Church for selection as a candidate for the ministry (in those days that was a simple process involving a brief interview with the Principal of New College, Prof J. H. S. Burleigh) and duly arrived at New College Residence on the Mound in October 1963 to study Divinity, supported by a postgraduate fellowship in the humanities.

The switch from Classics to Divinity was bewildering. With a very limited church background, I was convinced that all my fellow students knew much more about theology and church than I did—which was probably true. There were no family connections. I long thought that I was the first member of the family to attend a university—though, much later, my wife Elizabeth discovered a distant relative who had been a minister in the 1840s in Aberdeen, and had come to a very sticky end! The change from the precision of classical philology to theological speculation seemed hard to grasp. But I did well in the Christmas diet of papers and exams, and felt reassured. Once again, being a late starter was actually helpful, though it meant that as a student I spent too much time studying and too little on life. . . . I had originally envisaged specializing in New Testament—an obvious choice for a Classics graduate—but then opted for Church History with Professor Alex Cheyne, who, along with D. W. D. Shaw, later a professor in St. Andrews, was to be always immensely supportive. Alex Cheyne was an inspiration, meticulous and hugely understated. I was also very interested in systematic theology. But I was uncertain about how to negotiate the tensions that existed between the leading theologians—McIntyre and T. F. Torrance—and I was conscious that in Scotland at that time, somewhat uniquely, a previous degree in philosophy was thought almost mandatory for the proper understanding of systematic theology.

With Graeme Auld, a fellow student, who I had first met on a student expedition to Greece in 1961 and later Professor of Hebrew Scripture at Edinburgh, I was able to spend five months on a travel fellowship in the summer of 1964, visiting Orthodox monasteries in Greece and archaeological sites in Turkey and the Middle East. In Easter 1965 I was in Tübingen with the support of Peter Matheson, later Master of Ormond College Melbourne—Moltmann's *Theologie der Hoffnung* had just appeared. The summer semester 1965 was spent in Heidelberg, much facilitated by one of our German visiting students in New College, Martin Schweigler. I met Professor Hans Freiherr von Campenhausen, and contemplated a thesis in patristics. (In New College I had taken a basic German course.) Germany seemed like a more exciting option than Oxbridge for theology, and was a traditional destination for Scots students. There was a long standing exchange between the Tübingen Stift and New College. Connections were to be maintained, notably with Martin, Walter Sparn, Dieter de Lazzer, and Uli Wahl. (There was to be a delightful reunion in the Stift in the summer of 2010, and in 2013 in Edinburgh.) In the summer of 1966, I graduated with a First again and another postgraduate scholarship. By now I was pretty much set on the idea of an academic career in theology. Oxford for graduate study was suggested, but I was sure that Germany must be the exciting place to be. America was unknown—Scots tended to do ThM's at Princeton Seminary or STMs at Union, and I wanted to produce a doctorate. Unlike Oxbridge, we seemed to have had, and still have, no strong connections with such centres as Yale and Harvard.

October 1966 brought me back to Heidelberg. I was still interested in ecclesiastical history, but also in systematic theology. Patristics seemed like a good beginning. Hilary of Poitiers was potentially interesting. T. F. Torrance was interested in Hilary, but I also wanted to explore the hermeneutic questions, which seemed to lie behind the current explosive Barth/Bultmann debate. Hermeneutics again suggested Germany rather than Oxbridge. I had no knowledge of America, and was unaware of what it might have to offer. In view of my Classics background, von Campenhausen, always a hugely kind supervisor, suggested a thesis on the form of the commentary in the early church, with particular reference to Hilary's commentary on St. Matthew's Gospel. I was able to spend two months around Easter 1967 in Paris at the Sorbonne, to hear Marrou and Courcelle on patristics—given the state of my French, this was an interesting exercise.

Elizabeth and I were married in September 1967 and set off for Heidelberg, where we lived in the Oekumenisches Studentenheim in Plankengasse and I was tutor. After three semesters, I came to feel that the evidence for commentary form was so fragmentary that the project was becoming elusive, and also that this philological study was not contributing to my continuing interest in systematic theology. At the same time, exposure to Lutheran theology and worship suggested a theological universe in some ways more congenial than the Reformed school in Edinburgh—more *theologia crucis* rather than *theologia gloriae*, more *simul iustus et peccator* than one of the elect. I acquired studies by Lutherans also influenced by Barth—Ernst Wolf, Otto Weber. In Heidelberg, I attended lectures by Schlink, Gadamer, von Rad, Gunther and Heinrich Bornkamm, Toedt, and others. I travelled to Tübingen to hear Käsemann.

The Barth/Bultmann controversy seemed to centre on conflicting hermeneutics of word and faith—Jüngel's *Paulus und Jesus* had been a stimulating guide to the hermeneutical tensions. I had left New College well versed in Barth, but I shared the skepticism about aspects of that perspective held by some of my teachers, and had a sense that theology should move in a more liberal direction. (Few could then have predicted that Barth studies would create a vast new industry in Reformed circles in the twenty-first century!) It was important to me to see what Barth was really like, and in the winter semester of 1966/67 I drove down from Heidelberg to Basel, to Barth's Saturday seminars, with some friends from the Studentenheim—a Dutchman, an American, and a Swiss friend. We visited Le Corbusier's famous chapel at Ronchamps, covered in snow. That semester Barth examined the section *De Verbo Divino* from Vatican II. Barth was always at pains to resist the predicable "Barthian" interpretations. In 1967, I was involved as a graduate assistant in a WCC conference in Heidelberg on hermeneutics, with James Barr, Erich Dinkler, and Hendrik Berkhof. Moltmann had switched the emphasis to hope. Eberhard Bethge's *Dietrich Bonhoeffer* was important. In the spring of 1968, Ronald Gregor Smith lectured in Heidelberg on *Sekularisierung*.

What did I make of Karl Barth, the patron saint of New College, Edinburgh, where I studied, and of Princeton Theological Seminary, where I have enjoyed much generous hospitality as a visiting scholar? In New College in the 60s it sometimes seemed that Barth was not the question but the answer. The subject for our first essay in doctrine was Barth's Doctrine of the Word of God in its threefold form. In Heidelberg I began to read Luther and Lutheran theology. By 1966 Karl Barth was eighty, an immensely genial old man who was driven to the seminar in an Austin 1100 by his wife. He interpreted the text charitably, and was clearly excited about the council. Though he did think that despite the biblical references, there was still too much influence of Aquinas. Barth was still Barth, and quite right too. Talking about justification one day, he asked whether we should choose Christ or his benefits. Ever seeking the *via media*, I diffidently suggested *Christus cum beneficiis suis indutus*, which I seemed to remember came from Calvin and might be OK. The great man would have none of it! In the winter semester of 1968, he welcomed Elizabeth and me to his sadly incomplete Schleiermacher seminar in the winter of 1968, by which time we were in Zurich. His final very irenic thoughts on Schleiermacher were published as an introduction to a Schleiermacher selection shortly after he died in December 1968.

What do I think about Barth? (Harvard Symposium 2009.) I have suggested to that reading Barth was like a good glass of red wine. Nothing like it at the right time, but there's no point in adding to the world's population of Barthian alcoholics. It's all a question of balance and discernment, and each of us must strike our own balance here. More than this, I don't think one can have a solid appreciation of modern theology without a careful reading of Barth. It will only take you a couple of weeks to read through the *Church Dogmatics*—especially if you don't stop to eat or drink.

In Heidelberg there was much stimulus from Von Campenhausen's *Sozietaet* on Augustine, which included Ulrich Duchrow, Gerhard Beiser, and Gerhard May. But I decided to continue the thesis in a direction closer to hermeneutics, and we spent summer semester 68 in Zurich, with the help of our friends, the Schaedelins. I attended Jüngel's lectures and his *Sozietaet*, which studied Wittgenstein's *Philosophical Investigations.*

What then? We saw T. F. Torrance, Elizabeth's uncle, and he suggested Cambridge with Donald Mackinnon to finish the thesis and learn some more philosophical theology. In summer 1968, we arrived in Selwyn Road Cambridge and I became a member of the new Churchill College, a science-based institution. I attended lectures with Mackinnon, and with Bernard Williams in philosophy. Contemporaries among graduate students were John Clayton, Patrick Sherry, Barry Richards, and Robert Holyer. We attended Churchill's new chapel, welcomed by the indomitable chaplain, Noel Duckworth. At this time I was trying to develop an approach to theology based on the theme of the love of God. Mackinnon suggested producing two doctorates, one on Hilary and one on the love of God. This was a good idea, but I thought it would have extended graduate life considerably, and finance might also become an issue. It was also time to consider the church dimension.

II

In the autumn of 1969, Elizabeth and I both took up posts as assistant ministers in Edinburgh, in solid working class parishes. Here was this "real world" with which I was very familiar as a child, and which I hoped to engage with a relevant theology. But very soon the opportunity arose of a lectureship in Glasgow, technically in the philosophy of religion. Such openings were rare, and we moved to Glasgow, commuting back to the Edinburgh parishes. In Glasgow the new Professor of Divinity was Allan Galloway, a generous and supportive mentor who had studied with Tillich. The school of Bultmann and Gregor Smith was continued by my colleague Iain Nicol, soon to move to Toronto, and the faculty included William Barclay, Murdo Ewan Macdonald, and William Frend. This was a time of much teaching and the establishment of a family. In October 1970, I was ordained to the ministry of the Church of Scotland in the University Chapel. We became members of Wellington Parish Church, then led by the excellent Stuart MacWilliam. I became involved in the Society for the Study of Theology, which I had first attended through the invitation of Tom Torrance in 1965, and in a small group of scholars who hoped to produce an essay collection and comprised Stewart Sutherland, Stephen Sykes, Dan Hardy, Robert Morgan, Richard McKinney, and myself.

In 1973, out of the blue came a suggestion from Stephen Sykes that I should apply for a University Lectureship in Divinity—modern theology and patristics were specified. To my surprise—and that of others—I was appointed. We moved back to Cambridge. John Morrison, chair of the appointments committee, generously suggested that I should succeed John O'Neill as one of the informal chaplains to Wolfson College, and, in 1975, I became a Fellow. Many new lecture courses had to be written, there was a great deal of undergraduate and graduate supervision, with high quality students including Sarah Coakley, David Ford, John Webster, John Sentamu, and an old Churchill friend, Tom Broadbent. We were much occupied with establishing a house in Cambridge and looking after three small sons, on very little money. Another small theological discussion group was formed—originally by Brian Hebblethwaite, Keith Ward, and myself, and then, including Julius Lipner and others. I joined the Triangle Club, a theology-philosophy-science group, getting to know Mary Hesse and Arthur Peacocke. I served as Secretary of the Faculty Board. In 1978, I finally published *Hilary of Poitiers—Theology and Exegetical Method*, and in 1980, *Theology of the Love of God*.

It seems likely that I was invited to Cambridge partly as a representative of the Edinburgh/Barth/Mackinnon perspective in theology, which I in many ways endorsed. But in time I became sympathetic also to the more liberal stream of theology followed by Geoffrey Lampe, Arthur Peacocke, and others. This was not dissimilar to the liberal orthodox thought of Alex Cheyne, Bill Shaw, and the Baillie tradition in Scotland. Cambridge, which in the time of Bucer, "burned the dead as well as the living," was not always an easy place for such digression.

In the late 1970s, I applied for chairs back in Scotland. This avenue was effectively blocked by the famous Committee of Nomination to Theological Chairs, a Church of Scotland body at that time influential in academic appointments, for whom my recent dalliance with liberalism was hardly a recommendation.

In 1982, largely on the recommendation of Brian Hebblethwaite and the outgoing Dean, Keith Ward, Sir Maurice Sugden invited me to become Dean of Trinity Hall. Though a medieval foundation (1350), the Hall had nineteenth-century statutes, which did not specify that the Dean of Chapel had to be an Anglican clergyman, though a member of the college was technically required to say Matins and Evensong daily. It seemed to me that it was not wise to offer Presbyterian communion in a college where most of the members were Anglican. We had worshipped in Great St. Mary's for some years and in my view there was no *theological* superiority of either Presbyterian or Anglican polities over one another. Through the kindness and understanding of Peter Walker, Bishop of Ely, I was ordained deacon and priest in September, in time to take up the post of Fellow and Dean in October 1982. The Trinity Hall years were delightful—the life of the chapel community and the choir, the fellowship, all kinds of pastoral activity. I was briefly the world's most improbable Senior Treasurer of the Boat Club. (I only sat in a boat once, but became expert at firing water pistols at Boat Club dinners—not quite the context of traditional Scottish ministry. The only empirical evidence of concrete achievement in my career is to be found in the Ladies' loos which I managed to get installed in the Boathouse.) On the other hand, frequent absence from home throughout the week as University Lecturer and college Dean put a strain on Elizabeth and the young family, and there were significant changes in the faculty, including the death of Geoffrey Lampe. On the retirement of Donald Mackinnon, Nicholas Lash became the Norris–Hulse Professor. In 1984, I published a short book on *The Church of God*, and in 1985 *Making Christian Decisions*, a study in Christian Ethics.

1985 brought a vacancy in the Chair of Divinity back in Glasgow. John Macquarrie and John McIntyre were the external assessors. I applied and was appointed in the summer of 1985, though I did not take up the appointment till April 1986. My mother and Elizabeth's parents were in Scotland: on the other hand, Elizabeth had developed a successful business career and this was hard to abandon. For a period I commuted between Cambridge and Glasgow by car at weekends. I was readmitted to the Church of Scotland when I returned to the Presbytery of Glasgow and retained and exercised permission to officiate in the diocese of Glasgow—a position not universally appreciated on either side of the ecclesiastical divide.

Glasgow meant immersion in new tasks—teaching and research, administration almost immediately, as head of department, dean of the faculty, and through my involvement on various university committees. In the Church of Scotland, I worked on the European Committee of WARC, on Education for the Ministry, and, soon, on the Panel on Doctrine, eventually as Convener, and on the Church and Nation Committee. From 1991 to 1997, and again from 2001 to 2008, I was Principal of Trinity College, another pastoral role. In 2006, we enjoyed a memorable celebration on the 150th anniversary of Trinity College.

Returning to Glasgow, I worked on turning the fruits of my teaching and reflection on earlier work into a work on systematic theology. This eventually appeared in 1994, after much frustrating negotiation with T. & T. Clark, as *God in Christian Perspective*.

An attempt I made some years ago to characterize my publications as a continuous development looked like this:

My research centres on substantive issues of constructive theology, and particularly on interpreting the love of God. The focus is on the multi-layered impact of a Christology of divine love, developed through five monographs. (I began to look at concepts of love as key to exegesis in theology in my PhD thesis, published as *Hilary of Poitiers—A Study in Theological Method* (1978). *Theology of the Love of God* (1980) explores concepts of the love of God as the basic structuring element of Christian theology. In engagement with interpretations of love in the tradition, and with contemporary use of concepts of faith, hope, and history, it is proposed that the nature of God as love shapes every aspect of theology. This is exemplified through analysis of the relationship between creation and redemption, understood as one dynamic movement, disrupting boundaries of redemption.

In *God in Christian Perspective* (1994) the enterprise is developed further. An understanding of God as a multi-faceted model draws on Christology and Trinity, faith and practice in community. God is personal, self-differentiated being, transcendent, yet also immanent in the created order as hidden divine presence. The core elements of faith and revelation, divine action and Christology, are reappraised in the light of current theological proposals. Doctrines interact in a web of connection to shape Christian practice. A Christian understanding retains the basic core of unconditional love, Christologically characterized. A contemporary concept of God draws upon these core elements, and upon a retrieval of the historical traditions from which they arise. It can be articulated in language intelligible to contemporary citizens, and its consequences spelled out within the complexity of contemporary cultures.

Generosity and the Christian Future (1997) carries this thesis to a further stage through engagement with the emancipatory theologies, postmodernity, and political theory. The study re-imagines the framework of the divine love conceived as generosity. The need to be as alert to potential futures, as to past developments, and to relate doctrine to political theory and cultural issues, is grounded in the theological, more precisely kenotic, Christological argument. Attention is paid to issues of human rights, violence, gender, and the power structures of the churches themselves.

John and Donald Baillie Transatlantic Theology (2002), built on first access to the Baillie Papers, lies at the heart of this submission. I regard the work of the Baillies as seminal to the understanding, justification, and revisioning of a progressive Christian theology. This is a theological biography of the Baillie brothers. It traces in detail the interaction of their theology within the cultures in Europe and America, in which they worked notably in the circle of the "critical realists." It sheds light on the huge influence of the Baillies in Scotland. This tradition is a trajectory against the stream today. I judge it to offer significant resources, combining conceptual plasticity with distinctive direction, for the future.

The Transformative Imagination: Rethinking Intercultural Theology (2004). This comparative study of connections between theology and culture, through the arts, the sciences, political and human rights issues, shapes reflection on the mystery of God in a postfoundational frame. Reciprocity between ethical issues and questions of transcendence are explored. This yields a re-conception of theological methodologies, in which theology, and paradoxically Christology, is seen as a catalyst rather than a trump card in interdisciplinary projects exemplified through specific instances in the humanities, the sciences, and in politics.

The central theme of the divine love is spelled out in two shorter studies in less technical style. *The Church of God* (1984) comments critically on traditions of church, ministry, and sacraments, in denominational cultures, stressing the Christological imperative to be an always outward looking church. *Making Christian Decisions* (1985) assesses Christian input into specific ethical issues. My work includes the jointly produced collections *Studies in Scottish Church History* (2000), produced as a Festschrift for Alex Cheyne, with Stewart J. Brown, *Believing in the Text* (2004), an exploration of theology and literature edited with David Jasper, *Explorations in Theology 8* (1981), a collection of Geoffrey Lampe's papers, and *Fifty Key Christian Thinkers* (2004), with Peter McEnhill, together with a volume of published articles, *Traces of Liberality*, (2006). This sketch attempts to document a project with a distinctive accent on the love of God as Christological leitmotif. It conceives theology as a generous approach to the transcendence of God and the consequences of incarnation. This continues in *Christ and Human Rights* (Ashgate 2006), *Faith and Human Rights* (Fortress 2008), with Richard Amesbury, and *Hospitable God* (Ashgate 2010), with Allen Smith.

It has been good to be able to contribute a number of essays to celebratory collections for friends—Alex Cheyne, Bill Shaw, Geoffrey Lampe, Brian Hebblethwaite, Duncan Forrester, Wentzel van Huyssteen, Henk Vroom, Peter Matheson, John Macquarrie, Dan Migliore, John Webster, and Werner Jeanrond. It was good too to see former students in chairs in various places—in Harvard, Cambridge, Aberdeen, and Belfast, and to remain in touch with many others.

Much less writing would have been done had I not had the good fortune to spend a number of terms of study leave away from the responsibilities of Glasgow. Since 1987, I had begun to attend AAR conferences in the USA. In 1995 I was able to spend a few weeks in Princeton and Chicago. In 1998, Elizabeth and I spent a semester at the Centre of Theological Inquiry in Princeton and, in 2001, a semester at Claremont School of Theology, close to Los Angeles where our son Craig was a graduate student at UCLA. In 2005 we were able to return to Princeton Seminary, to discover that Elizabeth's cousin, Iain Torrance, was to be the new President—Iain was to be very supportive throughout our visits. In

2009, just after I retired and completed the work of the RAE 2008 panel, we were able to spend a final semester at Payne Hall in Princeton. Also, in 1999 I had taught (eight hours a week in German!) theology as a Visiting Professor in Mainz, through the good offices of our old Heidelberg friend Gerhard May. These semesters were immensely stimulating and brought us good friends—notably, Wentzel and Hester van Huyssteen, and Bob and Jane Maclennan in Princeton, Richard and Amy Amesbury in Claremont, and Renate and Thomas Kiworr-Ruppenthal in Mainz. The presence of Glasgow students completing ThMs in Princeton was also a welcome support, bringing us stimulating student connections. In 2007, I was very honored to receive, at AAR in San Diego, a Festschrift volume, *The God of Love and Human Dignity*, edited by a Glasgow/Princeton alum, Paul Middleton, with essays from old friends and colleagues. I became a Fellow of the Royal Society of Arts and then of the Royal Society of Edinburgh—these things are somewhat serendipitous!

Life in Glasgow had continued over the years in the usual academic round, with a large number of changes in the departmental staff. Norman Shanks became leader of the Iona Community, William Storrar, a Professor in Edinburgh and then Director of the Center of Theological Inquiry in Princeton. There were sad losses as well, Robert Carroll and Douglas Murray. In Glasgow too there were some highly talented students. The church candidates, with some notable exceptions, were to become much more conservative in the twenty-first century. Later, the quality of life was greatly enhanced by the presence of a group of close colleagues, especially David Jasper (from 1999 to 2002 I directed the Centre for Theology and Literature which he had founded), Mona Siddiqui, Professor of Islamic Studies (a new departure for a department which had concentrated on Christian studies since 1451), Lloyd Ridgeon, also in Islamic Studies, and Allen Smith, a post-doctoral research associate with whom I discussed and wrote *Hospitable God*.

Some further areas of professional involvement should perhaps be noted. In 1996, 2001, and in 2008, I was part of the Theology and Religious Studies team on the UK Government's Research Assessment Exercise, chairing the 2008 panel and, in 1999, involved in a similar exercise in the Netherlands. In all of these very illuminating experiences I was lucky to be supported by able and perceptive colleagues, not least Duncan Forrester, David Fergusson, Ronald Piper, and Wentzel van Huyssteen. All of these experiences help to enrich and broaden one's professional engagement. Later I was to conduct many departmental assessments with a view to the REF of 2014.

On the Panel on Doctrine (and also, perhaps rather unusually, on the Church of England Archbishops' Commission on Doctrine—*We Believe in God*—and the Scottish Episcopal Church's Doctrine Committee—*The Incarnation*, etc.) there was much to learn about theology and church. The Panel produced a report on *The Interpretation of Scripture*, unanimously adopted by the Church, which recognized that there were a number of legitimate different approaches to the interpretation of Scripture. There followed, in 1994, a report on marriage, which considered same-sex relationships and opened up a vigorous discussion, parallel to similar debates in other churches. In Trinity Hall I had become aware of the hurt caused by ecclesiastical disapproval of same-sex affection, and this was reinforced by pastoral experience, as Principal of Trinity College, of the discrimination encountered by ministerial candidates who would otherwise have been considered excellent candidates for ordination. It was impossible for openly gay Christians to speak in the General Assembly. In 2006, I was co-founder of *Affirmation Scotland*, an organization dedicated to supporting gay and lesbian Christians in the Church of Scotland, and an advocate in public debate. This concern stimulated my interest in the attitudes of the churches to human rights and to justice—an area which became a recurring theme in my writing, underlined, in a very different context, by a deeply unpleasant encounter with discrimination experienced by Elizabeth in a short period of employment with the Church Offices in Edinburgh, and its aftermath for us as non-persons in Presbyterian circles.

Another long-time concern was ecumenical theology and engagement. In 2005 I joined the SCIFU talks—Scottish Churches Initiative for Unity—a project for union between the Church of Scotland and the Episcopal, Methodist and United Reform Churches, and was involved in drafting material. The overwhelming rejection of the final report by the church was not perhaps surprising. However, the tone of the final debate was astonishingly hubristic, and, in my view, represented a clear indication that all was not well with the theological wisdom of the church. A growing gap between church and academy was reflected in the almost complete absence of ordained Church of Scotland ministers in the university departments.

Hospitable God, much of which was written in Princeton, developed the concept of human rights to encompass the whole created order as the purpose and goal of God who is the source of hospitality, love, and justice, and also addressed these themes of discrimination and ecumenical action. Later I produced articles, mainly for Festschrifts, and reviews. I was delighted to have Werner Jeanrond from Lund as an ideal successor. Links with the department were maintained as an Honorary Professorial Research Fellow, and an honorary Fellow in the School of Divinity in Edinburgh, where I did some teaching and examining. Living in Edinburgh and in Cambridge, it was possible to take up again links with Trinity Hall and St. Edward's Church, and to develop appreciated links with a younger generation of theologians, not least through the Society for the Study of Theology.

This is a tale of accident rather than substance. And, again unlike with Bede, it has fortunately been possible to write down these things with the benefit of Microsoft Word.

—Cambridge, March, 2014.

Author Biography and Bibliography

Rev. Prof. George McLeod Newlands, Professor of Divinity, University of Glasgow, 1986–2008, Professorial Research Fellow 2008–, Principal, Trinity College, Glasgow, 1991–97, 2002–7, Honorary Fellow, School of Divinity, University of Edinburgh, 2010–12th July 1941, son of George and Mary Newlands, married 1967, Mary Elizabeth Wallace; three sons.

Education

Perth Academy, University of Edinburgh (M.A. 1st Class Classics), (Vans Dunlop Scholar, 1963), B.D. 1st Class. Ecclesiastical History, (Cunningham Fellow, 1966); PhD (1970), D.Litt. (2005); University of Heidelberg; University of Zurich, Churchill College, Cambridge (M.A.). Ordained minister, Church of Scotland, 1970, and priest, Church of England, 1982, Assistant Minister, Muirhouse, Edinburgh, 1969–70; Lecturer in Divinity, University of Glasgow, 1969–73, Cambridge University; Lecturer in Divinity, 1973–86; Fellow, Wolfson College, 1973–82, Fellow and Dean, Trinity Hall, 1982–86; University of Glasgow: Dean, Faculty of Divinity, 1988–90, Director, Centre for Theology, Literature, and the Arts, 1999–2002, Hensley Henson Lecturer, Oxford, 1995, Visiting Professor, University of Mainz, 1999, Visiting Scholar, Claremont School of Theology, California, 2002, Visiting Scholar, Princeton Theological Seminary, 2005, 2009. Member, Doctrine Committee Church of England, 1983–86, Convener Panel on Doctrine, Church of Scotland, 1995, Doctrine Commission SEC 2008–12, Member, European Committee, World Alliance of Reformed Churches, 1987–95, Reformed Churches, 1987–95; Church and Nation Committee, Church of Scotland, 1992–96, Unity, Faith and Order Committee, Action for Churches Together in Scotland, 1995–, Scottish Churches Initiative for Unity, 1999–2003; HEFCE RAE

Panel for Theology and Religious Studies, 1996, 2001, 2008 (Chairman), AHRC Peer Review College, from 2004, strategic reviewer, Member, Center of Theology Inquiry, Princeton, 1998; Netherlands RAE Panel, 1999, FRSA (2005), FRSE (2008), President, Society for the Study of Theology, 2013-14. Member Editorial Board, Theology in Scotland, 1996, Conversations, 2002, Trustee, Hope Trust (Chairman), VISOR, Netherlands from 2008.

Bibliography (Continued from *Traces of Liberality*, 2005)

Books

Christ and Human Rights. London: Ashgate, 2006
Traces of Liberality: Collected Essays. New York: Lang, 2006
Faith and Human Rights, by Amesbury and Newlands. Minneapolis: Fortress, 2008. (Chinese trans. 2013.)
Hospitable God: The Transformative Dream. London: Ashgate 2010.

Articles

"John Baillie." In *Dictionary of Historical Theology*, edited by T. Hart, 48–49. Carlisle, UK: Paternoster, 2000.
"Spirituality and Human Rights." *The New Theologian* 14.2 (2004) 4–7.
"John and Donald Baillie." *A Time for Trumpets*, edited by N. Blackie, 17–27. Edinburgh: St. Andrew Press, 2005.
Quisquilia Princetoniana. Princeton Seminary Review NS XXVI.1. (2005) 2–7.
"John Macquarrie in Scotland." In *In Search of Humanity and Deity, Festschrift for John Macquarrie*, edited by R. Morgan, 17–24. London SCM, 2006.
"Salvation—Personal and Political." In *Oxford Handbook of English Literature and Theology*, edited by D. Jasper, 829–38. Oxford: Oxford University Press, 2006.
"The Church and the Gay Issue." *The Scotsman*, May 24, 2006.
"Postfoundational Theology and Public Policy." In *The Evolution of Rationality. Festschrift for Wentzel van Huyssteen*, edited by F. Leron Shults, 394–417. Grand Rapids: Eerdmans, 2006.
"John McIntyre and History." *Theology in Scotland* 14.2 (2007) 19–32
"Luther's Ghost—Ein gluehender Backofen voller Liebe." In *Theology as Conversation: Festschrift for Daniel Migliore*, 373–93. Grand Rapids: Eerdmans, 2009.
"Donald Baillie, John Baillie." In *Blackwell Companion to the Theologians* II, edited by Ian Markham, 3–22. Oxford: Blackwell, 2009.
"I am the True Vine": Sermon. *Expository Times* 120.7 (April, 2009) 339–40.

"Christianity and Culture: WARC at the Millennium." In *Crossroad Discourses, Festschrift for Hendrik Vroom, Rodopi*, edited by J. Gort et al., 563–78 Amsterdam, 2010.

"Incarnation." In *Grosvenor Essay* No. 7, edited by G. Newlands, 1–7. Edinburgh: Scottish Episcopal Church, 2011.

"Humane Spirit—Towards a Liberal Theology of Resistance and Respect." In *Religious Pluralism and the Modern World*, edited by S. Sugirathaja, 152–63. London: Palgrave Macmillan, 2012.

Reviews

2005

Calvin's Christology. By Stephen Edmonson. *Journal of Theological Studies* 56.2 (2005) 747–48.

2006

God and Enchantment of Place. By David Brown. *Journal of Theological Studies* 57.1 (2006) 400–401.

Reason and the Reasons of Faith, Edited by Paul J. Griffiths and Reinhold Hutter. Theology Today 63.4 (2006) 549–50.

Christ in Focus. By Charles Marsh. *Epworth Review* 33.3 (2006) 91.

A Short Course on Christian Doctrine. By George Pattison. *Expository Times* 117.11 (2006), 480.

Theological Fragments. By Duncan Forrester. *Expository Times* 118.1 (2006) 45–46.

Theology in the Public Square. By Gavin D'Costa. *Journal of Theological Studies* 57.2 (2006) 817–19.

2007

Christ and Horrors. By M. M. Adams. *Journal of Theological Studies* 58.2 (2007) 782–84.

The Gift of Story. Edited by E. Griesinger and M. Eaton. *Literature and Theology* 20.4 (2007) 477–78.

On the Scope and Truth of Theology. By Robert Neville. *Conversations in Theology and Religion* 5.1 (2007) 31–32.

2008

Thou Who Art. By J. A. T. Robinson. *Expository Times* 119.11 (2008/9) 556.

2010

The Ultimacy of Jesus. By Trevor Williams. *Journal of Theological Studies* 61.1 (2010) 459–60.

Faith and its Critics. By David Fergusson. *Theology in Scotland* 17.1 (2010) 83–85.

Authorising Marriage. By Mark Jordan. *Scottish Journal of Theology* 63.4 (2010) 496–98
Human Rights and the Image of God. By Roger Ruston. *Scottish Journal of Theology* 63.4 (2010) 488–90.

2011

An Introduction to Christian Theology. By R. Plantinga, T. Thomson, and M. Lundberg. *Journal of Theological Studies* 62.1 (2011) 408–10.
Evoking Lament. Edited by E. Harasta and B. Brock. *Scottish Journal of Evangelical Theology* ? (2011) ?–?.
Against the Tide. By Miroslav Volf. *Scottish Journal of Evangelical Theology* 29.2 (2011) 278–79.
Visions of Agape. Edited by C. Boyd; and *Divine Love*. Edited by J. Levin and S. Post. *Modern Believing* 52.4 (2011) 55–57.
Human Rights or Religious Rules. By J.van der Ven. *Journal of Empirical Theology* 24 (2011) 15–16.

2012

Reshaping Ecumenical Theology. By Paul Avis. *Journal of Reformed Theology* 6.3 (2012) 15–16.
God and Being: An Enquiry. By George Pattison. *Journal of Theological Studies* 63.1 (2012) 399–400.
Divine Humanity: Kenosis Explored and Defended. By David Brown. *Journal of Theological Studies* 63.1 (2012) 400–402.
Theology and Human Flourishing: Essays in Honour of Timothy J. Gorringe. Edited by Mike Higton et al. *Journal of Theological Studies* 63.2 (2012) 803–4.

2013

Spirit of Love. By Amos Yong. *Modern Believing* 54.1 (2013) 68–69.

Papers:

This material is held at Glasgow University Archive Services
    Reference Number(s)   GB 0248 ACCN 3772.

Website:

www. georgenewlands.com

Bibliography

Adams, G. *Christ and the Other.* Farnham, UK: Ashgate, 2010.
Adams, J. *Hallelujah Junction.* San Francisco: Harper, 1966.
Aicher-Scholl, I. *Die Weisse Rose.* Frankfurt am Main: Fischer 1993.
Alison, J. *Broken Hearts and New Creations.* London: Darton, Longman and Todd, 2010.
———. *On Being Liked.* London: Darton, Longman & Todd, 2003.
Amesbury, R. "Force of Law." In *Deconstruction and the Priority of Justice*, edited by D. Cornell, 3–67. New York: Routledge, 1992.
———. *Morality and Social Criticism.* New York: Palgrave Macmillan, 2005.
Amesbury, R., and G. Newlands. *Faith and Human Rights.* Minneapolis: Fortress, 2008.
Amis, K. *The Letters of Kingsley Amis.* Edited by Z. Leader. London: HarperCollins, 2001.
Badcock, G., ed. *John McIntyre: Theology After the Storm.* Grand Rapids: Eerdmans, 1997.
Badiou, A. *St Paul—The Foundation of Universalism.* Stanford: Stanford University Press, 2003.
Baillie, D. *God was in Christ.* London: Faber and Faber, 1948.
Barr, J. *The Scope and Authority of the Bible.* Explorations in Theology 7. London: SCM, 1980.
Barth, K., "Extra nos–pro nobis–in nobis." In *Hoeren und Handeln, Festschrift für E. Wolf*, edited by H. Gollwitzer, 15–27. Munich: Kaiser, 1962.
———. *Kirchliche Dogmatik 4/4.* Zürich: EVZ, 1967.
———. *Letters, 1961–68.* Edinburgh: T. & T. Clark, 1981.
———. *Theology of the Reformed Confessions.* Translated by D. L. Guder and J. J. Guder. Louisville: Westminster John Knox, 2002.
Beeson, T. *Windows on Westminster.* London: SCM, 1983.
Berthrong, J. "Human Rights and Responsibilities: A Confucian Perspective on the Universal Declaration of Human Rights." In *Human Rights and Responsibilities in the World Religions*, edited by J. Runzo et al., 199–208. Oxford: One World, 2002.
Blanchoff, T., ed. *Democracy and the New Religious Pluralism.* Oxford: Oxford University Press, 2007.
Bonhoeffer, D. *Ethics.* London: Collins, 1963.
Bultmann, R. *Das Evangelium des Johannes.* Güttingen: Vandenhoek & Ruprecht, 1964.
Burghardt, W. *Justice: A Global Adventure.* Maryknoll, NY: Orbis, 2004.

Caputo, J. D. "Olthuis's Risk: A Heretical Tribute." In *The Hermeneutics of Charity*, edited by J. K. A. Smith and H. I. Venema, 41–51. Grand Rapids: Brazos Press, 2004.
Chapman, M. *Ambassadors of Christ*. Aldershot, UK: Ashgate, 2004.
———. *The Future of Liberal Theology*. Aldershot, UK: Ashgate, 2001.
Chopp, R. "A Feminist Perspective: Christianity, Democracy and Feminist Theology." In *Christianity and Democracy*, edited by J. Witt, 111–29. Boulder, CO: Westview, 1993.
Cobb, J. "The Holy Spirit and the Present Age." In *The Lord and Giver of Life: Perspectives on Constructive Pneumatology*, edited by D. H. Jensen, 147–62. Louisville, KY: Westminster John Knox, 2008.
Coleman, J. A. "Not Democracy but Democratization." In *A Democratic Catholic Church: The Reconstruction of Roman Catholicism*, edited by E. C. Bianchi and R. R. Ruether, 13–22. New York: Crossroad, 1992.
Critchley, Simon. *The Ethics of Deconstruction: Derrida and Levinas*. Purdue: Purdue University Press, 1999.
Daniels, N. "Democratic Equalities." In *Cambridge Companion to John Rawls*, edited by S. Freeman, 241–76. Cambridge: Cambridge University Press, 2006.
Deneen, P. *Democratic Faith*. Princeton: Princeton University Press, 2005.
Derrida, J. *Adieu to Emmanuel Levinas*. Stanford: Stanford University Press, 1999.
———. "Force of Law." In *Deconstruction and the Priority of Justice*, edited by D. Cornell, ?–?. New York: Routledge, 1992.
———. *Given Time*. Chicago: University of Chicago Press, 1992.
———. *On Cosmopolitanism and Forgiveness*. London: Routledge, 2001.
Derrida, J., and A. Dufourmantelle. *On Hospitality*. Stanford: Stanford University Press, 2000.
Dworkin, R. *Is Democracy Possible Here?* Princeton: Princeton University Press, 2006.
Falconer, A., J. Schaefer, and C. John. "Theology and Human Rights." *Reformed World* 48.2 (1998)
Fergusson, D. "Beyond Theologies of Resentment." *Scottish Journal of Theology* 59 (2006) 183–92.
———. *Faith and Its Critics*. Oxford: Oxford University Press, 2008.
Ford, D. "Flamenco, Tai Chi and Six-Text Scriptural Reasoning: Report on a Visit to China." *Cambridge Interfaith Programme Papers*. Cambridge: 14 November 2012.
Foxgrover, D. ed. *The Legacy of Calvin*. Grand Rapids: Calvin Studies Society, 2000.
Freeman, S., ed. *Cambridge Companion to Rawls*. Cambridge: Cambridge University Press, 2003.
Friedman, T. *Hot Flat and Crowded*. New York: Farrer, Strauss and Giroux, 2008.
Gamwell, F. *Politics as a Vocation*. Cambridge: Cambridge University Press, 2005.
Gerrish, B. "John Calvin on Luther." In *Interpreters of Luther*, edited by J. Pelikan, 67–96. Philadelphia: Fortress, 1968.
———. "The Pathfinder—Calvin's Image of Luther." In *The Old Protestantism and the New: Essays on the Reformation Heritage*, edited by B. Gerrish, 27–48. Edinburgh: T. & T. Clark, 1982.
Glick, W. *Adolf von Harnack*. New York: Harper and Row, 1967.
Gorringe, T. *Discerning Spirit: A Theology of Revelation*. London: SCM, 1990.
Gort, J. D., et al., eds. *Crossroad Discourses between Christianity and Culture*. Amsterdam: Rodopi, 2010.
———. *Religions View Religion*. Amsterdam: Rodopi, 2006.

Graf. F. *Kirchendaemmerung*. Munich: Beck, 2011.
Haight, R. *The Future of Christology*. New York: Continuum, 2005.
———. "The Holy Spirit and the Religions." In *The Lord and Giver of Life: Perspectives on Constructive Pneumatology*, edited by D. H. Jensen, 55–70. Louisville, KY: Westminster John Knox, 2008.
Harink, D. *Paul among the Postliberals*. Grand Rapids: Brazos, 2003.
Harnack, A. von. *The Apostles' Creed*. Translated by S. Mears and T. Bailey. London: A. & C. Black, 1901.
———. "Die Aufgabe der theologischen Fakultaeten und die allgemeine Religionsgeschichte." In *Reden und Aufsaetze II*, 172–98. Giessen: Toepelmann, 1910.
———. *Aus der Friedens-und Kriegsarbeit*. Giessen: Toepelmann, 1916.
———. *History of Dogma*, Volumes 1–8. London: Williams & Norgate, 1894–99.
———, ed. *Jahre des Wiederstands*. Weinsberg: Neske, 1989.
———. *Luke the Physician*. Translated by J. R. Wilkinson. London: Williams & Norgate, 1907.
———. *Marcion*. Durham, NC: Labyrinth, 1990.
———. *The Sayings of Jesus*. Translated by J. R. Wilkinson. London: Williams & Norgate, 1908.
———. *What is Christianity?* London: Williams & Norgate, 1902.
———. *What is Christianity?* Philadelphia: Fortress, 1986.
Harnack, G-A. von, ed. *Ernst von Harnack, Jahre des Widerstands, 1932–45*. Weinsberg: Neske, 1989.
Hebblethwaite, B. *The Incarnation*. Cambridge: Cambridge University Press, 1989.
Heclo, H. *Christianity and American Democracy*. Cambridge: Harvard University Press, 2007.
Helmick, G., and Petersen, R. *Forgiveness and Reconciliation*. Radnor, PA: Templeton, 2001.
Herdt, J. *Religion and Faction in Hume's Moral Philosophy*. Cambridge: Cambridge University Press, 1997.
Hewitt, D. *Getting Rich First: Life in a Changing China*. London: Vintage, 2008.
Heyd, D., ed. *Toleration*. Princeton: Princeton University Press, 1996.
Hick, J. ed. *The Myth of God Incarnate*. London: SCM, 1977.
Hodgson, P. *Winds of the Spirit*. London: SCM, 1994.
Holl, K. *Gesammelte Aufsaetze*, Volume 1. Tübingen: Mohr, 1928.
Horner, R. *J-L Marion: An Introduction*. Aldershot, UK: Ashgate, 2005.
Hunter, A., and K. Chan. *Protestantism in Contemporary China*. Cambridge: Cambridge University Press, 1993.
Husbands, M., and D. Treier. *Justification—What's at Stake in the Current Debate?* Downers Grove, IL: IVP Academic, 2004.
Israel, J. *The Dutch Republic*. Oxford: Oxford University Press, 1995.
Jeanrond, G. *A Theology of Love*. London: T. & T. Clark, 2010.
Jenkins, D. *The Contradiction of Christianity*. London: SCM, 1977.
Jensen, D., ed. *The Lord and Giver of Life*. Louisville: Westminster John Knox, 2008.
Jieren, Li. "In Search of the Via Media between Christ and Marx: A Study of Bishop Ding Guangxun's Contextual Theology." PhD diss., Lund University, 2008.
Johnson, E. *Women, Earth and Creator Spirit*. New York: Paulist, 1993.
Johnson, M. S. "Calvin's Ethical Legacy." In *The Legacy of Calvin*, edited by D. Foxgrover, 63–83. Grand Rapids: Calvin Studies Society, 2000.

Kaltenborn, C-J. *Adolf von Harnack als Lehrer Dietrich Bonhoeffers*. Berlin: Evangelische Verlagsanstalt, 1971.
Kearney, R. *Anatheism*. New York: Columbia University Press, 2011.
———. "Philosophizing the Gift." In *The Hermeneutics of Charity*, edited by J. K. A. Smith and H. I. Venema, 52–72. Grand Rapids: Brazos Press, 2004.
Keating, P. "The Conditioning of the Unconditioned: Derrida and Kant." *Borderlands e-journal* 3.1 (2004). Online: http://www.borderlands.net.au/vol3no1_2004/keating_conditioning.htm.
Kelsey, D. *Eccentric Existence: A Theological Anthropology*. Louisville: Westminster John Knox, 2009.
Klemm, David. "Theology at the End of Art." Glasgow University Seminar, November, 2005. Unpublished.
Lactantius. *Divinarum Institutionum*. In *Fathers of the Church* vol. 49. Translated by Mary McDonald OP. Washington, DC: Catholic University of America Press, 1964.
Lakeland, P. *Postmodernity*. Minneapolis: Fortress, 1997.
Lampe, G. *God as Spirit*. Oxford: Clarendon, 1977.
———. *I Believe*. London: Skeffington, 1960.
Langford, T. *In Search of Foundations: English Theology 1900–1920*. Nashville: Abingdon, 1969.
Lijphart, A. *Patterns of Democracy*. New Haven: Yale University Press, 1999.
Lovin, R. *Christian Realism and the New Realities*. Cambridge: Cambridge University Press, 2008.
Macquarrie, J. *On Being a Theologian*. London: SCM, 1999.
———. *Theology, Church and Ministry*. London: SCM, 1986.
Mannermaa, T. *Christ Present in Faith*. Minneapolis: Fortress, 1985.
Marion, J-L. *The Idol and the Distance*. New York: Fordham University Press, 2001.
McCormack, Bruce. "Iustitia Aliena." In *Justification in Perspective*, edited by Bruce McCormack, 161–96. Grand Rapids: Baker Academic, 2006.
———. "What's at Stake in the Current Debate over Justification?" In *Justification: What's at Stake in the Current Debate?* edited by M. Husbands and D. Treier, 81–117. Downers Grove, IL: IVP Academic, 2004.
McIntyre, J. *The Christian Doctrine of History*. Edinburgh: Oliver and Boyd, 1957.
McKim, D., ed. *Cambridge Companion to Luther*. Cambridge: Cambridge University Press, 2003.
May, G. *Markion: Gesammelte Aufsätze*. Edited by K. Greschat and M. Meiser. Mainz: von Zabern, 2005.
Meister, C., and J. Beilby. *Routledge Companion to Modern Christian Thought*. London: Routledge, 2013.
Migliore, D. *Called to Freedom*. Louisville: Westminster John Knox, 1981.
———. *Faith Seeking Understanding*. Grand Rapids: Eerdmans, 1991.
———. "Participatio Christi: The Central Theme of Barth's Doctrine of Sanctification." *Zeitschrift für Dialektische Theologie* 18.3 (2002) 286–307.
Milbank, J. "Against Human Rights." Online. Nottingham: Centre of Theology and Philosophy, 2009.
Min, A. *The Solidarity of Others in a Divided World: A Postmodern Theology after Postmodernism*. London: T. & T. Clark, 2004.
Minow, M. *Between Vengeance and Forgiveness*. Boston: Beacon, 1998.
Morgan, R., ed. *Christ Alive and At Large*. Norwich, UK: Canterbury, 2010.

———, ed. *In Search of Humanity and Deity*. London: SCM, 2006.
———, ed. *The Religion of the Incarnation*. Bristol, UK: Bristol Classical Press, 1989.
Moule, C. G. W. H. *Lampe—A Memoir by Friends*. London: Mowbray 1982.
Moyn, S. *The Last Utopia: Human Rights in History*. Cambridge: Harvard University Press, 2010.
Müller, J. "HIV/AIDS, Narrative Practical Theology and Postfoundationalism." 2004. Online: www.julianmuller.co.za/emergence_story.pdf.
Murphy, A. *Conscience and Community*. University Park, PA: Penn State University Press, 2001.
Nainggolan, B. *The Social Involvement of Adolf von Harnack*. Regensburg: Roderer, 2005.
Nederman, C. *Worlds of Difference: European Discourses of Toleration, c. 1100–1550*. University Park, PA: Penn State University Press, 2000.
Newlands, G. *Christ and Human Rights*. Aldershot, UK: Ashgate, 2006.
———, ed. *Explorations in Theology*, 8. London: SCM, 1979.
———. *God in Christian Perspective*. Edinburgh: T. & T. Clark, 1994.
———, ed. *Grosvenor Essay No. 7*. Edinburgh: Scottish Episcopal Church, 2011.
———. *Hospitable God*. Farnham, UK: Ashgate, 2010.
———. *John and Donald Baillie—Transatlantic Theology*. New York: Lang, 2002.
———. "John McIntyre and History." *Theology in Scotland* XIV.2 (2007) 19–32.
Niebuhr, H. *The Responsible Self*. New York: Harper and Row, 1963.
Nimmo, P. *Being in Action*. London: T. & T. Clark, 2007.
Noll, M. "Battle for the Bible. The Impasse over Slavery." *Christian Century*, 2 May 2006, 20–25.
———. *The Civil War as a Theological Problem*. Chapel Hill, NC: University of North Carolina Press, 2006.
Nottmeier, H. *Adolf von Harnack und die deutsche Politik, 1890–1930*. Tübingen: Mohr, 2002.
Nussbaum, M. "Radical Evil in Liberal Democracies: The Neglect of the Political Emotions." In *Democracy and the New Religious Pluralism*, edited by T. Blanchoff, 171–202. Oxford: Oxford University Press, 2007.
Nyomi, S. "Life in Fullness for All." *Reformed World* 58.1 (2008) 3–11.
O'Neill, J. "Adolf von Harnack and the Entry of the German State into War." *Scottish Journal of Theology* 55.1 (2002) 1–18.
Oduyoye, M. "Talitha Qumi." *Reformed World* 58.1 (2008) 82–89.
Olthuis, J. "Crossing the Threshold." In *The Hermeneutics of Charity*, edited by J. Smith and H. Venema, 23–40. Grand Rapids: Brazos, 2004.
Pannenberg, W. *Jesus, God and Man*. London: SCM, 1983.
———. *Revelation as History*. New York: Macmillan, 1968.
Pauck, W. *Harnack and Troeltsch*. New York: Oxford University Press, 1968.
Pearson, C., ed. *Faith in a Hyphen: Crosscultural Theologies Down Under*. 2004. Reprint. Adelaide: Open Book, 2009.
Peston, R. *Who Runs Britain?* London: Hodder and Stoughton, 2008.
Phillips, K. *Wealth and Democracy*. New York: Broadway, 2002.
Placher, W. *Narratives of a Vulnerable God*. Louisville: Westminster John Knox, 1994.
Polkinghorne, J., ed. *The Work of Love*. Grand Rapids: Eerdmans, 2001.
Putnam, H. *Ethics without Ontology*. Cambridge: Harvard University Press, 2004.
Pye, M. *Maximum City*. London: Picador, 1993.
Rahner, K. *Theological Investigations* XVI. London: Darton, Longman and Todd, 1979.

Rawls, J. *Justice as Fairness: A Restatement*. Cambridge: Harvard University Press, 2001,
———. *A Theory of Justice*. Cambridge: Harvard University Press, 1971.
Richards, D. "Toleration and the Struggle against Prejudice." In *Toleration*, edited by D. Heyd, 127–46. Princeton: Princeton University Press, 2006.
Rogers, E. *After the Spirit*. London: SCM, 2006.
Rumscheidt, M. *Revelation and Theology: An Analysis of the Barth-Harnack Correspondence of 1923*. Cambridge: Cambridge University Press, 1972.
Saarinen, R. *God and the Gift: An Ecumenical Theology of Giving*. Collegeville, MN: Liturgical, 2005.
Scholl, Inge. *The White Rose, Munich 1942-1943*. Translated by A. Schultz. Middletown, CT: Wesleyan University Press, 1983.
Schrag, C. *God as Otherwise than Being*. Evansston, IL: Northwestern University Press, 2002.
Schwoebel, C. *Karl Barth–Martin Rade: Ein Briefwechsel*. Guetersloh: Mohn, 1981.
Sen, A. *The Idea of Justice*. New York: Allen Lane, 2009.
Shults, F. *The Evolution of Rationality. Festschrift for Wentzel van Huyssteen*. Grand Rapids: Eerdmans, 2006.
———. *The Postfoundational Task of Theology*. Grand Rapids: Eerdmans, 1999.
Siddiqui, M. "Between God's Mercy and God's Law: Human Dignity in Islam." In *The God of Love and Human Dignity*, edited by P. Middleton, 51–64. London: T. & T. Clark, 2007.
———. *Islam*. 4 vols. London: Sage, 2010.
Simpson, J. B. *Simpson's Contemporary Quotations*. New York: Houghton Mifflin, 1988.
Slenczska, R. *Die "Murren" des Hans Freiherr von Campenhausen*. Books on Demand. GmbH, 2005.
Smith, J. K. A., and H. I. Venema. *The Hermeneutics of Charity*. Grand Rapids: Brazos, 2004.
Sobrino, J. "A Critique and Unmasking of Present-day Democracies." *Concilium* 4 (2007) 69–82.
Spufford, F. *Unapologetic*. London: Harper Collins, 2012.
Stout J. *Democracy and Tradition*. Princeton: Princeton University Press, 2004.
Sugirathaja, S., ed. *Religious Pluralism and the Modern World: An Ongoing Engagement with John Hick*. London: Palgrave Macmillan, 2012.
Talbott, W. *Which Rights Should be Universal?* Oxford: Oxford University Press, 2005.
Tracy, D. "Form and Fragment: The Recovery of the Hidden and Incomprehensible God." *Reflections* 3 (1999) 62–88.
Tutu, D. *God Has a Dream*. New York: Doubleday, 2004.
———. *No Future without Forgiveness*. New York: Doubleday, 1999.
———. "To Be Human Is to Be Free." In *Christianity and Democracy*, edited by J. Witt, 311–320. Boulder, CO: Westview, 1993.
Twiss, S. B. "Confucian Values and Human Rights." In *Human Rights and Responsibilities in the World Religions*, edited by J. Runzo et al., 283–300. Oxford: One World, 2002.
Van Huyssteen, J. W. *Essays in Postfoundational Theology*. Grand Rapids: Eerdmans, 1997.
———. *The Shaping of Rationality*. Grand Rapids: Eerdmans, 1993.
———. *Theology and the Justification of Faith*. Grand Rapids: Eerdmans, 1989.

Van Huyssteen, J. W., et al. *The Authority of the Bible.* Church Report. Stellenbosch, SA: Dutch Reformed Church, 1983.
Veldsman, D. "Revisiting the Implications of Contemporary Epistemological Models for the Understanding of Religious Experience." *Religion and Theology* 11.3 & 4 (2004) 278–97.
Vroom, H. "The Dignity of 'I' and 'Me.'" In *The God of Love and Human Dignity*, edited by P. Middleton, 35–50. Edinburgh: T. & T. Clark, 2007.
———. *No Other Gods.* Grand Rapids: Eerdmans, 1996.
———. "Theology of Religions: Observations." In *Religions View Religions*, edited by J. Gort et al., ?–?. Amsterdam: Rodopi, 2008.
Wallis, J. *God's Politics.* Oxford: Lion, 2005.
Walzer, M. *Spheres of Justice.* New York: Basic, 1983.
Webster, J. "The Identity of the Holy Spirit: A Problem in Trinitarian Theology." *Themelios* 9.1 (1983) 1–7.
———. "Barth and the Reformed Confessions." *Zeitschrift für Dialektische Theologie* 21 (2005) 6–33.
Welker, M. *God the Spirit.* Minneapolis: Fortress, 1994.
———, ed. *The Work of the Spirit: Pneumatology and Pentecostalism.* Grand Rapids: Eerdmans, 2006.
Williams, B. "Toleration, an Impossible Virtue." In *Toleration*, edited by D. Heyd, 18–27. Princeton: Princeton University Press, 1996.
Williams, R. *On Christian Theology.* Oxford: Blackwell, 2000.
Wischmeyer, W., ed. *Aus der Werkstatt Harnacks: Transkription Seminarprotokolle Hans von Sodens (Sommersemester 1904-Wintersemester 1905-6).* Berlin: de Gruyter, 2004.
Witte, J. *Christianity and Democracy in Global Context.* Boulder: Westview, 1993.
———. *God's Joust, God's Justice.* Grand Rapids: Eerdmans, 2006.
———. "A Short History of Western Rights." In *God's Joust, God's Justice*, 31–48. Grand Rapids: Eerdmans, 2006.
Witte, J., and J. Van den Wyver, eds. *Religious Human Rights in Global Perspective.* Dordrecht: Nijhoff, 1996.
Wolf, E. *Peregrinatio.* Munich: Kaiser, 1962.
Wolterstorff, N. *Justice—Rights and Wrongs.* Princeton: Princeton University Press, 2008.
———. "The Grace that Shaped My Life." *Reformed World* 56 (2006) 6.
Wright, D., and Badcock, G., eds. *Disruption to Diversity.* Edinburgh: T. & T. Clark, 1996.
Yong, A. "Guests, Hosts and the Holy Ghost." In *The Lord and Giver of Life: Perspectives on Constructive Pneumatology*, edited by D. H. Jenson, 71–86. Louisville, KY: Westminster John Knox, 2008.
———. *Spirit, Word and Community.* Aldershot, UK: Ashgate, 2002.
Zahl, S. *Pneumatology and Theology of the Cross in the Preaching of Christoph Friedrich Blumhardt: The Holy Spirit between Wittenberg and Azusa Street.* London: T. & T. Clark, 2010.
Zhibin, Xie. *Religious Diversity and Public Religion in China.* Aldershot, UK: Ashgate, 2006.

Index of Names

Adams, Graham, 9
Adams, John, 2n2
Akinola, Peter, 134
Alesius, Alexander, 38
Alison, James, 9, 30, 103
Allison, Anthony, x
Altizer, Thomas, 23
Amesbury, Richard, 63n3, 91, 133
Amis, Kingsley, 201
Amis, Martin, 190
Andrewes, Launcelot, 5
Aquinas, Thomas, 28
Auld, Graeme, 225

Badcock, Gary, 116–17
Badiou, Alain, 122
Baillie, John, 209, 232
Banks, Iain, 108n20
Barr, James, 119, 227
Barth, Karl, 7, 31, 32, 43–47, 156–58, 227
Bateman, William, 184
Beale, Charles, 193
Berthrong, John 20n32
Blount, Brian, 170–71
Bonhoeffer, Dietrich, 23, 140, 158
Bultmann, Rudolf, 32

Calvin, John, 6, 37–39, 187
Campenhausen, Hans von 60, 61–62, 153, 215, 226
Caputo, John, 50
Chapman, Mark, 213, 216, 221
Cheyne, Alex, 115
Chopp, Rebecca, 126n3
Cobb, John, 10, 87

Coleman, John, 78, 79n2
Collier, John, 193
Copland, Aaron, 187

Dawkins, Richard, 23, 25
Deneen, Patrick,, 135
Derrida, Jacques, 48–50, 128
Dorrien, Gary, 60
Dworkin, Ronald, 141n34

Ebeling, Gerhard, 38
Ellacuria, Ignacio, 126n5

Fergusson, David, 24, 25, 112, 127n6
Ford, David, 14n26
Forrester, Duncan, 234
Friedman, Thomas, 137–38

Gamwell, Franklin, 139
Gerrish, Brian, 40, 41n14, 42
Goehr, Alexander, 26
Gorringe,Tim, 8
Graf, Friedrich, 23n1
Guangxun, Dang, 17
Gunnarson, Gretar, 127n6

Hamilton, Patrick, 37
Harnack, Adolf von, 149–61
Harnack, Ernst von, 149
Hebblethwaite, Brian, 230
Hegel, Friedrich, 32
Herdt, Jennifer, 122
Hewitt, Duncan, 16
Hick, John, 58–59, 69
Hodgson, Peter, 9

Holl, Karl, 39
Huyssteen, Wentzel van 85–87, 88, 90, 92, 94–95

Jeanrond, Werner, 236
Jeffs, Thelma, 193
Jenkins, David, 5n3
Jenkins, Philip, 89
Jensen, David, 10
Johnson, Elizabeth, 9
Jordan, Mark, 30
Jun, Ma, 1n1

Kearney, Richard, 50
Keller, Catherine, 30
Kelsey, David, 33
Klemm, David, 51
Kueng, Hans, 44

Lampe, Geoffrey, 8,9, 62, 215
Las Casas, Bartholome, 164
Li, Jieren, 17
Lincoln, Abraham, 135
Loisy, Alfred, 154
Lossky, Vladimir, 9
Luther, Martin, 6n3, 37–47, 55–56

Mackinnon, Donald, 228
Macquarrie, John, 110–14
Mannermaa, Tuomo, 46
Marion, Jean-Luc, 53
May, Gerhard, 161
McCormack, Bruce, 45
McIntyre, John, 115, 117–19, 124
Messer, Donald, 169
Middleton, Paul, 234
Migliore, Daniel, 37, 47, 56–57
Milbank, John, 64
Miller, Calum, 72
Min, Anselm, 9
Minow, Martha, 103
Morgan, Edward, 209, 210
Moule, Charles, 8
Muller, Julian, 109
Murphy, Andrew, 120–22

Newlands, George, 222–36
Niebuhr, Richard, 123

Niemoeller, Martin, 149
Nimmo, Paul, 47
Noll, Mark, 175
Nussbaum, Martha, 30, 129n14
Nyomi, Setri, 83

Oduyoye, Mercy, 83n6
Olthuis, James, 51

Pannenberg, Wolfhart, 119–21
Pastorius, Francis, 165
Penn, William, 164
Plato, 6
Polkinghorne, John, 10, 104
Putnam, Hilary, 129

Rad, Gerhard von, 27
Rahner, Karl, 8, 31, 113
Rawls, John, 129
Richard, Lucien, 172n11
Robinson, Gene, 206
Robinson, John, 22, 224
Rogers, Eugene, 9
Rorty, Richard, 91, 133
Runcie, Robert, 207, 215, 220
Rust, Godfrey, 211–12

Saarinen, Risto, 54
Schillebeeckx, Eduard, 31
Schleiermacher, Friedrich, 31, 152
Scholl, Sophie, 211
Schrag, Calvin, 51–52
Sen, Amartya, 141n34
Shaw, Douglas, 72, 225
Siddiqui, Mona, 65
Smith, Allen, 12n25
Smith, Gregor, 60
Soden, Hans von, 60, 61
Stout, Jeffrey, 127–28
Sugden, Marian, 192
Sykes, Stephen, 229

Talbott, William, 133
Torrance, Iain, 38n1, 233
Torrance, Thomas, 228
Tracy, David, 43
Troeltsch, Ernst, 152, 155
Turing, Alan, 29

index of names

Tutu, Desmond, 27, 55, 102, 126n4, 169, 173
Twiss, Sumner, 20n32

Veldsman, Daniel, 87n1
Vroom, Hendrik, 70, 83–84

Walker, Peter, 230
Wallis, Jim, 136–37, 189
Wang, Hai, 1n1
Ward, Keith, 104
Warhol, Andy, 67
Webster, John, 8
Weir, Stuart, 9
Weiwei, Ai, 20

Welker, Michael, 3, 9
Williams, Bernard, 120
Williams, Rowan, 8
Wit, Johan de, 125
Witte, John, 126, 168
Wolterstorff, Nicholas, 82, 130n16

Xiabao, Liu, 20
Xie, Zhibin, 16

Yong, Amos, 9, 10, 12

Zahl, Simeon, 6n4
Zhang, Zhongwen, 1n1

www.ingramcontent.com/pod-product-compliance
Lightning Source LLC
Chambersburg PA
CBHW050348230426
43663CB00010B/2040